The Art of Social Engineering

Uncover the secrets behind the human dynamics in cybersecurity

Cesar Bravo

Desilda Toska

BIRMINGHAM—MUMBAI

The Art of Social Engineering

Copyright © 2023 Packt Publishing

All rights reserved. No part of this book may be reproduced, stored in a retrieval system, or transmitted in any form or by any means, without the prior written permission of the publisher, except in the case of brief quotations embedded in critical articles or reviews.

Every effort has been made in the preparation of this book to ensure the accuracy of the information presented. However, the information contained in this book is sold without warranty, either express or implied. Neither the authors, nor Packt Publishing or its dealers and distributors, will be held liable for any damages caused or alleged to have been caused directly or indirectly by this book.

Packt Publishing has endeavored to provide trademark information about all of the companies and products mentioned in this book by the appropriate use of capitals. However, Packt Publishing cannot guarantee the accuracy of this information.

Group Product Manager: Pavan Ramchandani
Publishing Product Manager: Prachi Sawant
Book Project Manager: Ashwin Dinesh Kharwa
Senior Editor: Isha Singh
Technical Editor: Nithik Cheruvakodan
Copy Editor: Safis Editing
Proofreader: Safis Editing
Indexer: Rekha Nair
Production Designer: Ponraj Dhandapani
DevRel Marketing Coordinator: Marylou De Mello

First published: October 2023

Production reference: 1270923

Published by Packt Publishing Ltd.
Grosvenor House
11 St Paul's Square
Birmingham
B3 1RB

ISBN 978-1-80461-364-1

www.packtpub.com

To our beloved son, Thomas.

This book, born during the wondrous days of your arrival, symbolizes the power of dedication and passion. We want you to know, dear Thomas, that you are the very spark that ignited the flames of commitment and purpose within our hearts.

Just as we watched you take your first steps, stumble, and then rise with unyielding determination, so too did this book evolve through countless revisions, fueled by our relentless dedication. It stands as a testament to the incredible potential that resides within us all when we pursue our dreams with unwavering passion.

Thomas, you are the embodiment of inspiration. Your boundless curiosity and fearless exploration of the world around you remind us daily that anything is possible with dedication and perseverance.

This book is dedicated to you, our little motivator, to encourage you to dream without limits, to reach for the stars, and to remind you that your passion can set the world ablaze.

May it serve as a living testament to the limitless possibilities that await you, and as a constant reminder that, with dedication, there are no heights you cannot reach. Your presence has filled our lives with immeasurable joy, and we dedicate this book to you as a token of our love and belief in your limitless potential.

With all our love, Mom and Dad

Cesar and Desilda

Foreword

It's my privilege to introduce *The Art of Social Engineering*, written by Cesar Bravo and Desilda Toska. Both authors are not just scholars in cybersecurity but also inventors who have pioneered some of the most groundbreaking tools and methodologies we use today. Their combined expertise provides an unparalleled depth of understanding of the intricate dance of human psychology and digital security.

Over the years, as I've navigated the ever-evolving corridors of cybersecurity, it has become clear that no firewall or encryption protocol can offer a foolproof defense against a hacker armed with a deep understanding of human behavior. The most complex security system can crumble with misplaced trust, a single innocent click, or an unsuspecting reply. Social engineering is, in essence, the act of manipulating people into divulging confidential information, not necessarily through technical means but through the power of persuasion, deception, and psychological manipulation.

This book offers more than just a glimpse into the techniques used by social engineers; it serves as a comprehensive guide, a deep dive into the intricate web of tactics, strategies, and real-world examples. Whether you're a seasoned security expert, a business owner trying to safeguard your assets, or just a curious reader, there's something in these pages for you.

Bravo and Toska have not merely presented a manual; they've crafted a masterpiece. They have blended their profound knowledge with engaging narratives, making complex concepts digestible and relatable. It's a journey through the delicate balance between trust and caution, intuition and investigation, safety and vulnerability.

As our world further intertwines with technology, and as the lines between the digital and the physical continue to blur, understanding the art and science of social engineering becomes paramount. This book isn't just about understanding the threats; it's about fostering a culture of vigilance, critical thinking, and continuous learning.

Humans are and will continue to be our most important defense.

In the hands of Cesar Bravo and Desilda Toska, you're not just reading about social engineering; you're delving into the minds of masters. Prepare to be enlightened, to be astounded, and most importantly, to be prepared.

Stay safe, stay informed, and always remember – the most important line of defense is an educated mind.

Rhonda Childress
VP and Chief Innovation Officer Security and Resiliency at Kyndryl
Kyndryl Fellow
IBM Fellow Emeritus

Contributors

About the authors

Cesar Bravo is a researcher who has created and patented more than 100 inventions related to cybersecurity in the US, Germany, China, and Japan.

Cesar has been working with several universities across the world to teach cybersecurity at all levels, including a master's degree in cybersecurity (in which he also served as thesis director).

In recent years, Cesar has become a recognized speaker (including a TEDx talk) with international presentations in the UK, Germany, Mexico, the US, and Spain.

His last book, *Mastering Defensive Security*, was translated into several languages, and with thousands of copies sold around the world, it is widely recognized as a must-read book in cybersecurity.

Desilda Toska (de Bravo) embarked on her professional journey as a QA engineer, honing her skills through years of dedicated work. Starting out as a consultant, she quickly ascended the ranks to become a first-line manager and eventually assumed the role of the head of the automation practice at IBM CIC Italy. During her tenure at IBM, Desilda discovered her fervent passion for crafting innovative programs using IoT technologies. This enthusiasm led her to become a prominent female inventor with several inventions patented in the ever-evolving field of technology, particularly in the realm of cybersecurity. Equipped with an unquenchable thirst for knowledge, Desilda earned her MSc degrees from the University of Tirana, Albania, and a Doctorate Magistrale degree from the University of Milan, Italy, both in computer science. Desilda has expanded her horizons yet again as a university teacher.

This book is dedicated to those who stand as sentinels against the crafty architects of social engineering.

To the bold souls venturing into the cybersecurity journey, this book is a call to action, a testament to the indomitable human spirit, and a reminder that in the face of ever-evolving threats, we possess the power to do what's right and protect the world.

May this book serve as a shining example of wisdom, empowering you to thwart the schemes of those who seek to exploit the human element. Together, we can fortify the digital landscape and protect the innocent from the cunning wiles of social engineering.

Our hope is that this book will inspire you to embrace the same dedication and passion that we poured into its creation.

About the reviewer

Anton Belik has worked in the cybersecurity field for more than 15 years. He was the CEO of a security start-up, Pyrobox, and helped build security teams from scratch at several high-load projects, start-ups, and big manufacturing companies. He is passionate about the web, network, cloud, hardware security, and social engineering. He is a certified Offensive Security Certified Professional and a member of the JBFC security community.

I'd like to thank my family and friends who understand the time and commitment it takes to research and test data that is constantly changing. Working in this field would not be possible without the supportive community.

Table of Contents

Preface — xiii

Part 1: Understanding Social Engineering

1

The Psychology behind Social Engineering — 3

Technical requirements	4	Complimenting	12
Disclaimer	4	Supporting other points of view	13
Understanding the art of manipulation	4	Leveraging empathy	13
Examining the six principles of persuasion	7	Leveraging influence for defensive security	14
Developing rapport	11	Summary	15
Using appropriate body language	11	Further reading	15
Using your knowledge to help	12		

2

Understanding Social Engineering — 17

Technical requirements	17	Fake investment	23
Detecting social engineering attacks	17	Fake advertisements	25
Social media attacks	18	Social engineering and the crypto scam	28
The lost passport	19	Summary	35
The federal government grant	21		
Romance scam	21		

3

Common Scam Attacks — 37

Technical requirements	37	Avoiding these scams	47
What is a scam?	38	**Other scams**	**48**
The Nigerian scam (419)	38	The investor scam	48
The history of the scam	39	The Business Email Compromise scam	48
Identifying the Nigerian scam	41	Fraud compensation	49
Types of Nigerian scams	44	**Scambaiting**	**50**
Funny Nigerian scams	45	**Summary**	**51**

4

Types of Social Engineering Attacks — 53

Technical requirements	**54**	**Quid pro quo**	**73**
Disclaimer	**54**	Free tech support	73
Phishing attacks	**55**	Free software to download	74
History of phishing attacks	55	How to protect yourself against quid pro quo attacks	74
Famous phishing attacks	56	**Pretexting**	**74**
Types of phishing attacks	59	Fake job offers	74
Baiting	**70**	False charities	75
Physical baiting	70	**Watering hole**	**76**
Cyber baiting	71	Crypto mining	76
Protecting yourself against baiting	71	**Summary**	**76**
Dumpster diving	**72**	**Further reading**	**76**
Tailgating	**73**		

Part 2: Enhanced Social Engineering Attacks

5

Enhanced Social Engineering Attacks — 79

Technical requirements	80	Disclaimer	80

Table of Contents   ix

Targeted attacks	80	Fake updates	86
Identifying high-value targets	81	Scareware	87
		Fake pages	89
OSINT	**82**	Magic-ware	92
OSINT tools	82	Hacking-ware	93
OSINT methods	83	Gaming-based attacks	94
OSINT use cases	84	Forum-based attacks	95
Web-based attacks	**84**	Adware	98
Fake logins	84	**Summary**	**99**

Social Engineering and Social Network Attacks   101

Disclaimer	102	WhatsApp-based attacks	110
Social engineering through mobile applications	**102**	Instagram-based attacks	112
		Other attacks	**114**
Malicious apps and app-based attacks	103	Sextortion	114
Exploiting app permissions for data access	106	Fake news attacks	116
The challenges in identifying and mitigating such attacks	107	Forex scams	119
Social engineering via social networks	**108**	**Summary**	**121**
Clickbait attack	108		

AI-Driven Techniques in Enhanced Social Engineering Attacks   123

Technical requirements	**124**	Strengthening collaboration and information sharing	130
Artificial intelligence in social engineering attacks	**124**	**Understanding deepfakes**	**130**
The growing role of AI in social engineering	124	Deepfake videos	132
AI-driven social engineering techniques	125	How to detect deepfake videos	133
Strategies for combating AI-enhanced social engineering attacks	**125**	Deepfake audio	133
		Implications for social engineering attacks	136
Understanding the threat landscape	126	**Other AI attacks**	**137**
Implementing effective security measures	127	**Summary**	**143**
Fostering a culture of security and awareness	129		

8

The Social Engineering Toolkit (SET) — 145

Technical requirements	146
SET	146
Importance of understanding SET in cybersecurity	147
Installing and setting up SET	148
System requirements for SET installation	148
Downloading and installing SET	148
Executing SET	149
Understanding the main components and modules of SET	150
Social-Engineering Attacks	152
Penetration Testing (Fast-Track)	159
Other options	159
Mitigation and defense against SET attacks	160
Technical controls and vulnerability management	160
User awareness and training	160
Email and web filtering	161
IR and TI	161
Access controls and privilege management	161
Continuous monitoring and response	161
Summary	162
Further reading	162

Part 3: Protecting against Social Engineering Attacks

9

Understanding the Social Engineering Life Cycle — 165

Technical requirements	166
Disclaimer	166
The history of the social engineering life cycle	166
The iconic Kevin Mitnick	167
The social engineering life cycle	168
Reconnaissance	169
Target selection	170
Pretext development	171
Engagement	172
Exploitation or elicitation	172
Execution (post-exploitation)	175
How to stay protected	176
Control your social media posts	176
Configure your privacy settings on social media	176
Beware of fake profiles	177
Be cautious	177
Be careful with dating sites	177
Avoid social media bragging	177
Be mindful of your posts	177
Remove image metadata	177
Implement awareness campaigns	178
Summary	178

10

Defensive Strategies for Social Engineering — 179

Technical requirements	180	Enhanced cybersecurity training	188
Disclaimer	180	Assessing the effectiveness of existing cybersecurity training programs	189
Importance of defensive strategies	180	Identifying gaps and areas for improvement	189
Recognizing social engineering red flags	181	Case studies and lessons learned	190
Employee awareness campaigns	182	Analyzing real-world social engineering incidents	190
Phishing campaigns and countermeasures	184	Extracting valuable lessons from past experiences	191
CTF exercises	187	Summary	195

11

Applicable Laws and Regulations for Social Engineering — 197

Technical requirements	198	Convictions for social engineering – lessons learned from notable cases	201
Examples of laws and regulations around the world	198	Summary	202

Index — 203

Other Books You May Enjoy — 212

Preface

Social engineering is one of the most common methods used by attackers to steal data and resources from people, companies, and even governments.

This book, *The Art of Social Engineering*, provides readers with a comprehensive understanding of social engineering attacks and how to protect against them. It starts by explaining the psychological principles behind social engineering attacks and the current threat landscape and providing a series of examples to help you identify those attacks.

After that, you will learn about the most interesting psychological principles used by attackers, including influence, manipulation, rapport, persuasion, and empathy. You will also understand how attackers leverage technology to enhance their attacks by using fake logins, impersonating emails, displaying fake updates, and even using social media as their favorite means to execute attacks.

Of course, the book will also teach you how to develop your own defensive strategy, including awareness campaigns, phishing campaigns, cybersecurity training, capture the flag, and many more tools and techniques.

By the end of this book, you will have a good knowledge of social engineering, which will enable you to easily identify, prepare, and protect against the ever-growing threat of social engineering attacks and keep you and your organization safe!

Who this book is for

This book is for cybersecurity professionals who want to expand their knowledge of the tools, strategies, and mechanisms used in social engineering attacks.

It is also suitable for professionals who want to change their mindset to increase their level of awareness against social engineering attacks, IT specialists who want to understand how to prevent social engineering attacks, and students who want to improve their knowledge of social engineering attacks and their relevance in the current context of social media.

It is also useful to managers and other decision-makers who want to understand the impact of social engineering on their companies, HR managers who want to create strategies to reduce the possibility of social engineering attacks, and government officials who want to understand the impact of social engineering attacks on politics.

What this book covers

Chapter 1, The Psychology behind Social Engineering, provides a deep dive into the art of manipulation and how attackers leverage psychological principles to influence the actions of victims.

Chapter 2, Understanding Social Engineering, provides an overview of the most common social engineering attacks on social media, how to spot them, and how to avoid them.

Chapter 3, Common Scam Attacks, provides a comprehensive overview of the most common types of scams and how to avoid them.

Chapter 4, Types of Social Engineering Attacks, provides a comprehensive examination of the most common social engineering attack types, coupled with guidance about how to recognize and prevent them.

Chapter 5, Enhanced Social Engineering Attacks, helps you discover how technology is being used by attackers to elevate their social engineering techniques and learn effective methods for the detection and prevention of these attacks.

Chapter 6, Social Engineering and Social Networks Attacks, provides an exploration of the wide-ranging landscape of social engineering attacks through social networks and mobile apps, including comprehensive guidance on how to protect against those attacks.

Chapter 7, AI-Driven Techniques in Enhanced Social Engineering Attacks, explores the intersection of AI and social engineering in cybersecurity, covering AI's role in advanced attacks, the impact of deepfakes, and AI-driven phishing attacks.

Chapter 8, The Social Engineering Toolkit (SET), provides a deep dive into the SET framework, including its installation and configuration and a comprehensive review of its components, plus invaluable insights into mitigating and defending against SET-driven attacks.

Chapter 9, Understanding the Social Engineering Life Cycle, provides a thorough exploration of the social engineering life cycle, meticulously unveiling its distinct stages while equipping you with indispensable knowledge to protect you and your organization against these attacks.

Chapter 10, Defensive Strategies for Social Engineering, helps you discover modern defensive strategies against social engineering threats, including employee awareness, phishing countermeasures, practical exercises, capture-the-flag exercises, cybersecurity training, and real-world case studies.

Chapter 11, Applicable Laws and Regulations for Social Engineering, helps you navigate the legal landscape, uncovering the protective measures and regulatory frameworks designed to combat social engineering, plus lessons learned from notable legal cases.

To get the most out of this book

While this book is self-contained and there are no prerequisites, basic cybersecurity knowledge is a plus.

Software/hardware covered in the book	Operating system requirements
The **Social Engineering Toolkit (SET)**	Linux

You can complement the knowledge in this book by also reading *Mastering Defensive Security* by Cesar Bravo, as that will give you a more in-depth understanding of the cybersecurity field.

Conventions used

There are a number of text conventions used throughout this book.

`Code in text`: Indicates code words in text, database table names, folder names, filenames, file extensions, pathnames, dummy URLs, user input, and Twitter handles. Here is an example: "This patent shows a cognitive system capable of identifying and preventing scam attacks: `https://patents.google.com/patent/US10944790B2/en?inventor=cesar+bravo`."

Any command-line input or output is written as follows:

```
$ sudo apt install set -y
```

Bold: Indicates a new term, an important word, or words that you see onscreen. For instance, words in menus or dialog boxes appear in **bold**. Here is an example: "Then, to make this even more attractive, notice that the button says **One-click transfer without password**."

> Tips or important notes
> Appear like this.

Get in touch

Feedback from our readers is always welcome.

General feedback: If you have questions about any aspect of this book, email us at `customercare@packtpub.com` and mention the book title in the subject of your message.

Errata: Although we have taken every care to ensure the accuracy of our content, mistakes do happen. If you have found a mistake in this book, we would be grateful if you would report this to us. Please visit `www.packtpub.com/support/errata` and fill in the form.

Piracy: If you come across any illegal copies of our works in any form on the internet, we would be grateful if you would provide us with the location address or website name. Please contact us at `copyright@packt.com` with a link to the material.

If you are interested in becoming an author: If there is a topic that you have expertise in and you are interested in either writing or contributing to a book, please visit `authors.packtpub.com`.

Share Your Thoughts

Once you've read *The Art of Social Engineering*, we'd love to hear your thoughts! Scan the QR code below to go straight to the Amazon review page for this book and share your feedback.

`https://packt.link/r/1804613649`

Your review is important to us and the tech community and will help us make sure we're delivering excellent quality content.

Download a free PDF copy of this book

Thanks for purchasing this book!

Do you like to read on the go but are unable to carry your print books everywhere?

Is your eBook purchase not compatible with the device of your choice?

Don't worry, now with every Packt book you get a DRM-free PDF version of that book at no cost.

Read anywhere, any place, on any device. Search, copy, and paste code from your favorite technical books directly into your application.

The perks don't stop there, you can get exclusive access to discounts, newsletters, and great free content in your inbox daily

Follow these simple steps to get the benefits:

1. Scan the QR code or visit the link below

```
https://packt.link/free-ebook/9781804613641
```

2. Submit your proof of purchase
3. That's it! We'll send your free PDF and other benefits to your email directly

Part 1: Understanding Social Engineering

Part 1 is about acquiring a comprehensive understanding of social engineering, the types of attacks, as well as the psychological concepts used by attackers.

This part has the following chapters:

- *Chapter 1, The Psychology behind Social Engineering*
- *Chapter 2, Understanding Social Engineering*
- *Chapter 3, Common Scam Attacks*
- *Chapter 4, Types of Social Engineering Attacks*

The Psychology behind Social Engineering

You have probably heard the term **social engineering** before, either in the news (as part of a big scam) or even in your job as part of the annual security awareness program.

But what is social engineering? Well, to make it simple, we can just say that social engineering is the art of manipulating people to perform an action that will provide a benefit for the attacker. That action could be in the form of disclosing information, executing an action (such as executing a command), or even disabling or bypassing a security measure.

In other words, social engineering is focused on "hacking" the users, not the systems.

Now, to better understand social engineering, it is imperative to understand the psychology, principles, and tactics behind those attacks. Attackers will leverage a set of psychological concepts, principles, and tactics to successfully manipulate the victim. They will then use the art of manipulation to influence the victim to either reveal sensitive information (passwords, users, etc.) or even perform a given action (such as disabling the antivirus).

Understanding those tactics will help you to identify when you are a target and avoid falling into these elaborate attack vectors. For this reason, in this chapter, we will cover the following main topics:

- The art of manipulation
- Tactics and principles used to influence the victims
- Developing rapport
- The weakness behind the empathy
- Leveraging influence tactics for defensive security

Technical requirements

There are no technical requirements for this chapter.

Disclaimer

All characters in the illustrations are fictional characters.

Illustrations are inspired by real attacks; therefore, the language used (including spelling and grammatical errors) is intentional.

Understanding the art of manipulation

Social engineering is the art of manipulating users to perform actions or divulge confidential information for the benefit of the attacker.

Examples of those actions can be as follows:

- Install a given software (which may contain malware)
- Remove some security settings or applications (disable the antivirus, firewall, etc.)
- Execute an unknown command that may impact the confidentiality, integrity, or availability of data (for example, delete a table using SQL commands)
- Create or edit an active user (that will provide access to the attacker)
- Change system configurations (to facilitate access to data)

Additionally, examples of the types of information that the attacker may want to gather from the victims are as follows:

- User credentials (usernames, passwords, etc.)
- Trade secrets
- Organizational information (which can be used later for whaling attacks)
- Financial information
- Corporate sensitive information (clients, price lists, etc.)
- Sensitive personal information (used for impersonation attacks)

While most people believe they will never fall victim to this type of attack, the truth is that we are all susceptible to a social engineering attack.

In fact, social engineering attacks have evolved into well-fabricated scenarios that are carefully crafted to leverage a series of physiology paradigms to effectively trick and manipulate the victim without them even noticing that they are under attack.

Therefore, organizations must invest time and resources to include social engineering awareness campaigns as part of their cybersecurity strategy to reduce the risks of employees falling into these types of attacks.

A common mistake is to focus social engineering awareness campaigns on IT people, while in reality, attackers prefer to attack other employee profiles, as follows:

- **Non-IT employees**: Attackers assume that non-IT personnel are less aware of the consequences of executing a given command. The following figure shows a typical example of how an attacker can manipulate an employee into executing a command to delete hundreds and even thousands of records in a database:

Figure 1.1 – Manipulating non-IT employees

- **Overwhelmed users**: We all know that some companies are happy to assign overwhelming workloads and job responsibilities to some employees. This is, of course, a terrible business practice, but it can also become a vulnerability that attackers may want to exploit. For example, as shown in the following figure, an attacker can manipulate an overwhelmed employee to gather access to a restricted location (which will enable the attacker to perform a super dangerous physical attack):

Figure 1.2 – Manipulating overwhelmed users

- **Sales teams**: Sales teams are normally overstretched to achieve sales quotas at the end of the quarter. Attackers can leverage that stress to manipulate the victim to perform a restricted action, as highlighted in the following figure:

Figure 1.3 – Manipulating sales teams

- **Executive assistants**: Executive assistants handle a lot of sensitive information that is a potential target for attackers. Therefore, executive assistants are a common target that attackers may try to manipulate to gain access to that information. The following figure shows an example of how an attacker can impersonate an IT manager to obtain a password reset code to gain access to the senior manager's account:

Figure 1.4 – Manipulating executive assistants

Of course, those are only a few examples of groups that are more prone to be attacked by a social engineering attack, but in the end, what we want to highlight is the importance of ensuring that the organization is well-trained and aware of the threats of social engineering attacks.

The bottom line is that users are the biggest layer of defense to prevent those attacks in your organization, therefore, ensuring that everyone is well-trained to recognize those attacks should be a key component in your cybersecurity strategy.

Now, while manipulation is the art used by attackers, there are a lot of psychological principles behind this that enable the attacker to successfully manipulate users not only to perform those actions but to do it without doubting the intention of the attacker. Now, let's review them in detail.

Examining the six principles of persuasion

As mentioned, social engineering is an *art*, an art that can be improved with time but can also be learned by applying several tactics.

Those tactics were highlighted by Robert Cialdini (behavioral psychologist) in the book *The Psychology of Persuasion*, in which he divides those tactics into six key principles, as shown in the following figure:

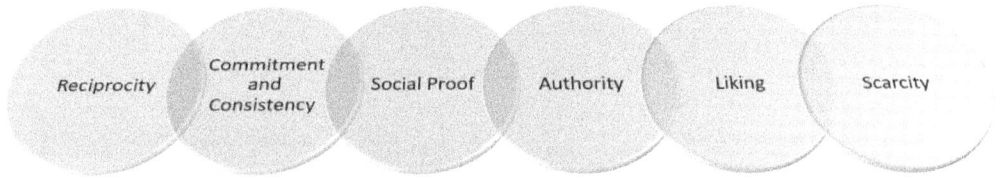

Figure 1.5 – Key principles of influence

Now, let's review each of those principles:

- **Reciprocity**: There is a strong sense of payback when we receive something from others. Therefore, an attacker may use this technique by giving you something or doing a favor for you to influence your brain to do something form them later.

Figure 1.6 – Example of using reciprocity to influence a victim

- **Commitment and consistency**: If you commit to something, it is likely that you will honor that commitment, even if the original commitment or incentive slightly changes. That is exactly what the attacker wants. First, the attacker will make you commit to something reasonable and then slightly change it at the last minute to something you may have doubts about, but due to the previous commitment, you are likely to accept and proceed. The following figure shows an example of how an attacker can use this to gather physical access:

Figure 1.7 – Example of using commitment to influence a victim

- **Social proof**: This principle is based on the fact that people's behaviors are influenced by what others do in a given place (the culture of the place). For example, in companies with a mature cybersecurity culture, tailgating is seen as an unacceptable behavior. However, the same action (tailgating) can be seen as just being polite in other companies with less cybersecurity awareness as illustrated in *Figure 1.8*:

Figure 1.8 – Example of using social proof to influence the victim

- **Authority**: It is more likely that people will follow an order when it is given by a person with authority (or at least pretending to have it). Impersonating a cybersecurity expert, influencer, or any other credible or known person is a typical case of using authority to influence the victim into executing a questionable action. As seen in *Figure 1.9*, the attacker calls the victim, impersonating someone from the IT or security department. Then, the attacker requests the victim to provide a code that they supposedly sent to them. However, what the victim does not know is that the code they are giving to the attacker is actually a password reset code that will give full access to the attacker:

Figure 1.9 – Example of using authority to influence the victim

- **Liking**: People are more willing to trust others they like, and an attacker may use that principle to influence a victim. Liking is not limited to physical attraction; in fact, there are many other methods that attackers may use to gain your trust, as follows:

    - By sharing some characteristics in common (such as saying we live or grew up in the same city or have similar ancestors)

    - By sharing the same passion (for example, the same series, the same idols, the same favorite music group, etc.)

    - By following the same team or groups (in sports, politics, etc.)

The following figure shows an example of how an attacker can use some compliments to like the victim and gain their trust:

Figure 1.10 – Example of using liking to influence the victim

- **Scarcity**: This tactic is commonly used in marketing to influence you to purchase something (which, most of the time, is something that you don't need). This tactic is incredibly powerful, which is why it is present in almost all social engineering attacks. Here, the attacker will push the victim by making them believe that they will lose a big opportunity if they do not leverage it right now!

Figure 1.11 – Example of using scarcity to influence the victim

Now, there are other key tactics and techniques used in social engineering attacks that are not included in that list such as developing rapport, empathy, and pretexting, so let's review them in detail.

Developing rapport

While similar to the principle of liking, rapport goes beyond that by creating a relationship or bond with the victim.

In fact, building rapport is about creating a trusting relationship with the victim with the objective to make the victim feel comfortable and thus more prone to execute a given task or to give some sensitive information. As humans, we tend to share data freely with people we trust, and thus for an attacker, developing an instant rapport is key.

There are many tactics that an attacker can leverage to create rapport, so let's see the most used tactics to develop rapport.

Using appropriate body language

To develop rapport, it is key that the victim doesn't perceive you as a potential threat; instead, you should represent a friendly figure that is there to help and listen. For example, for an attacker, a stressed or nervous attitude may cause distrust in the victim, while a relaxed attitude will be reflected in a more friendly body language that will make the victim feel more engaged and comfortable.

Figure 1.12 – Example of using body language to influence the victim

As seen in the preceding figure, a person with relaxed body language gives confidence to the victim to perform a dangerous action (in this case, to provide a security PIN).

Using your knowledge to help

Being arrogant by presuming deep technical knowledge will not help to build rapport. Instead, attackers will look for opportunities to help others with their technical knowledge. This tactic will help to build an almost instant rapport with the victim because first, the victim is now in debt to the attacker, but also because the attacker unconsciously set themselves as a technical expert in the eyes of the victim.

Figure 1.13 – Using your knowledge to build rapport

As seen in the preceding figure, the attacker uses their knowledge to build rapport with the victim while also setting themself as an expert. Then, they leverage it to execute the attack by giving a false link to the victim that will collect the victim's credentials.

Figure 1.14 – Example of using compliments to influence the victim

As seen in the preceding figure, the attacker compliments the victim by stating that they are very smart and cares about security. That compliment creates rapport and the attacker will leverage that to trick the user to put their password into a non-secure page, allowing the attacker to capture the victim's credentials.

Supporting other points of view

There are people that may feel discriminated against because their opinion is part of a minority group. In those cases, an attacker may leverage that to create instant rapport by supporting that point of view in front of the victim. As mentioned, this needs to seem genuine and to achieve that, the attacker must understand the topic they are supporting very well in order to be able to drive a friendly conversation with the victim to further their relationship of trust.

Figure 1.15 – Example of influencing the victim by creating a rapport

As seen in the preceding figure, an attacker would take the opportunity of someone complaining about security policies to agree with the victim (to build rapport) and then to offer a "solution" to avoid that security policy, which, in the end, will enable the attacker to access data and corporate systems.

Leveraging empathy

Empathy is defined as the ability to understand and share the feelings and emotions of others. In this case, an attacker will put themselves in a difficult situation in the hope that the victim will feel empathy and then be more vulnerable to fall into a trap to give information, perform a questionable action, or even bypass a security process to help the attacker during the difficult situation.

Figure 1.16 – Using empathy to bypass some security controls

The preceding figure shows a great example of how an attacker can leverage empathy to bypass a security control.

Notice that to enhance the chances of success, the attacker will search for a victim that is more likely to feel empathy for a given situation. For example, in this case, the attacker targeted a victim that is a mom and, therefore, is more likely to feel empathy for a situation in which a supposedly pregnant girl is suffering, and thus the victim would be willing to bypass a security process to help the pregnant girl.

Leveraging influence for defensive security

The good news is that you can also apply those psychological principles (such as influence) to enhance the cybersecurity culture in your organization.

In fact, here are some examples of how you can leverage some social engineering concepts in your organization:

- **Social proof**: You can leverage influential people in your company to promote cybersecurity best practices. A good implementation example is to provide a hands-on cybersecurity awareness workshop to those influential employees and name them *Cybersecurity Advocates*. This will help you motivate those influencers to enhance cybersecurity awareness across the organization and also to bring more to join your program as Cybersecurity Advocates.

> **Important note**
> Those kinds of programs work better if people are also awarded a digital badge that highlights their new Cybersecurity Advocate title.

- **Scarcity**: You can apply scarcity in many ways to enhance your cybersecurity programs, such as the following examples:

    - Announce that only X number of employees are eligible for the Cybersecurity Advocate title
    - Limit the number of people that can attend awareness training (which brings the feeling that they will attend an exclusive training)
    - Make users think that installing a given cybersecurity tool is not an obligation but a privilege that they need to pursue (because they are getting a license for free)

    As mentioned before, this technique is more powerful when combined with other tactics.

- **Authority**: One of the biggest challenges of cybersecurity campaigns is to get users involved. People are normally busy doing their day-to-day activities, and additional assignments (such as cybersecurity awareness training) are not a priority for most of them. However, you can leverage the principle of authority by asking a C-suite executive (CEO, CTO, etc.) to be the sponsor of the initiative. That sponsorship means recording a video or sending an email to the entire organization to highlight the importance and relevance of the cybersecurity initiative. Another great way to deliver this message is during a corporate event such as a Town Hall meeting. This will surely help to bring people's attention to your cybersecurity awareness program.

> **Important note**
> Some authors suggest that the executive should also highlight the consequences of not attending the required training; however, that may bring a negative connotation to your initiative, and from experience, it is better for people to be motivated to learn rather than forced by fear.

All other principles can also be used (and mixed) to support your cybersecurity initiatives, and now, it is up to your imagination to create the perfect blend to improve your cybersecurity strategy.

Summary

In this chapter, we learned the art of manipulation and how attackers leverage a number of techniques to influence the actions of the victims. We also reviewed the most common profiles targeted by attackers using social engineering.

Then, we moved to a deep dive into the actual tactics and principles used by attackers to influence the victims during a social engineering attack, which included key topics such as scarcity, liking, social proof, and others.

Additionally, we explained what developing rapport means and why this is relevant during a social engineering attack. After that, we moved to a new section in which we explained how attackers leverage people's empathy to manipulate the victims to bypass some security processes.

We then closed an amazing chapter by reviewing how we can also leverage those principles to support our cybersecurity strategy.

Now, get ready because, in the next chapter, we will acquire a deeper understanding of social engineering by reviewing the different types of social engineering attacks.

Further reading

To further your knowledge of the various topics discussed in the chapter, refer to the following resource:

- *System and Method to Prevent Scams* by Cesar Bravo, Peter Bahrs, and David Blyler. This patent shows a cognitive system capable of identifying and preventing scam attacks: `https://patents.google.com/patent/US10944790B2/en?inventor=cesar+bravo`.

2
Understanding Social Engineering

In the previous chapter, we learned how criminals leverage some psychological principles to execute successful social engineering attacks. Now, it's time to understand social engineering attacks in depth by looking at how attackers leverage the popularity of social media to execute some of those attacks at scale, hitting as many victims as possible.

Attackers use a clever combination of social engineering techniques as well as ingenuity to create very interesting attacks that are designed to fool even the most experienced users. This chapter will give you the required skills to easily identify those attacks and understand how you can avoid them.

In a nutshell, the following topics will be discussed:

- Detecting social engineering attacks
- Exploring social media attacks
- The crypto scam

Technical requirements

There are no technical requirements for this chapter.

Detecting social engineering attacks

We can define social engineering as a non-technical attack vector that aims to exploit psychological principles to manipulate users to obtain access to physical places, data, and systems. As mentioned previously, social engineering is an art and while it may not require technical skills, it requires a lot of manipulation skills to successfully trick the victim. Successful social engineers are charismatic, smart, and empathic, and know how to read the victim to act and react according to the situation without blowing their cover.

Before executing a social engineering attack, the attacker will fabricate a story that supports the selected manipulation technique.

To create the story, the attacker will study the victim, the company, and even the person that they are trying to impersonate. This is done to enhance their credibility, build trust, and avoid raising any suspicions from the victim.

However, there is a good technique that you can use to spot a social engineering attack that consists of asking the attacker several questions to blow their cover. This technique is very effective because it can make the attacker nervous, which may influence the attacker to abandon the attack.

To apply this defensive technique, you need to ask questions that only the real person knows. Another technique is to repeat a similar question with a different context to confuse the attacker and potentially destroy their cover by providing different answers to the same question. You can also ask for unexpected (or false) information from the attacker to discourage them from continuing with the attack for fear of being caught, as illustrated in *Figure 2.1*:

Figure 2.1 – Detecting a social engineering attack

> **Important note**
> If you find that someone is impersonating another person and that you are facing a social engineering attack, you must remain calm and provide wrong answers to encourage the attacker to stop the attack. Confronting the attacker (especially when face to face) could represent a threat to your security, so using a subtle technique to discourage the attacker is your best choice.

Social media attacks

Back in the 90s, many social engineering attacks were executed in person, including manipulating people to get unauthorized physical access to an office or physically retrieving papers with data from the office trash bins (a technique known as dumpster diving). However, in-person attacks carry a higher risk of being caught or identified if the attack is not successfully executed.

On the other hand, virtual attacks came with the advantage of anonymity, in which the risk of being identified or caught is less likely to happen. And now attackers are also leveraging the popularity of social media sites as a channel to impersonate people and execute a plurality of scams.

With billions of active users, **Facebook** is one of the most popular social media sites, which also makes it one of the favorite platforms used by attackers to scam people using social engineering. However, the following attacks are not limited to Facebook since attackers use other platforms such as Instagram, Twitter, and more. *Figure 2.2* shows the high number of hours that Facebook users spend on this platform every month:

Figure 2.2 – Average time spent by Facebook users each month

The best way to prevent social engineering attacks is by spreading awareness, so let's look at the most common social engineering attacks that are executed on social media sites.

The lost passport

This is an interesting attack with two types of victims: the person who got their social media account stolen and all their contacts, who will be the ones scammed by the attacker.

To achieve this, the attacker first needs to compromise a social media account. This can be done using a plurality of methods:

- **Phishing**: This is a social engineering attack that consists of sending emails, SMSs, or phone calls impersonating a real user identity to steal the personal information of victims
- **Man in the middle**: This is an attack that consists of a "*threat actor*" that captures the data of the interaction between a user and an application
- **Malware**: This consists of downloading or installing malicious software that is programmed to steal victims' personal information
- **Keylogging**: This type of attack is designed to record all the interactions the victim does with a computer keyboard and send this information to attackers
- **Social engineering**: In this type of attack, the attacker plays with the psychology of the victims to make them perform some actions that will allow the attacker to steal their confidential information

Once the attacker has access to the account, they start *phase two* of the attack, which consists of sending a message to all the contacts. This message is part of an elaborate plot that consists of manipulating the victim by using empathy and trust, as follows:

1. The attacker analyzes the recently hacked social media account to have a clear profile of the person who they will be impersonating.
2. The attacker then identifies and classifies the person's friends based on their relation with the victim (family, friends, work friends, and so on).
3. The attacker will then attack a group of the victim's friends who are not close enough to know personal details, such as whether the person is traveling or not. This may involve avoiding close family members who should be aware of any trip, and instead, targeting other friends who may not be aware of whether the victim is traveling or not.
4. The attacker contacts the second victim in a very friendly way to start the conversation.
5. Once rapport is created, the attacker *injects* the scam by telling a compelling and sad story about how their dream trip to Europe was just ruined because a criminal stole their wallet with their passport.
6. Then, they continue by saying that they are OK but are now facing a problem because, to get a new passport, they need some money.
7. To make the history even more credible, the attacker requests that the victim use a secure transfer method (because, you know, a criminal may intercept it), so they ask to send the money under their name using an international service such as Western Union.
8. Once the money has been transferred, the attacker will use a fake ID to collect the money.
9. *Figure 2.3* shows a real example of the lost passport attack.

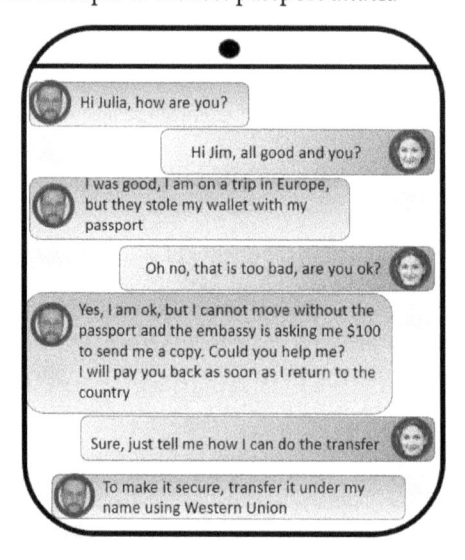

Figure 2.3 – Example of the stolen passport scam

Remember that this is only an example and attackers may tweak the conversation a bit to keep the attack relevant and undetected.

The federal government grant

This attack starts like the previous one – that is, by hacking a real social media account. Then, the attacker contacts some of the victim´s friends with a friendly chat. Once rapport is created, the attacker will start talking about a very interesting government assistance program that they (the person who is being impersonated) are enjoying.

If the victim shows any interest, then there are two possible attacks:

- **The link**: The attacker sends a link to the victim to enroll in this *amazing* program. The link then will either inject malware (to gain remote access to the system) or show a fake login screen to capture the victim's credentials.

- **The fake agent**: Once the victim shows interest in the governmental program, the attacker will put the victim in contact with a *friend* who "runs" that program to help the victim enroll faster and easier. Then, the fake government employee will request the victim to pay a little money to cover some administrative costs or taxes. We say little money because to manipulate the user, the amount required is less than 10% of the promised money, which is designed to be very tempting for the victim.

Keep in mind that the attacker may use other techniques, such as adding a sense of urgency to push the person to make a decision faster and without much analysis.

Romance scam

In this attack, the attacker creates a fake social media account to impersonate an attractive person (either male or female). Here, the main goal of the attacker is to use social engineering techniques to manipulate the person to *fall in love* and enter a virtual relationship.

> **Note**
> Be aware that attackers now leveraging **Generative Artificial Intelligence (GEN AI)** tools to create images of attractive people to create eye-catching profiles.

This type of attack requires time and dedication from the scammer; however, scammers are willing to invest time in creating this relationship because the chance of this scam´s success very high.

In fact, this is considered one of the most common and lucrative scams that grew by 80% in 2021. Additionally, authorities estimate that more than $547 million was lost in this scam, which confirms that this is a very lucrative scam (`https://consumer.ftc.gov/articles/what-know-about-romance-scams`).

Let's look at how this attack works:

1. The attacker starts by sending a friend request to the victim.
2. Once the victim accepts the friend request, the attacker starts a friendly conversation with the victim.
3. Then, the attacker charms the victim and starts a *virtual relationship*.
4. Once the victim is *in love*, the attacker will plan a visit to meet the victim (in person) and formalize the relationship (it is important to highlight that, in most cases, the scammer claims to be in a different country).
5. In some cases, the attacker will even send fake tickets to trick the victim and create an illusion of commitment.
6. As with many other scams, there are different methods to achieve the final scam. The most common are as follows:
    A. Call the victim from the airport, saying that the airline is requesting some extra money. Then, the attacker requests the victim to transfer that amount of money to continue the trip to meet the love of their life.
    B. Call the victim from the airport saying that authorities are asking for some extra money (related to a visa or taxes) and that it must be paid immediately because otherwise, they will lose the flight.
    C. Call the victim saying that they missed the connecting flight and that some money is needed to pay for that ticket to reach the final destination.
7. In most cases, if the victim performs the transfer, the attacker will find another excuse to continue with the scam and obtain more money.

Now that we know how this type of scam works, let's look at how we can identify and avoid falling for it.

Avoiding the romance scam

As with other scams, there are several red flags that you can look for to identify this scam:

- The person (scammer) is out of the country
- Special interest in speeding up the relationship
- Requesting money (either by transfer, gift card, etc.) with a sense of urgency

The following figure illustrates additional red flags to identify the romance scam:

Figure 2.4 – How to identify the romance scam

Keep in mind that the attacker also uses the romance scam as a way to perform different types of extorsions, as we will review in depth in *Chapter 6*.

Fake investment

This scam consists of investment posts on social media sites that offer very good returns without any skill, education, or experience required.

There are several variations of this scam, but in general, the scammer will use some social engineering tactics to gain the trust of the victim, persuade the victim, and then steal the victim's money. Let's look at each of them in detail:

- **Gaining trust**: Once the victim contacts the scammer, the attacker will try to gain the user's trust using any of the following methods:

    - Show pictures of the payslips of other investors (as proof of potential income)
    - Deposit the payment of the first day of work
    - Show pictures of luxury offices
    - Show testimonials from other investors

    Here, the attacker will show (and fabricate) as much evidence as needed to convince the victim that the company is real.

- **Persuading the victim**: Here, the attacker needs to use some extra social engineering skills to persuade the victim that this is a unique opportunity to make easy money.

  Additionally, the attacker also needs to persuade the victim to join them as soon as possible as this will prevent the victim from diving deeper into the company or contacting any government agency to validate the veracity of the company.

- **Gathering the money**: The final step is to take the money from the victim. This is especially complicated because *hey, who pays to work?*

  However, here is where social engineering comes into play: convincing the victims to willingly deposit hundreds (even thousands) of dollars to get the promised returns.

Here are some social engineering concepts that are used by attackers in this type of scam:

- **Sense of urgency**: *Do it now or you will miss this opportunity.*
- **Pressure**: *If you don't do it now, I will give this to another person waiting in the queue.*
- **Manipulation**: *Sorry, this amazing opportunity is only for people who can afford it.*
- **Empathy**: *I know you really want this investment. I spoke with my manager and he authorized me to give you a 50% discount if you join us now! But you need to hurry up because he needs to approve the transaction and he is leaving in 30 minutes.*
- **Social pressure**: They will transfer you to another person to convince you that if you don't pay now, you will lose the opportunity of your life.

The following figure shows an example of a fake investment scam:

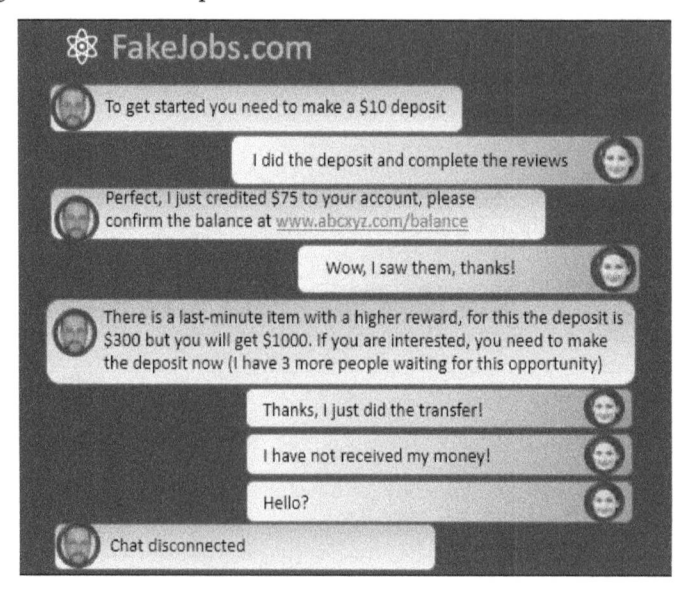

Figure 2.5 – Fake investment scam

As seen in *Figure 2.5*, the scammer gives the victim a *bait* to show that the investment involves high rewards; then, they offer a higher reward to get a higher amount of money from the victim. Also, as shown in this example, several social engineering tactics were used, such as manipulation (the $75 bait), sympathy and empathy (*I will give this great opportunity to you*), and a sense of urgency (*do it now or someone else will take advantage of this opportunity*).

Another item to highlight here is that, in most cases, the first deposit that's given to the victim (the $75 bait) is normally reflected on the dashboard of the scammer's website, as illustrated in the following figure:

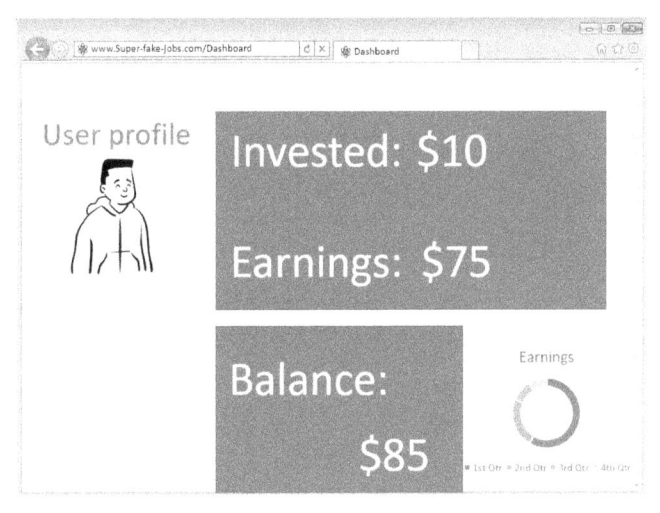

Figure 2.6 – Fake dashboard

However, the user will not be able to retrieve any money because the website is fake. In fact, in cases when the user requests to withdraw the first deposit, the attackers will provide a plurality of excuses to delay the user request, such as *the deposit to your bank is in transit, we did the deposit, please contact your bank*, and many more.

If the user insists, the account on the fake web page will be deleted, and all access to the scammer's social accounts will be blocked.

Fake advertisements

A common scam involving social engineering techniques is the fake advertisements (ads) scam. This scam is based on publishing ads on social media with incredible deals. The most common examples are as follows:

- Discounted electronics
- Refurbished goods
- Return pallets

As an example, the following figure shows some of the fake ads that are published on social media sites:

Figure 2.7 – Fake ads scam

Again, this type of scam also involves social engineering techniques:

- **Social proof**: To make the trap more credible, attackers use fake accounts to like the post and give more credibility to the scam. In some cases, attackers may even purchase likes to increase the credibility of the post. Also, sometimes, they use those fake accounts to post positive experiences to trick the victims into believing this is a real bargain, as shown in the following figure:

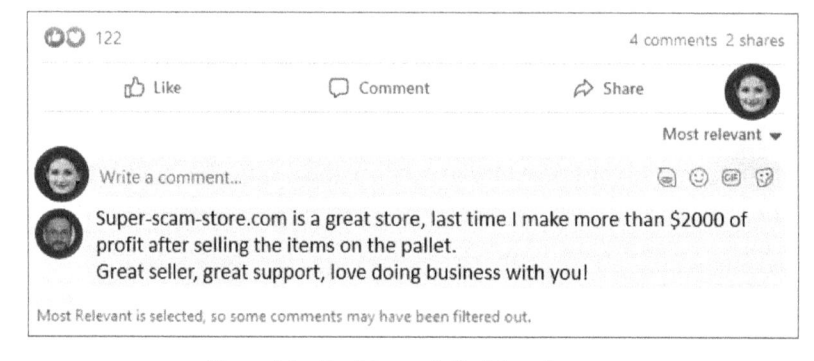

Figure 2.8 – Social proof of a fake ads scam

- **Reciprocity**: Once the victim contacts the scammer, they will try to make the user purchase the product they are selling. However, if the user does not seem to be interested in buying it, the scammer may use reciprocity by offering something to the user, thus influencing the victim into buying at least one product:

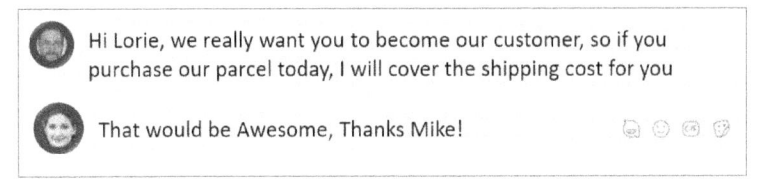

Figure 2.9 – Reciprocity of a fake ads scam

- **Scarcity**: To put pressure on the victim and ensure the victim falls into the trap, the attacker may use the scarcity tactic by saying that they have very few products available at a discounted price. Additionally, the attacker may also state that this is a one-time offer that ends soon, as illustrated in the following figure:

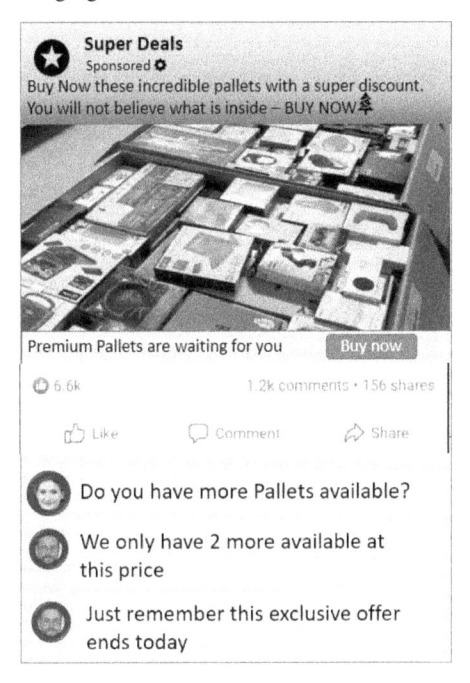

Figure 2.10 – Scarcity of a fake ads scam

As with other scams, the final execution of the fraud varies, but in general, there are two main types:

- The company just disappears and never sends anything to the victim.
- The seller sends low-quality items, empty boxes, or related materials. For example, instead of sending 10 iPhones, the attacker will send 10 iPhone cases; once the user claims that they were expecting the phone, then the scammer will either disappear or request more money to send the phones (which is only an extension of the original scam). Many victims fall into this trap with the hope of recovering part of the investment (but in the end, they just lose more money).

> **Market of likes**
>
> In social media, likes are seen as a way of endorsement, so there are companies that manage thousands of fake accounts and use them to sell likes. Prices vary from $10 for 200 likes to only $5 for 10,000 likes. However, as you may guess, some of those cheap services are a scam itself.

While some attacks may be carried across many social media sites, some attacks are more present on a given social network. Now, let's look at the crypto scam attack.

Social engineering and the crypto scam

This is a very interesting attack; in fact, the attack is so clever that even some experts have fallen for this well-crafted attack.

The attack is simple, yet brilliant. Here, the attacker sends a message to the victim, pretending it was sent by mistake as the intended recipient should be another person.

While this attack is not exclusively done via WhatsApp, the fact that WhatsApp is used by millions around the world as the main form of communication makes this platform one of the most commonly used for this attack. However, there is evidence of attackers using other social media platforms such as Twitter and even dating sites to execute this scam.

Now, to illustrate this attack, let's look at the following figure, which shows how the attacker engages the victim:

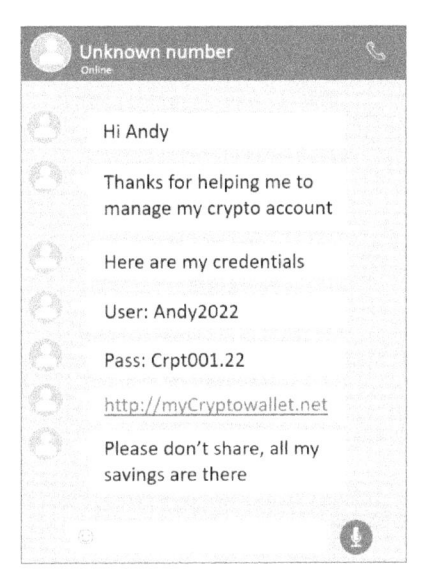

Figure 2.11 – Wrong message scam

Here, the attack is aimed at one of the oldest weaknesses in humans: **greed**. The message (which seems to have been sent to the wrong person) is a trap for the victim.

Once the user enters the site with the provided login information, a dashboard will be presented, showing an account with a lot of money (hundreds of thousands and even millions of dollars). Now, let's look at a real example to understand how this dashboard works and how the scam is executed.

Now, let's start with the main dashboard:

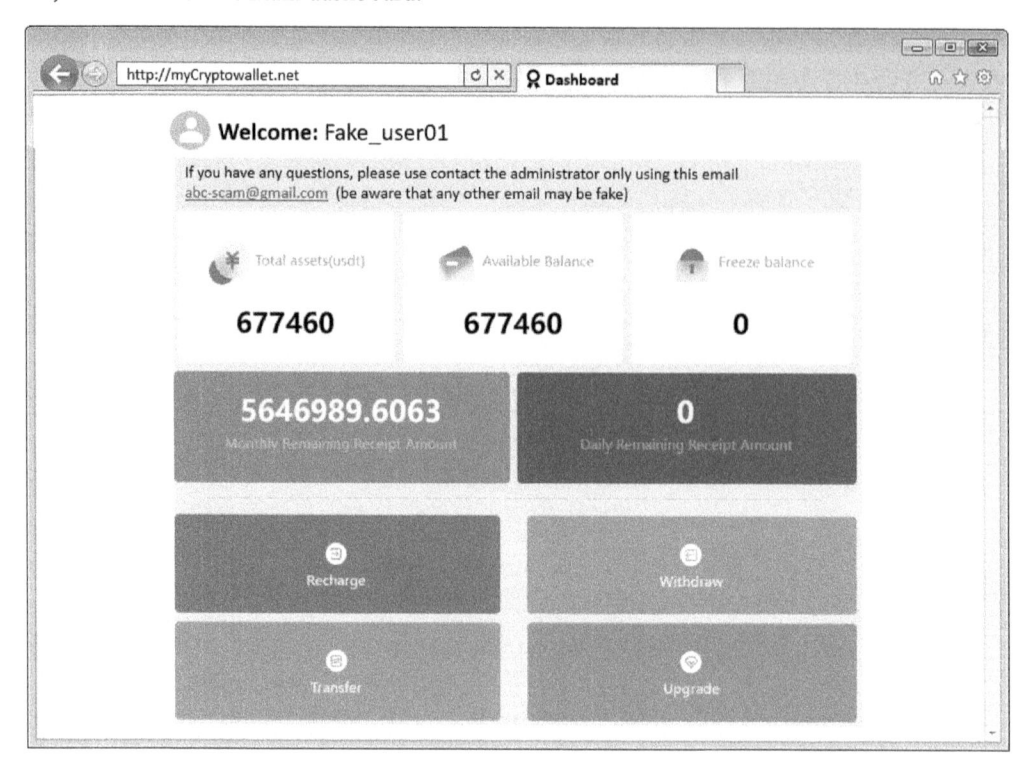

2.12 – Scam dashboard

Let's review the preceding figure from the point of view of the victim. First, the victim will be amazed to see that the credentials work and that they were able to log in to the user dashboard.

However, the victim is about to become astonished when they realize that the account balance is almost $1 million (in this case, it's $677.460).

> **Manipulating the user**
> To make the scam more credible, the dashboard is password protected and you will only be able to access it by entering the right username and password combination. This is a clever social engineering tactic to manipulate the user into thinking this page is real and not a scam.

Now, let's look at each of the options available:

- **Recharge**: This option allows the user to add funds to the account. It provides a Bitcoin address, plus detailed step-by-step instructions on how to perform the transfer. The following figure shows the recharge interface, which includes a QR code to make it easier for the victim to recharge funds:

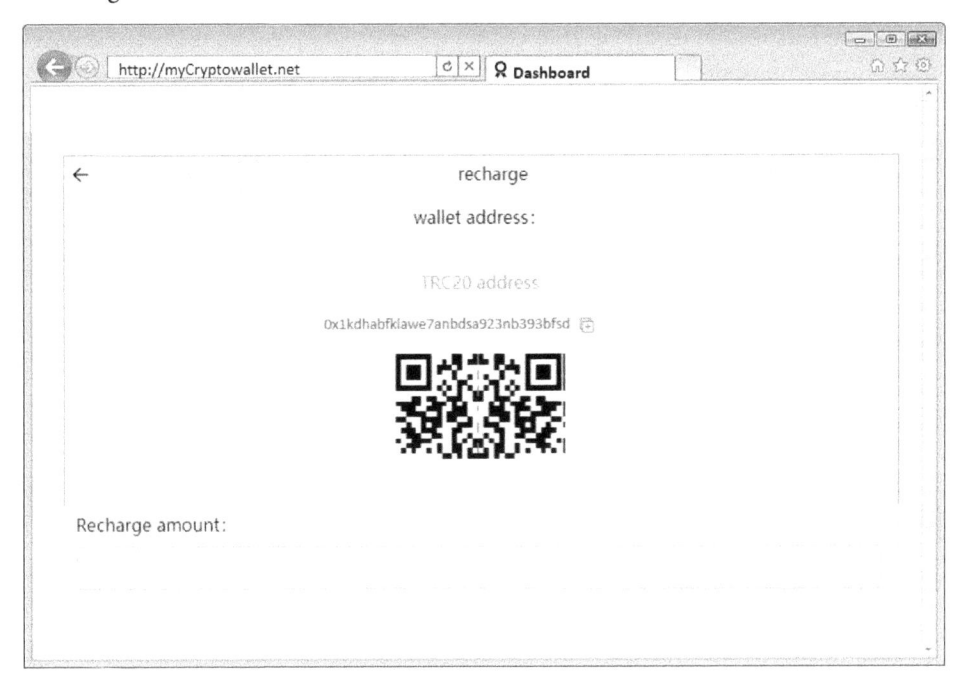

Figure 2.13 – Recharge dashboard

- **Withdraw**: This is probably the option that will immediately call the attention of the victim (*the gateway to easy money*) but not too fast – as shown in *Figure 2.14*, to do the withdrawal, the user needs a security key, which the victim doesn't have.

  However, this window is also full of items that have been carefully crafted to manipulate the victim, as highlighted here:

  - **Balance**: A subtle reminder of the potential gain. This serves as a motivation to ensure the victim stays on the page.
  - **Withdrawal success**: The attacker wants to manipulate the victim by showing that withdrawing money is possible and that more than $271,000 has already been withdrawn from the account. To make it even more realistic, the page also shows a withdrawal record that includes all *transactions*:

32 Understanding Social Engineering

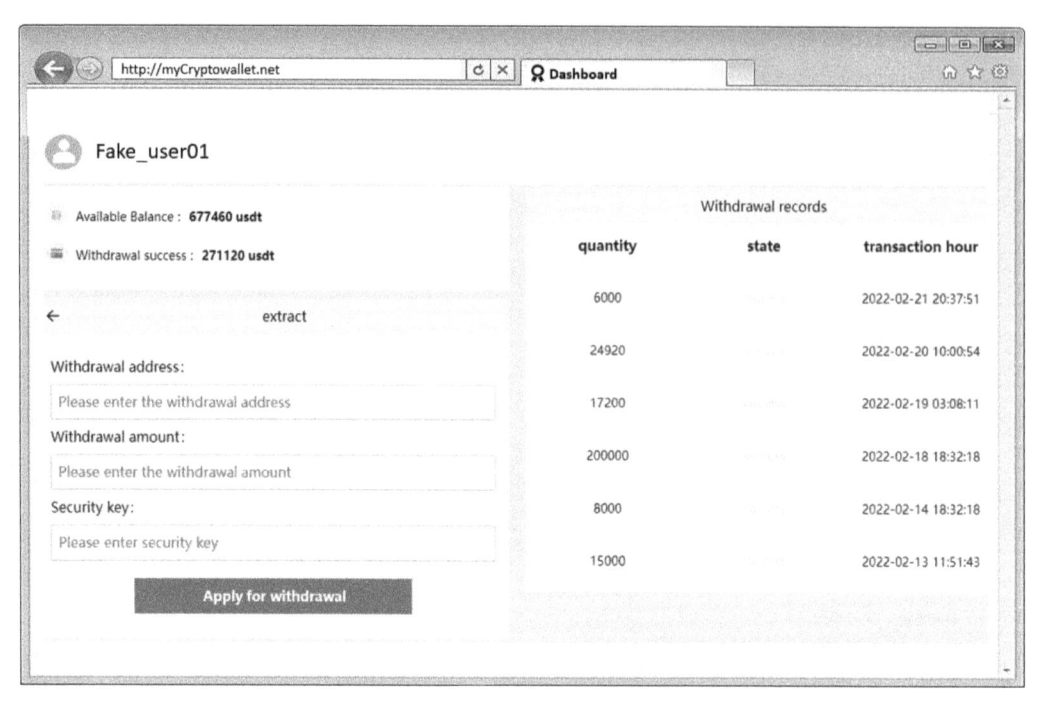

Figure 2.14 – Withdrawal dashboard

- **Transfer**: This option is a key part of the scam because, at first glance, this is the option that will grab the attention of the victim and make them think, *I can obtain the money here*. However, what the victim does not know is that this is exactly what the attacker wants you to think; let me explain why.

First, remember that this is social engineering at its best, and here, the attacker is playing with the victim's emotions because while the victim is feeling that they will win easy money, the reality is that they are about to lose some.

Now, as mentioned previously, this attack is simple but very clever because, as shown in *Figure 2.15*, the attacker shows the available balance in bold to make this more attractive and remind the victim of the potential price.

Then, to make this even more attractive, notice that the button says **One-click transfer without password**. *Now, you may be wondering, why is this important?* Well, this is telling the victim *This is the easiest way to get the money*, because here, you don't need the password (as in the previous option). In this case, you only need to select the destination account, add the amount, and boom – you are only one click away from becoming rich… however, it is not that simple.

One very interesting detail about this attack is that the attacker manipulates the victim by adding extra information – for example, the big button that says **without a password** or the other account field that says **you need at least a VIP level 1 account to receive the money**.

These are very subtle ways to manipulate the victim's brain and guide them to the trap. Now, the attacker already *injected* into your brain that you only need a VIP 1 account to become rich, so naturally, the victim's next step will be to find a VIP level 1 account:

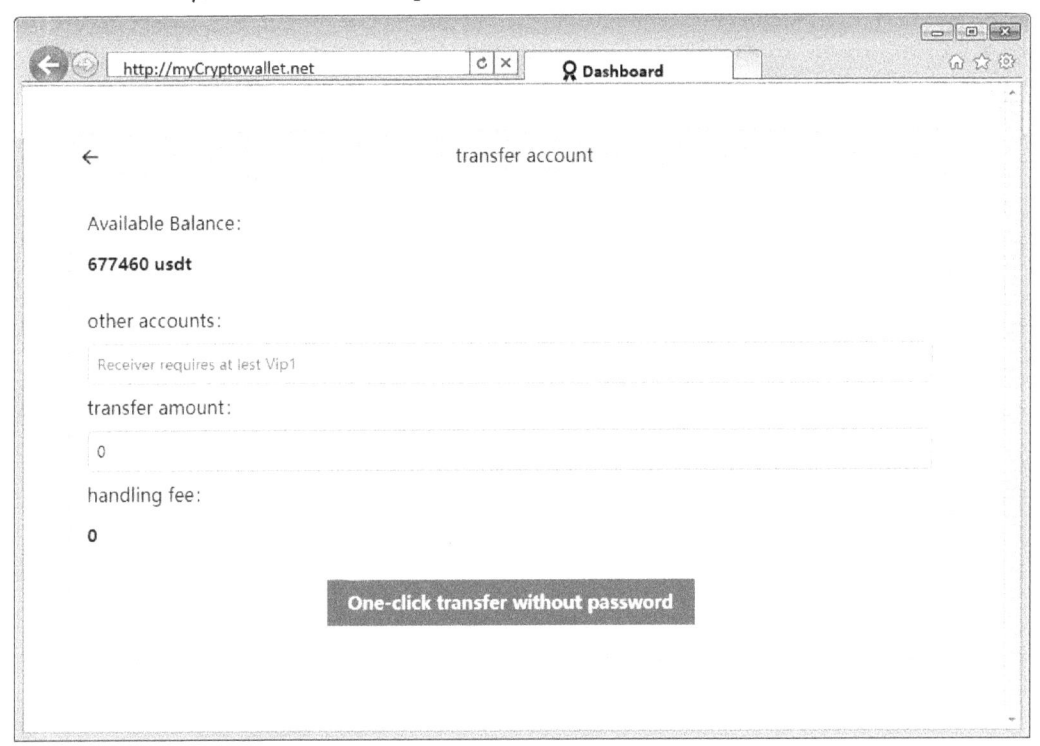

Figure 2.15 – Transfer dashboard

- **Upgrade**: As shown in *Figure 2.12*, the attacker even manipulates the victim with the placement of buttons because they were carefully placed to make the victim navigate through each of them until they arrived at their final destination: the **Upgrade** button.

> **Tip**
> Remember that, as shown in *Figure 2.15*, the only option to take the $600,000 out of this account is by having another account to transfer those funds. This is another manipulation method to ensure the user creates an account on the site.

As shown in *Figure 2.16*, the page starts by explaining (again) that you need at least VIP Level 1 to transfer funds to your account. Additionally, the page outlines the different types of VIP levels and the associated benefits and costs. Here, the attacker is also influencing the victim to purchase the most expensive VIP level because the higher the level, the higher the amount that can be transferred (in this example, the attacker is telling you that if you want to take all the money ($600,000), then you need to upgrade to Level 5):

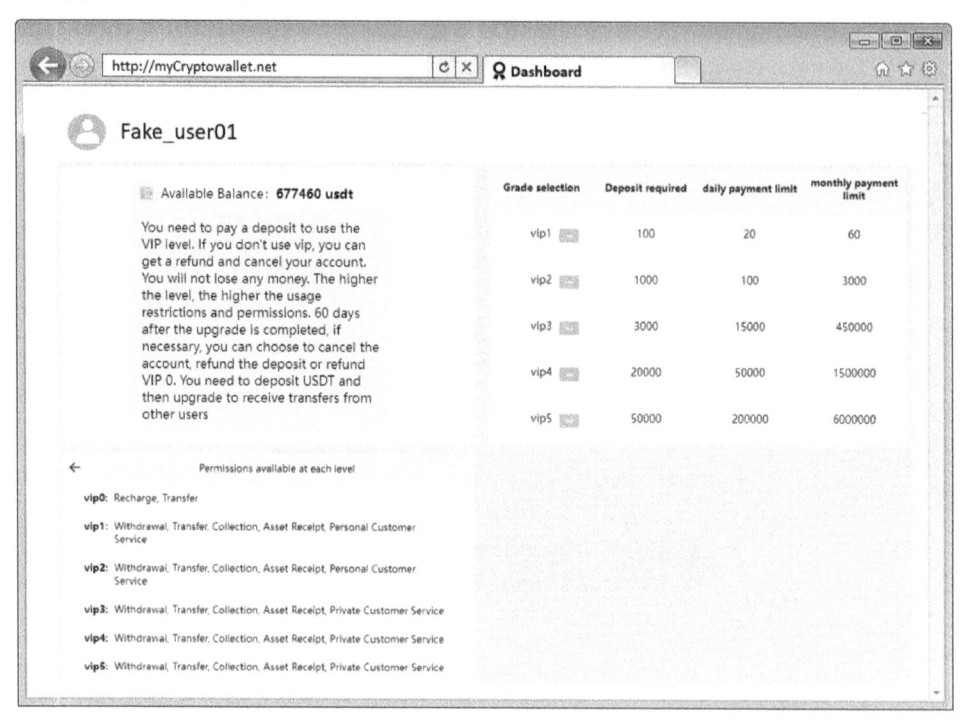

Figure 2.16 – Upgrade dashboard

And that's it! The victim then creates a new account, purchases a VIP level, and the attack is complete.

In most cases, it will take days for the victim to realize that it was a trap and that instead of *winning* $600,000, the reality is that they lost money.

But this is not all – the attacker can increase the impact of the scam by doing the following:

- Capturing the credit card information of the victim
- Getting access to the victim's crypto wallet (and stealing all their crypto assets)
- Using the password created by the victim (to create the new account) and testing whether it works on other user pages such as social media sites, banks, email, and more

In the end, this scam is a good example that we must be careful of when it's presented in a situation that seems too good to be true.

Additionally, this scam is also a great example of how a combination of social engineering techniques can easily manipulate a user to perform an action *unwillingly*, such as depositing money or crypto assets on an untrusted web page.

Summary

In this chapter, we understood the importance of detecting a social engineering attack and how people can securely avoid such threats. We also provided a comprehensive overview of the most common social engineering attacks on social media and how you can avoid them.

Additionally, you learned about the latest (and the most clever) social engineering attack, the crypto scam, which deceives the user into thinking that they are about to get access to the crypto account of a careless user, while in reality, they are about to get scammed.

In the next chapter, we'll review the most common types of scams and how to avoid them.

3
Common Scam Attacks

The evolution of the digital world has put humanity in front of different cyber risks and one of the most common is **scam attacks**. From fake emails and phone calls to elaborate online schemes, scammers are becoming cleverer in attacking their victims. A **scam attack** is a manipulation scheme that uses social engineering techniques to trick victims so that the attacker can steal the victims' personal or financial information.

Scam attacks can have serious consequences for victims, including financial loss and emotional distress. It's important to be aware of the different types of scams that exist, and the different methods available to protect yourself, such as being cautious of unsolicited offers or requests for personal information, and not responding to threatening or intimidating messages.

In this chapter, we will cover the following main topics:

- What is a scam?
- **Advance-fee fraud**, also known as the Nigerian scam (419 fraud)
- Other famous scams
- Scambaiting

As mentioned previously, we will cover different types of scams but with a deeper view of **advance-fee scams** since it is one of the most famous scams and has been around for decades; it has proven very successful in tricking people into giving their money or personal information.

Technical requirements

There are no technical requirements for this chapter.

What is a scam?

A **scam** is a fraudulent scheme or deception intended to deceive someone into performing an unwanted action (perform an action, release private information, and so on) or to achieve some financial gains. Scams can take many forms, including email scams, phone scams, phishing scams, pyramid schemes, investing scams, and more.

As a cybersecurity expert, it is of utmost importance to be aware of the most common types of scams, as well as the most common methods and practices aimed at protecting yourself and your clients from them.

Although there are thousands of different types of scams that are growing by the day, most of them are variations or modified versions of the classic and well-known scams.

> **Note**
> One common aspect in most scams is spelling and grammatical errors; therefore, we intentionally included some of those errors in the illustrations to reflect that common characteristic.

Now, let's carefully review the most notorious types of scams.

The Nigerian scam (419)

The Nigerian scam, also known as **advance-fee fraud**, or the **419 scam**, is a type of scam in which the attacker contacts the victim and offers a large sum of money (or a valuable prize).

> **Note**
> The reason why this scam is called the **419 scam** is because it violates section 419 of the Nigerian Criminal Code, which deals with fraud.

Once the victim is hooked by the possibility of making easy money, the attacker will request a small **advance fee** to pay some taxes or pay for some paperwork required to send the money.

> **Note**
> This scam is not always about money – there have been many cases in which the scammer will try to collect some personal information from the victim so that it can be used to impersonate that person or be sold on the black market.

One common aspect of this attack is that the attacker normally impersonates a royal member, a wealthy individual, a government official, or a businessperson. The following figure shows an example of a common Nigerian scam:

Figure 3.1 – Example of the Nigerian scam

Is important to highlight that while this type of fraud is commonly associated with Nigeria (and hence the name), it is currently used by criminals from all around the world. This is sad because this damages the name of a beautiful country, even when this scam is not exclusively executed in this amazing place. This scam originated more than 200 years ago, so let's see how it all started.

The history of the scam

The oldest record of this type of scam dates back to 1898, when the New York Times wrote an article about this *swindle*:

Figure 3.2 – Extract of the newspaper article about the Spanish Prisoner scam

Something interesting from the article is that it confirms that the scam has been around for more than a century but also that it did not start in Nigeria with a person sitting in an internet cafe. During those years (around the 19th century), the scams were done by postal mail. An example of a variation of this scam was the letter of the Spanish Prisoner, an example of which is shown in the following figure:

```
Fort of Barcelona – 1885
Dear sir
I am taking the liberty to trust you with a secret that I have not trust to anyone
but my current sufering in prison is pushing me to do it.
I was the captain of my regiment during the war and during one battle I hide
1.000.000 pesetas to avoid them being sized by the enemy.
I need to recover that money urgently before someone else find it.
The only person that knows the exact location is my daughter Mikela, so if you
promise me that you will take care of her, I will give you her address in Spain
where you must go to pick her up.
In exchange for taking care of my 2 treasures, I am willing to compensate you
with 500.000 pesetas.
The only thing that you need to do is to promise me to keep this secret and to
provide the expenses needed for her travel as I can not cover those expenses due
to my situation in jail.
I beg your pardon me if I cannot write english well.
Saludos,
Komandante Cesar de Tirana
```

Figure 3.3 – Example of the Spanish Prisoner scam

There were other variations of this scam. In one variation, the scammer impersonated a Marquis in exile after the French Revolution and a few others changed the country of origin to some faraway countries, such as Cuba.

> **Important note**
> Since this attack is popularly known as the Nigerian scam, we will use that name across the book (only to make it easier for you). However, we hope that it is clear to you that this advanced fee scam did not originate in Nigeria.

There are other documented cases, such as when a 14-year-old committed mail fraud by sending letters impersonating a Nigerian prince asking for a few dollars and a pair of jeans. The interesting fact about this mail scam is that it happened back in 1949 and it was not done by a person in Nigeria, but instead by a 14-year-old boy from the US. We can only guess that maybe this joke was the genesis of the Nigerian scam.

Now that we know how all this started, let's do a deep dive into the topic by understanding how to recognize these scams.

Identifying the Nigerian scam

Here are some characteristics that will help you to identify these types of scams:

- The sender is a political figure or a high-ranking officer who needs help to take out some money or values from their country, as shown in the following *Figure 3.4*:

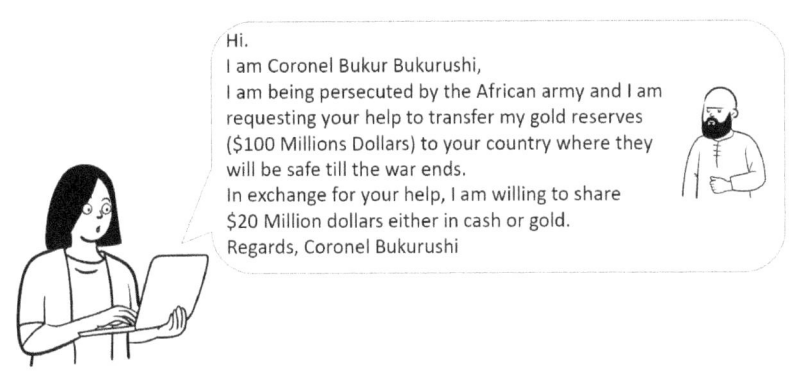

Figure 3.4 – Example of a scammer impersonating a high-ranking officer

- The sender is a very wealthy person in their last days and is looking for someone to donate their fortune to. The following figure shows an example in which the attacker offers generous compensation to whoever is willing to help them find a good charity to donate their money as illustrated in *Figure 3.5*:

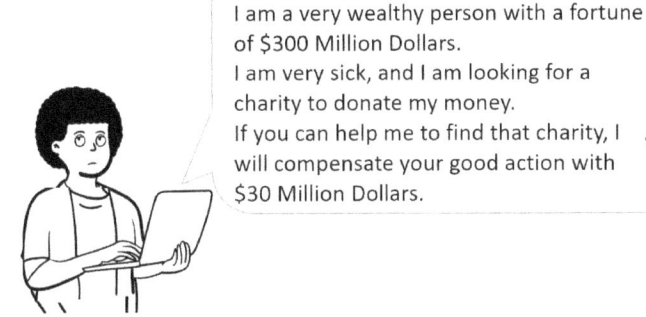

Figure 3.5 – A scammer impersonating a wealthy person

- The story presented by the attacker includes heartbreaking elements aimed to touch your feelings. As seen in the following *Figure 3.6*, in some cases their story is about the loss of a family member:

Figure 3.6 – A scammer using grief to create rapport

- They offer a ridiculous amount of money and, as seen in the following *Figure 3.7*, most of the time, the amount is expressed in millions of dollars:

Figure 3.7 – Scammer offering an incredible amount of money

- The sender asks the victim to be *discreet* and not to share the story with others. In the end, they know that other people are very likely to tell the victim that this is a scam, so for the attacker, the victim mustn't share this *million-dollar offer* with others. In some cases, once the victim transfers some money, the attacker will request the victim not to tell others, with the excuse that others may want to steal their millions, as illustrated in *Figure 3.8*:

Figure 3.8 – Scammer requesting discretion from the victim

- The attacker complements the victim, using statements such as *I am giving you this money because you are a good person*. Now, the attacker only wants to give compliments to hide their real intentions and create rapport, but these compliments are part of the pretext as the real intention of the scammer is to get money as soon as possible as illustrated in *Figure 3.9*:

Figure 3.9 – A scammer complementing the user to create rapport

- The email is about a sad history related to some personal or family tragedy (aimed to touch your sensitive side). For example, a Nigerian scam may involve the scammer impersonating a rich king in exile, asking for help to save his life and his kid. Notice that this example also shows other tactics, such as a sense of urgency and greed as seen in *Figure 3.10*:

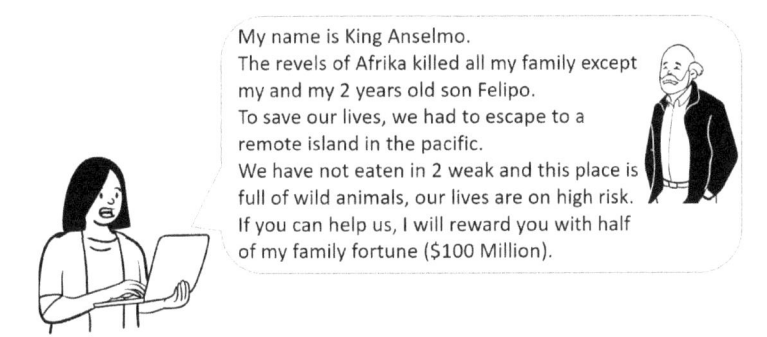

Figure 3.10 – A scammer impersonating a rich king needing help

- The following figure illustrates some additional characteristics that help identify these scams:

```
Email seems to target a          From: Company.com
group of people                  To: undisclosed recipients
The reply email is different     Reply to: <myfakemeail@arandompage.xyz>
from the one of the sender
                                 My name is King Anselmo.
The sender claims to be a        The revels of Afrika killed all my family except my and my 2
wealthy or powerful person       years old son Felipo.
They use certain words to        To save our lives, we had to escape to a remote island in
Touch your feelings and create   the pacific.
rapport
                                 We have not eaten in 2 weak and this place is full of wild
A sense of urgency               animals, our lives are on high risk.
                                 If you can help us, I will reward you with half of my family
Promise a huge amount of         fortune ($100 Million).
money
```

Figure 3.11 – Common items to identify a scam

Now that you've learned about the main characteristics of the Nigerian scam, it's time to dive deeper by understanding the different types and variations of the Nigerian scam.

Types of Nigerian scams

This scam has been around for decades, but it is still relevant and highly used by scammers. In fact, over the years, we have seen several variations of this scam. Here is a list of some of the most famous ones:

- **The Nigerian prince**: This is the classic Nigerian scam, where the scammer impersonates a wealthy Nigerian prince or government official who needs help transferring a large sum of money out of the country. In exchange, they ask either the victim to provide their bank account information or to pay a fee to release the funds.

- **The international transfer**: Here, the scammer offers the victim a portion of a large sum of money in exchange for their help in transferring the funds out of the country.

- **The lottery scam**: Here, the scammer tells the victim they have won a large sum of money in a lottery or raffle but must pay a small fee or provide personal information to claim the prize.

- **The inheritance scam**: Here, the scammer poses as the representative of a wealthy person who has died and left the victim a large sum of money but requires them to pay a fee to process the inheritance.

These are some of the most common scams that you may encounter; however, scammers are always creating new ingenious ways to evolve their attacks, so let's take a look at some of the more ingenious and craziest variations of the scams.

Funny Nigerian scams

Now, it is time to take a few minutes to look at some of the most interesting, crazy, and funny types of Nigerian scams.

The Ace Ventura scam

As crazy as this sounds, in the **Ace Ventura scam**, the attacker claims to be an exporter of exotic animals and offers a variety of animals for sale. The attacker claims that they collect and sell animals from all around Africa and offer monkeys, birds, and many other types of animals for a small fee.

There are two variations of this scam – one in which the attackers request the full payment of the animal (ranging from $100 to $1,000) and a new variation in which the attackers recognize the existence of some scammers affecting their business (yes, you read that right). To confirm that they are real, they offer for the animal to be paid for once it arrives at the victim's house.

However, there is always a catch and in the latter case, the attackers exchange several emails with the victim with the progress of the transaction and then request the victim to pay a small fee to bribe a customs official to send the animal.

Now, as you may imagine, there are no records of this scam being reported to the authorities because the victim is also doing (or conspiring to do) some unlawful actions, so this is an interesting case in which attackers do this attack with impunity as illustrated in *Figure 3.12*:

Figure 3.12 – An example of the animal scam

As shown in the preceding figure, the scammer will try to persuade the victim that this is a legitimate business and that this could be a way to make easy money.

The evil wife

This is a very rare scam, in which a wealthy old man is willing to give away a generous amount of his fortune in exchange for your help to take the money of his *evil* wife:

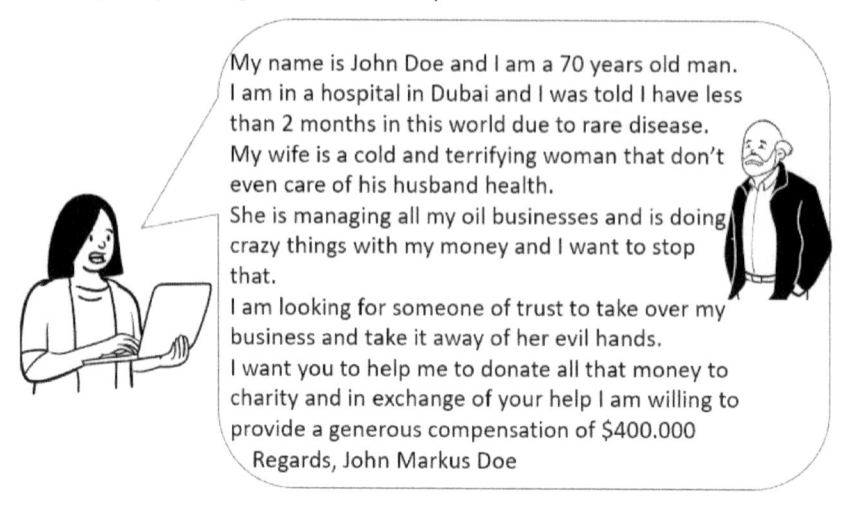

> My name is John Doe and I am a 70 years old man.
> I am in a hospital in Dubai and I was told I have less than 2 months in this world due to rare disease.
> My wife is a cold and terrifying woman that don't even care of his husband health.
> She is managing all my oil businesses and is doing crazy things with my money and I want to stop that.
> I am looking for someone of trust to take over my business and take it away of her evil hands.
> I want you to help me to donate all that money to charity and in exchange of your help I am willing to provide a generous compensation of $400.000
> Regards, John Markus Doe

Figure 3.13 – An example of the evil wife scam

Figure 3.13 illustrates a real example of the evil wife scam.

The Nigerian astronaut

Yes, you read that right – there is a new scam in which a supposed astronaut from the **Nigerian Space Research and Development Agency** (**NASRDA**) contacts you to ask for your help to come back to Earth.

The plot is that the astronauts were left behind in a special station in the 90s. Now, a group of government officials is trying to bring them back home, but to do that, they need to transfer $3,000,000 to the Russian space authorities to bring them back in a Soyuz spaceship.

The catch is that as government officials, they cannot do the direct transfer to the Russian space authorities, so they are looking for someone to help them do the transfer. In exchange for your help, the astronaut (who is eager to be back on Earth) is offering a juicy payment of $2,000,000. To make the plot sound more *credible*, the astronaut mentions that the government owes them all their salaries since 1990, which comes to a total of $15,000,000, so offering $2,000,000 is nothing for them. *Figure 3.14* shows an example of the astronaut scam:

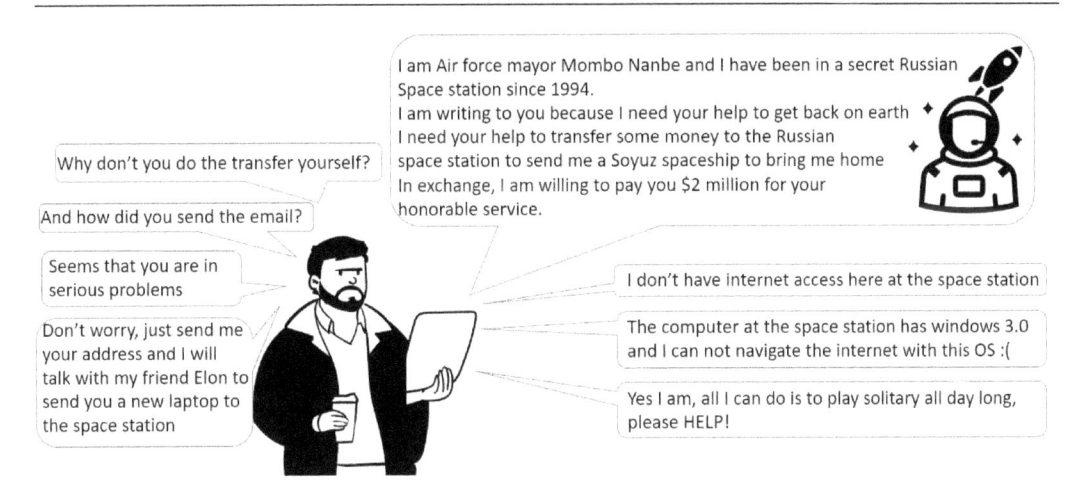

Figure 3.14 – An example of the Astronaut scam

As we can see, not all people fall for this scam, but a single victim lost 4.4 million yen in a single astronaut scam. You can read all about this incident here: https://www.yahoo.com/lifestyle/fake-russian-astronaut-scams-woman-112857866.html?guccounter=1.

Avoiding these scams

Knowing about all these types of scams is a great step to raise awareness, but here are some additional tips to prevent you from falling for these scams:

- Never disclose personal or sensitive information to unknown people via email (or social media), even if they claim to be a king or princess in distress.
- Do not reply to emails from unknown contacts.
- Distrust any request for a money transfer, even if it comes from one of your contacts. It could be a scammer that is impersonating their email or social media accounts.
- If you get an uncommon request via email from one of your contacts, then verify it by contacting your friend directly by phone (an early warning from the victim is key to preventing the attacker from scamming other friends).
- If an email is too good to be true, then it is a scam.
- Think twice! If you receive an email claiming that you won the lottery, ask yourself, *Did I participate in that lottery*?
- Don't reply to emails asking for more details – scammers are good and chances are that you will fall into their traps.

While the advance-fee scam is the most predominant scam, there are other very famous scams are worth reviewing, so let's take a look at them.

Other scams

There are hundreds of scams and is impossible to know all of them (in fact, scams are always evolving, so you may encounter a new attack every week).

However, let's review some additional scams that are currently on the rise and that you are very likely to encounter.

The investor scam

In the **investor scam**, the attacker claims to be from an investing company and offers you to join their investment scheme to double or triple your money. This is a very interesting scam because, in contrast to the Nigerian scam, those scammers sometimes have a real page and even a real office to provide confidence to the victims, they may even agree to meet in person to close the "*deal*". However, they will disappear after some time, leaving victims without their investments. *Figure 3.15* shows an example of this scam. In this example we added some typos and errors as it is common in many types of scams:

> we are not scammer, we hate scammer as you do.
>
> scammer make out life harder and harder, a lot of people think we are scammer, in fact, we are not!! please trustt us
>
> Open a sliver account: $1,000 to win and gain a maximum capital of $10,000

Figure 3.15 – Example of the investor scam

Figure 3.15 also shows a very interesting example in which their emails highlight that they are not scammers. That is in fact a technique used by the attackers to give some "validation" to the scam.

The Business Email Compromise scam

The **Business Email Compromise** (**BEC**) scam is considered by the FBI as *one of the most damaging online crimes*.

This scam targets companies and in most cases, the attacker will try to gather as much information as possible from the target company (using social engineering). Then, the attacker will impersonate either a business partner, a client, a provider, or even a high-ranking employee.

To perform the attack, the attacker will either spoof the email account of the person being impersonated or create a domain that is very similar to the one of the company, thus making the victim believe that the email is from a valid email account. The attacker will then request either confidential information or make a transfer to pay an urgent service or pending bill:

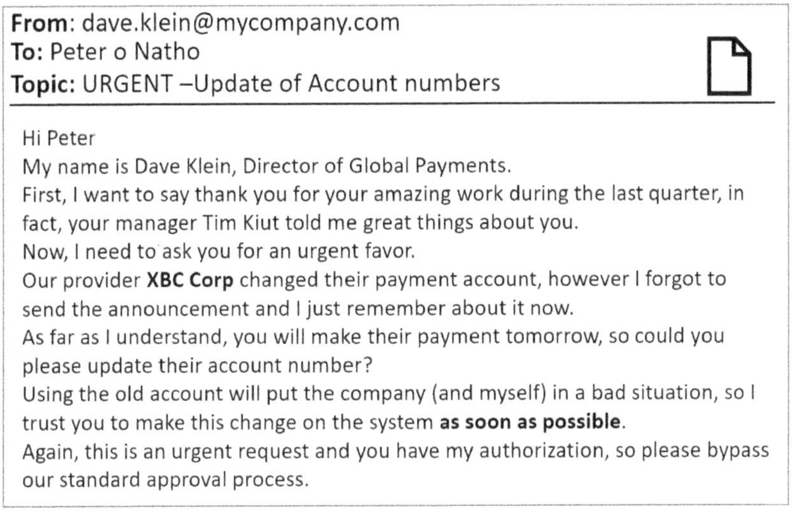

> **From**: dave.klein@mycompany.com
> **To:** Peter o Natho
> **Topic:** URGENT –Update of Account numbers
>
> Hi Peter
> My name is Dave Klein, Director of Global Payments.
> First, I want to say thank you for your amazing work during the last quarter, in fact, your manager Tim Kiut told me great things about you.
> Now, I need to ask you for an urgent favor.
> Our provider **XBC Corp** changed their payment account, however I forgot to send the announcement and I just remember about it now.
> As far as I understand, you will make their payment tomorrow, so could you please update their account number?
> Using the old account will put the company (and myself) in a bad situation, so I trust you to make this change on the system **as soon as possible**.
> Again, this is an urgent request and you have my authorization, so please bypass our standard approval process.

Figure 3.16 – Example of the BEC scam

As seen in the preceding *Figure 3.16*, the attack is full of social engineering techniques, including a sense of urgency, social pressure, liking, and authority, among others.

If you want to read more about this scam, I highly recommend this well-crafted article from the FBI: https://www.fbi.gov/how-we-can-help-you/safety-resources/scams-and-safety/common-scams-and-crimes/business-email-compromise.

Fraud compensation

This is a very malicious scam because it aims to trick people who have already been a victim of a scam.

Here, the scammer impersonates a government agency or organization that provides compensation to victims of scams. As with other scams, victims will fall prey to the temptation of obtaining a huge amount of money that, in some cases, they feel entitled to receive as compensation for the previous loss.

However, in the end, the scammer will either request some financial information or an advanced fee to proceed with the payment:

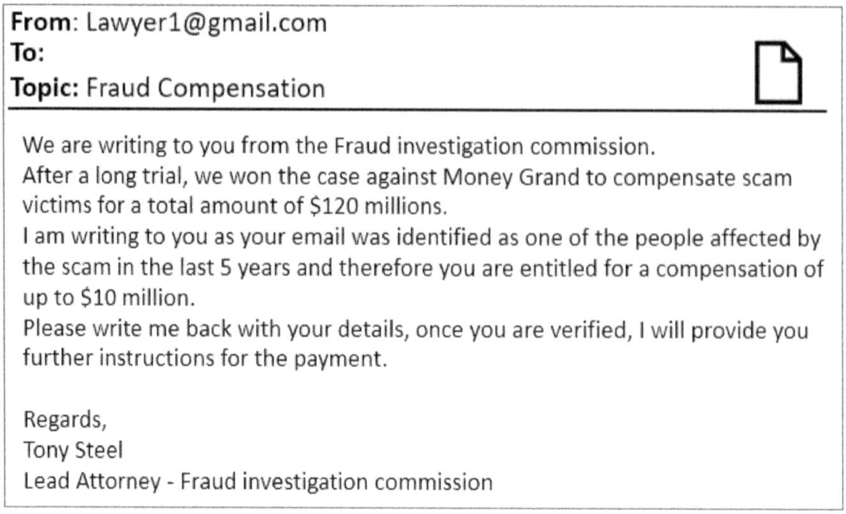

> **From**: Lawyer1@gmail.com
> **To**:
> **Topic**: Fraud Compensation
>
> We are writing to you from the Fraud investigation commission.
> After a long trial, we won the case against Money Grand to compensate scam victims for a total amount of $120 millions.
> I am writing to you as your email was identified as one of the people affected by the scam in the last 5 years and therefore you are entitled for a compensation of up to $10 million.
> Please write me back with your details, once you are verified, I will provide you further instructions for the payment.
>
> Regards,
> Tony Steel
> Lead Attorney - Fraud investigation commission

Figure 3.17 – Example of the fraud compensation scam

As shown in *Figure 3.17*, this is a very elaborate and dangerous scam.

Now that you have become an expert on different types of scams, let's look at an interesting technique that's used by the community to stop and prevent scams – **scambaiting**.

Scambaiting

Scambaiting is the art of scamming the scammer. Here, the idea is to make the scammer lose their time, which will prevent them from using that time to scam other potential victims. However, scambaiting can be dangerous, so this is not advised unless you have the proper training to do it.

There are several communities dedicated to scambaiting that provide tips on how to do it safely, forums with examples of scams, and even a wall of fame with funny pictures of the scammers.

You can gain access to some of the most recognized scambaiting communities at `https://www.419eater.com/` and `https://scammer.info/`.

Summary

In this chapter, we explored the different types of scams, including the famous **advance-fee fraud** and **investor scams**, before diving into newer forms of fraud, such as the **Business Email Compromise fraud**, which involves hackers gaining access to a business's email account and using it to send fraudulent requests for payments.

We also discussed other interesting types of fraud, such as **compensation fraud** and merciless scams, which target people who have already been victims of a scam and who are more likely to fall for this well-crafted secondary scam.

Additionally, we learned about the controversial practice of "scambaiting," and how this is used to fight back against scammers.

Overall, this chapter highlighted the importance of being aware of the different types of scams and the steps to protect yourself and your company from falling victim to them.

Join us in the next chapter, where we explore all the different types of social engineering attacks and how to identify and prevent them.

4
Types of Social Engineering Attacks

In this chapter, we are going to review the most common types of social engineering attacks to help you identify all the different types of attacks.

Understanding the different types of attacks is key because it will help you identify and apply the appropriate method or solution to avoid or mitigate that type of attack in your day-to-day life, as well as in your organization.

As mentioned previously, in this chapter, we will review the most common types of social engineering attacks, while also mentioning some unusual or unexpected types of scams such as dumpster diving, which, while they sound a bit silly, in reality, are very effective (in part because people don't expect those attacks, so they become more vulnerable).

Now, remember – it is important to keep your employees, peers, and friends aware of all these types of attacks because the first step in protecting yourself and your organization is to be able to identify those potential threats.

Also, keep in mind that these categories are not mutually exclusive, and many attacks can be categorized into multiple categories.

In this chapter, we will cover the following main topics:

- Phishing attacks:
  - History of phishing attacks
  - Famous phishing attacks
  - Types of phishing attacks:
    - Email phishing
    - SMS phishing (smishing)

- Voice phishing (vishing)
- Calendar phishing
- Technical support scam
- Baiting:
    - Physical baiting
    - Cyber baiting
- Dumpster diving
- Tailgating
- Quid pro quo:
    - Free tech support
    - Free software to download
- Pretexting:
    - Fake job offers
    - False charities
- Watering hole:
    - Crypto mining

Technical requirements

There are no technical requirements for this chapter.

Disclaimer

All the characters in this chapter's illustrations are fictional.

The illustrations are inspired by real attacks; therefore, the language used (including spelling and grammatical errors) is intentional.

There are many different types of social engineering attacks and the plurality of factors associated with each of them makes it a bit complicated to categorize them. For example, a technical support scam can be delivered by using a phishing email, a smishing message, or even a vishing attack, so in this chapter, we will try to explain the most common types of social engineering attacks in a way that is easy to understand to enable you to identify them successfully. In the end, the goal is not to be able to label the attack but to successfully recognize it while we are being targeted by any of them.

Now, let's start our journey and explore the most common types of social engineering attacks.

Phishing attacks

Phishing attacks are one of the most common types of cyberattacks and impact both individuals and corporations alike.

The attack is simple, and its name came from the word fishing as these attacks also use bait to make the victim fall into a trap. The difference is that, in this case, the bait is not a worm but a fraudulent email, text, voice, or call.

Normally, phishing attacks were used to gather sensitive information such as login credentials, credit card numbers, and other private information. However, over the last few years, phishing emails have become the method to deliver more dangerous (and complex) attacks, such as ransomware.

Phishing attacks became popular back in the 2000s when people started to massively adopt email as a day-to-day tool for personal and business use, allowing the attackers to attack a massive number of users with a single email.

History of phishing attacks

History tells us that this type of attack has existed since the mid-1990s, but in recent years, it has become more prevalent and sophisticated as this has become a very lucrative business for attackers and they keep reinventing the attacks to keep them relevant and effective.

It is impossible to talk about phishing attacks and not mention one of the first major attacks: **the 1995 America Online (AOL) attack**. AOL was one of the most powerful internet providers with millions of users and thousands of employees; however, the fact that it was a large company was what drew the attention of attackers and made it an appealing target.

> Note
>
> In retrospect, the attack may appear obvious, but during the 90s, the internet was a nascent technology, and people were still experimenting with it. Few were cognizant of the potential hazards associated with this new technology. As a result, techniques such as email attacks and forged (cloned) web pages were largely unfamiliar to the general public.

Going back to the attack, it was a very simple attack where the attackers sent an email to all AOL employees stating that their data had been compromised and asked them to update their personal information using the link in the email. The link redirected the victims to a fake AOL login page that seemed like the real thing but was only a fake page to steal the data.

As soon as the users entered their data, the attacker gained access to their AOL accounts and then used it to send spam or other malicious content to their contacts:

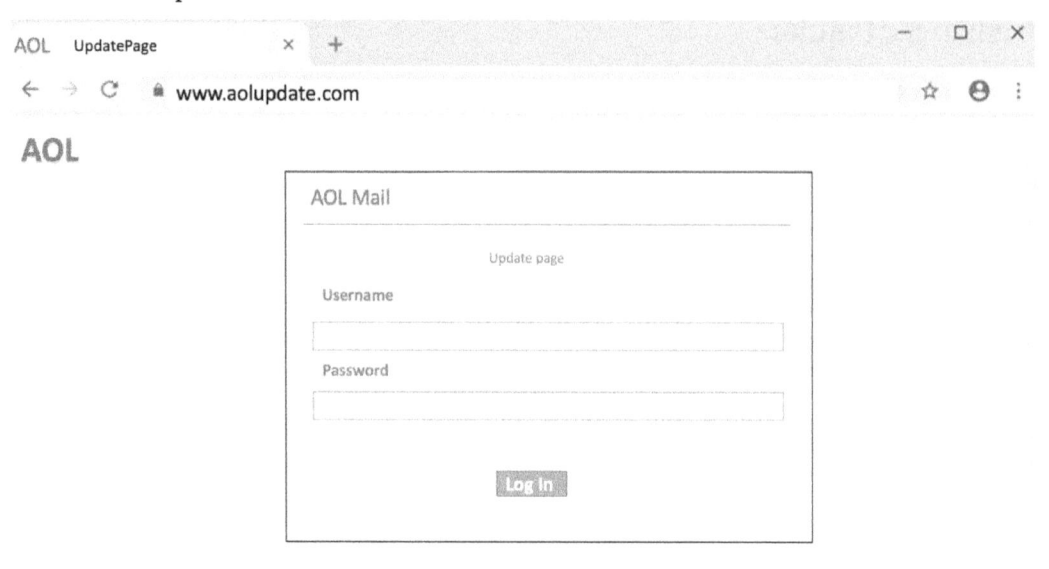

Figure 4.1 – Example of a cloned fake web page

Figure 4.1 shows an example of the AOL cloned fake web page used by the attackers to trick their victims.

Famous phishing attacks

As mentioned previously, AOL was only the beginning of a series of attacks on big internet companies. Now, let's review some of the most famous phishing attacks.

Yahoo! attack

Back in 2014, millions of Yahoo! users were attacked by receiving phishing emails that seemed like they were sent by Yahoo!.

In this case, the method that was used by the attackers was the same used in AOL – that is, using a fake login page to steal their data.

Figure 4.2 shows an example of the emails used by the attackers:

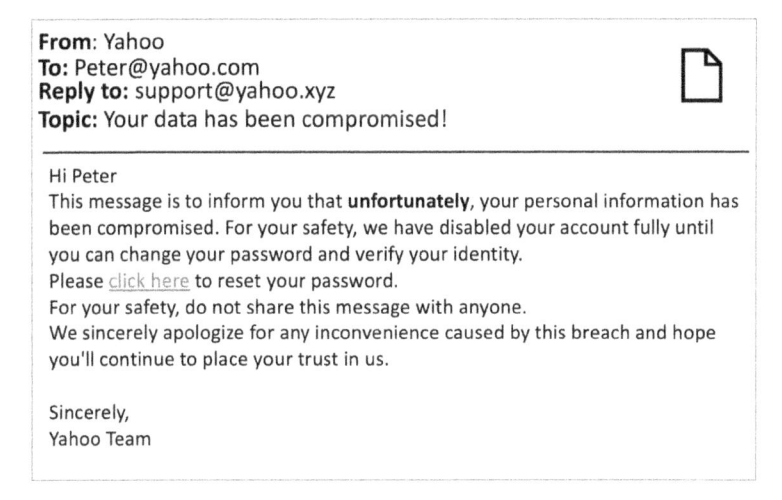

```
From: Yahoo
To: Peter@yahoo.com
Reply to: support@yahoo.xyz
Topic: Your data has been compromised!

Hi Peter
This message is to inform you that **unfortunately**, your personal information has
been compromised. For your safety, we have disabled your account fully until
you can change your password and verify your identity.
Please click here to reset your password.
For your safety, do not share this message with anyone.
We sincerely apologize for any inconvenience caused by this breach and hope
you'll continue to place your trust in us.

Sincerely,
Yahoo Team
```

Figure 4.2 – Example of phishing targeted at Yahoo! users

As you can see, the email seems to be real but contains a lot of details to help you not fall into attackers' traps:

- The sender's email is hidden
- Reply to is not a legitimate Yahoo! domain
- Grammatical errors in the email's text

Let's now see another famous phishing attack known as the Google attack.

Google attack

In 2017, there was another major phishing attack but, this time, the targets of the hackers were Google Docs users. The attack was based on an email that seemed to be sent from a legitimate Google email address, asking users to click on a link to access their Google Docs. Users were then redirected to a fake login page from where attackers stole user data, including usernames, passwords, and more.

Figure 4.3 shows an example of the email used in this attack:

From: Google
To: Thomas@google.com
Reply to: Troy@mail.xyz
Topic: Troy has shared a document on google doc with you!

Hi Thomas

Troy has shared a document on Google Doc with you.
To review the document, click on:

Open in docs

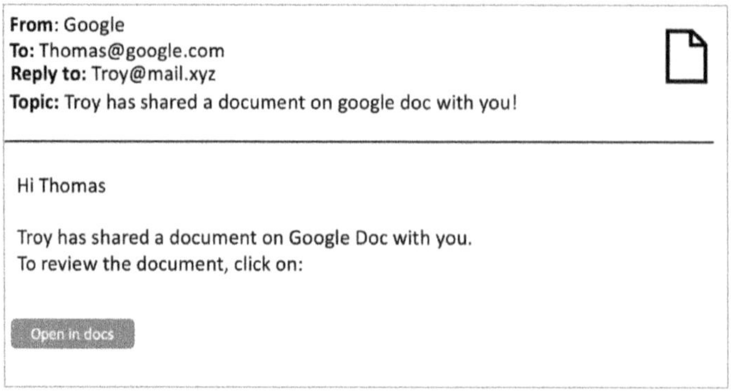

Figure 4.3 – Example of a Google Docs phishing attack

As in in the previous example of Yahoo! users, the email seems to be real but contains a lot of details to prevent you falling into the attackers' traps:

- The sender's email is hidden
- Reply to is not a legitimate Google domain
- Grammatical errors in the email's text

PayPal attacks

In 2020, PayPal users received emails saying that their accounts had been suspended and they needed to take immediate action to reactivate their accounts by clicking on the link attached to the email. The users were redirected to a fake login page where they were asked to enter their data to reactivate their accounts. This phishing attack is known as the **account suspension** scam and it affected millions of users.

Figure 4.4 shows an example of the email used in this attack:

From: PayPal
To: Thomas@PayPal.com
Topic: Your account has been suspended

Hello Dear Customer

Your account has been limited due to illegal uses. Please check your account by clicking on the button below:

Check it now

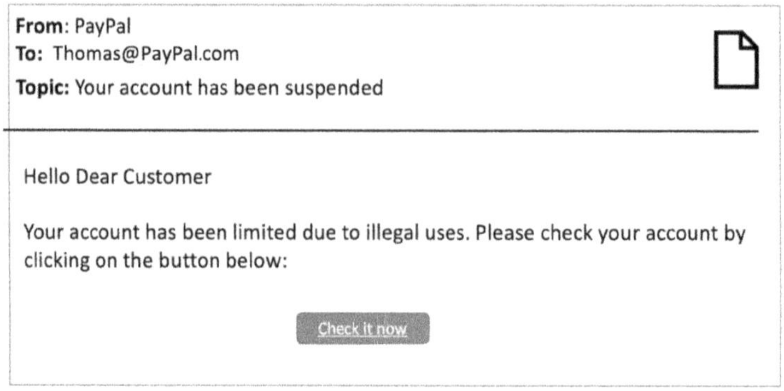

Figure 4.4 – Example of the PayPal "account suspension" phishing attack

However, this was not the only attack that occurred. Later that year, PayPal users were targeted in another email phishing attack by receiving an email with a fake invoice, asking the users to pay an amount of money to a seller or a service.

The email included a link that redirected the users to a fake PayPal payment website designed to capture the victims' credit card information.

Figure 4.5 shows an example of the email used for the attack:

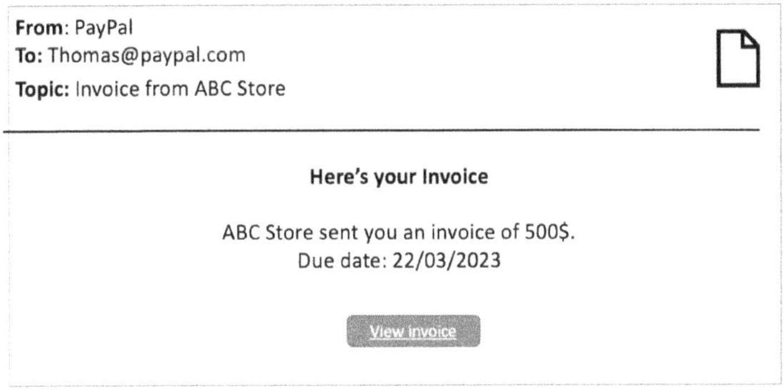

Figure 4.5 – Example of the PayPal invoice phishing attack

Now that we've covered some of the most famous phishing attacks, let's look at the different types of phishing attacks that exist.

Types of phishing attacks

As mentioned previously, there are many different types of phishing attacks, such as email phishing, SMS phishing, voice phishing, calendar phishing, and technical support scams.

Now, let's review them in detail.

Email phishing

Email phishing is one of the most common phishing attack methods and is where attackers send emails to users to steal their personal information. In this attack, the attacker tries to impersonate a trustworthy entity, a bank, an institution, or a form of social media to ask users to take immediate action. Here, attackers use several social engineering techniques, such as a sense of urgency and authority, to convince the user and make them fall for this attack.

Whaling

Whaling is a type of email phishing attack that's also known as **CEO fraud**. It's when the targets of the attackers are high-level executives, such as the CEOs or CFOs of an organization.

The attacker impersonates a trusted colleague or authority figure by sending an email to the victims while faking a trusted source and asking for personal information, such as their password, bank account details, or other sensitive data. In general, attackers add a sense of urgency to act by providing links that redirect to false web pages or attachments that contain malware.

Spear phishing

This attack is very different from normal phishing attacks because, while phishing attacks target a massive number of users in a single email, a **spear phishing** attack targets a single individual.

This means that, in this case, the attacker will study the victim to create a more elaborate email to increase the chances that the victim will fall into the trap.

Most of the time, this type of attack is used when the attacker wants to target a wealthy individual or when they are trying to get access to a given corporation.

Also, since this is a personalized attack, attackers tend to use more social engineering principles to increase the chance of success (such as impersonating a real person with a given authority over the victim).

Like other phishing attacks, the email will request the user to perform an action, such as opening an infected attachment, opening a link, or providing some sensitive information.

Detecting email phishing attacks

Detecting an email phishing attack is not an easy task since scammers are always looking for ways to improve their emails to make them look as legitimate as possible.

However, here are some tips that will help you to detect phishing emails:

- **Check the email address of the sender**: You can see the real sender by dragging your mouse on top of the email address or double-clicking it.
- **Check the language used**: Grammar and spelling errors are common in phishing emails.
- **Check the content of the email**: As seen in *Chapter 1*, these attacks will leverage some principles of persuasion, including a sense of urgency, authority, and others.
- **Check whether the email sounds too good to be true**: Most phishing attacks promise an attractive price or award to deceive users into clicking a malicious link or providing some sensitive information.
- **Check whether it is a generic email**: In most cases, phishing emails use generic words such as *Dear Friend* as they are sent to thousands of people (this does not apply to spear phishing attacks).
- **Check whether the email has a call for action**: At the end, the attacker wants you to perform some action, so all those emails will ask you to perform a given action to access the reward, such as clicking a link, calling a number, providing some information, and so on.

- **Check whether the emails are directed to undisclosed or hidden recipients**: As mentioned previously, attackers want to target hundreds of people in a single email. Therefore, to hide the address of the victims and avoid suspicions, they use *BCC* to obfuscate the list of recipients of the email (again, this does not apply to spear phishing attacks).

Figure 4.6 provides an example of how to identify an email phishing attack:

Annotation	Email content
The email seems to target a group of people	**From**: Thomas@centralbank.cyz **To:** undisclosed recipients
The **Reply to** area is different from the one of the sender	**Reply to:** <support@thisisnotcentralbank.xyz>
The sender claims to be a wealthy or powerful person	Hello My name is Thomas Tedua I am the general director of Central Bank. I am writing to inform that your Cousin Mr. Gink Biloba unfortunately lost his life last month.
They promise a huge amount of money	In his bank accounts he had let a big amount of money for you.
A sense of urgency	We need you to open an account today in our bank so we can be able to make this huge money transfer.
Call to action	To open your account please click on: [Open Account]
	Respectfully, Thomas Tedua

Figure 4.6 – Example of how to identify email phishing

As shown in *Figure 4.6*, the email is directed to a group of people, the reply address is different from the sender's address, and the content of the mail does not include any detail regarding the receiver (for example, the receiver's name). The email also shows some principles of persuasion, such as a sense of urgency and the promise for a large amount of money if you perform an action (in this case, opening the link). All these are clear trails of evidence that we are in the presence of a phishing email.

Protecting yourself from email phishing

Now, let's review some tips regarding how you can protect yourself from email phishing attacks:

- Avoid emails from unknown senders.
- Search for trails of scams and if there are any, delete the message immediately.
- If the emails seem to be from a trusted source, then use a secondary channel to contact the person to confirm whether the email is legitimate.
- Do not respond to suspicious emails.
- A real entity will never request your personal information over email, so avoid those messages.
- Avoid clicking on links contained in suspicious emails.
- Never open attached documents without verifying the source and the validity of the email.

- Always double-check the sender to verify their address.
- Remember that, sometimes, attackers will use a similar email domain to impersonate the address, so always double-check the sender's address. As an example, one common attack includes adding a letter to the domain – for example, `miicrosoft.com` (with a double i). Therefore, always double-check the email of the sender to avoid those types of attacks when the attacker uses a very similar domain.
- Implement rules to highlight emails that came from external domains to reduce the risks of attacks within an organization.
- Always use multi-factor authentication.
- Never reuse the same password on different accounts.
- Enable email security settings such as spam filters.
- Email authentication and security technologies such as SPF, DKIM, and DMARC are essential tools for protecting against email spoofing, phishing, and other malicious activities:
  - **Sender Policy Framework (SPF)**: Prevents email spoofing by checking whether the sending server is authorized to send emails on behalf of a domain. It uses DNS records to list authorized servers.
  - **DomainKeys Identified Mail (DKIM)**: Adds a digital signature to email headers to verify the email content's integrity and authenticity. It uses cryptographic keys.
  - **Domain-Based Message Authentication, Reporting, and Conformance (DMARC)**: DMARC builds on SPF and DKIM, allowing domain owners to set policies for handling failed authentication. It also provides reports to monitor email authentication.

SMS phishing (smishing)

SMS phishing, also known as **smishing**, is a type of social engineering attack where attackers try to steal the personal information of individuals by sending a personal SMS message asking them to perform an action such as entering a link, calling a number, or responding with some sensitive data.

There are several variations of this scam. Some of the most common are as follows:

- **Prize scamming**: An SMS comes to the victim's phone to inform them that they won a prize or reward and that to claim the reward, they need to open a link. Other variations include a request to call a number or respond to the message to engage in a conversation in which the attacker will later request some sensitive information.
- **Phishing links**: A message is received that contains clickable links that redirect the user to a fake website or to download some apps that will infect the user's device.
- **Spoofed SMS**: A message is received from a supposed trusted entity (for example, a bank) but in the end, it is just an attacker that is hiding their real number and impersonating a trusted entity.

- **Urgent SMS**: A message is received with a high sense of urgency to perform a given action, such as clicking on a link or calling a number.
- **Dark web services and SMS interception**: Dark web services offer the capability to intercept SMS messages destined for a specific phone number. These services essentially provide attackers with the ability to monitor and control SMS communication, potentially accessing sensitive information such as verification codes, passwords, and other personal data.
- **Inadequate security for multi-factor authentication (MFA)**: Many online services use SMS-based MFA to enhance account security. However, relying solely on SMS for MFA is not recommended due to its vulnerabilities. Attackers can intercept or redirect SMS messages, compromising the security of the MFA process. Techniques such as SIM swapping, where attackers trick mobile carriers into transferring a victim's phone number to their own SIM card, can be used to gain unauthorized access to accounts, even with SMS-based MFA enabled.

Figure 4.7 shows some examples of smishing:

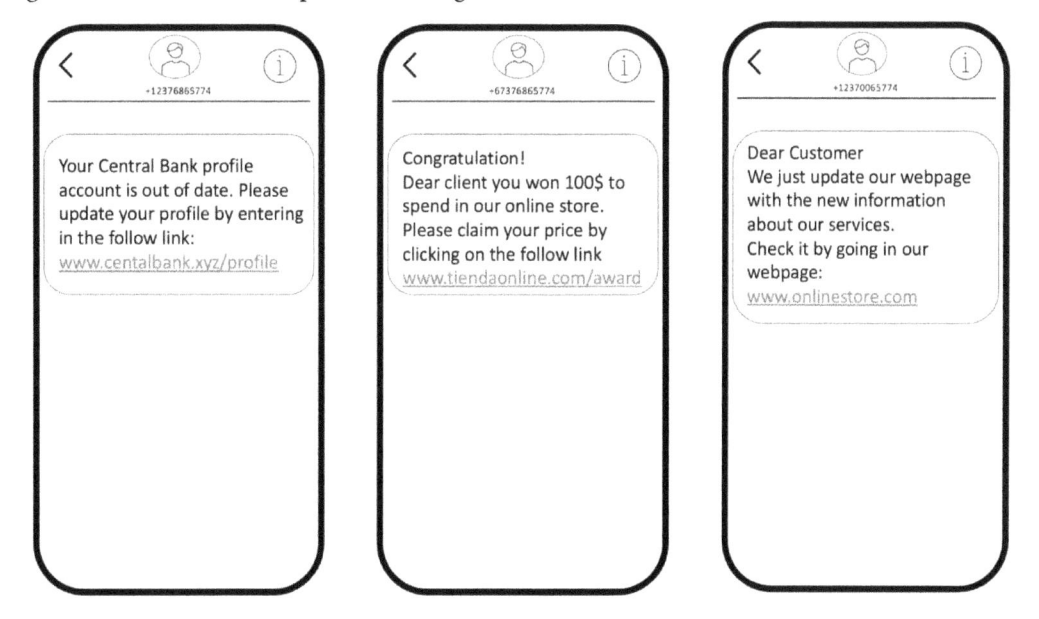

Figure 4.7 – SMS phishing examples

Now, let's consider some tips on how to detect that a received SMS might be a phishing attack.

Detecting SMS phishing attacks

Here is a list of tips that you can follow to detect potential smishing attacks:

- Check whether you get messages promising a reward from a store you never visited before

- Check whether the sender's number is a confirmed number for the society or person who is writing to you
- Check whether there are grammar and spelling errors as these are common in smishing
- Be suspicious of messages with a call for action, such as clicking a link, calling a number, and so on
- A real entity will never request your personal information over SMS, so avoid those messages

Protecting yourself from SMS phishing

Now, let's review some tips on how to protect ourselves from smishing attacks:

- Avoid SMSs from unknown senders
- Search for trails of scams and if there are any, delete the message immediately
- If the email seems to have come from a trusted source, then use a secondary channel to contact the person to confirm whether the SMS is legitimate
- Do not respond to suspicious SMS
- A real entity will never request your personal information over SMS, so avoid those messages
- Avoid clicking on links contained inside suspicious SMS
- Never open attached documents without verifying the source and the validity of the SMS
- Always double-check the sender to verify their number
- Enable SMS security settings such as spam filters
- Instead of SMS-based MFA, consider using more secure methods such as **time-based one-time passwords** (**TOTPs**) generated by authenticator apps such as Google Authenticator or hardware security keys
- For secure communication, consider using encrypted messaging apps such as Signal or WhatsApp, which offer end-to-end encryption to protect the content of your messages
- Use stronger authentication methods such as hardware tokens or biometric factors (fingerprint, face recognition, and so on) whenever possible, rather than relying solely on SMS-based codes
- Stay informed about the latest security practices and threats in the digital world to make informed decisions about the technologies you use and the security measures you implement

Voice phishing (vishing)

Voice phishing, also known as **vishing**, is a type of phishing attack where attackers use voice communication to trick people into revealing sensitive data. In most cases, the attackers fake a call from a bank or public institution, offering services or asking for personal data such as bank account numbers, usernames, passwords, security tokens, and other private information.

Using the tactic of **urgent calls**, attackers call the victim with justifications such as, "*Your bank account has been blocked*," "*Your personal bank information needs to be updated*," and many more. Most of the time, it is difficult to understand vishing since the attacker uses software that spoofs the phone number, making it seem like it's from a trusted organization or society.

There are different types of vishing:

- **Impersonation attacks**: In this type of vishing attack, the attacker pretends to be a family member, a friend, or a trusted person. Then, the attacker leverages social engineering techniques to manipulate the victim into sharing sensitive information (passwords, PINs, tokens, and so on) or sending/transferring some money.

- **Deep fake voicemail scam**: This is the newest type of vishing attack that is affecting thousands of users around the world. This is a very elaborate attack that has several phases. First, the attacker clones the voice of the person whom they are trying to impersonate by uploading a sample of the person's voice to an **artificial intelligence** (**AI**) voice cloning tool. Then, the attacker uses that AI-generated voice to record audio stating that the person is in a difficult situation and needs an urgent transfer of money (either to get out of jail, to board a plane to come back, and so on). Then, the recorded message is injected into the victim's voicemail. So far, this attack has been very effective for attackers because people believe the voice and because most people are not aware that a person's voice can be so easily cloned.

- **Robocall scam**: This type of attack uses a robotic voice to impersonate an automated system, from an institution such as a bank or government, to manipulate victims into sharing sensitive information or making a payment.

As shown in *Figure 4.8*, the attacker asking the victim to update some information:

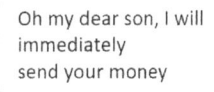

Figure 4.8 – Example of vishing

On the other hand; she was immediately willing to give her information.

Detecting vishing

Detecting vishing may be complicated, but here are a series of factors that you can consider to detect a vishing attack:

- The caller asks for personal information
- The caller requests that you take immediate action; for example, *"You need to urgently call this number to update your information," "You need to claim your prize in the next 2 hours; otherwise, it won't be available,"* and so on
- The call originates from an unknown number or country code
- There is an unusual request to avoid calling back
- Check the phone number that is calling; suspicious numbers are often attacks

Now, lets see how you can protect yourself from this type of attack.

Protecting yourself from voice phishing

Here are some tips on how to protect yourself from vishing attacks:

- Activate a spam call filter.
- Never give out personal information; a legitimate organization will never ask for your personal information over the phone.
- Always ask questions to verify the identity of the person calling. For example, you can ask for their name, surname, and company details and check them independently.
- Try to ask the same question in different ways and check that the answer is always the same; it's easy for an attacker to fall into this trap.
- Check the tone of voice of the person calling and ensure their way of communication is aligned with the profile of the caller.
- Be on the lookout for potential trails of social engineering principles. For example, a sense of urgency is always a good indicator of a smishing attack.

Calendar phishing

Calendar phishing, also known as **calendar hijacking**, is a type of phishing attack in which the attacker sends a calendar invitation that seems to be from a trusted source but it contains a malicious link or requests some sensitive information.

Here, the victim can be exposed to two different threats:

- When the user accepts the invite, it will redirect them to a page that aims to harvest some sensitive information (including login credentials, tokens, and more).
- When the user accepts the invite, it contains Trojan malware that gets activated when the invite is accepted, causing malware to be downloaded onto the victim's device (ransomware, keyloggers, and remote control, among other threats).

This is a very dangerous attack and attackers are using it more often because calendar invitations bypass most filters and security measures, making the attack more likely to succeed. Additionally, this attack is less known by users, thus making it also more effective for attackers; therefore, we must make an effort to educate users on this type of attack to reduce the risk of users falling prey to this social engineering attack.

Here are some examples of calendar phishing:

- **Fake appointment**: Attackers send an invitation to a person or group of people with a fake appointment link that, as soon as it's clicked, will install malware on the victim's device.
- **Spoofed event**: Attackers send an invitation to a group of people with a link to register for a big event such as a workshop, a webinar, or training. During registration, some sensitive information is required and that information will be captured by the attacker.
- **Malware attack**: Attackers send a link or an attachment alongside the invitation that will install malware on the victim's device to steal personal data.
- **Ransomware attack**: Attackers send invitations with a link or downloadable document that will encrypt the victim's device and obtain the decryption code the victim needs to pay.

Figure 4.9 shows an example of a calendar phishing attack:

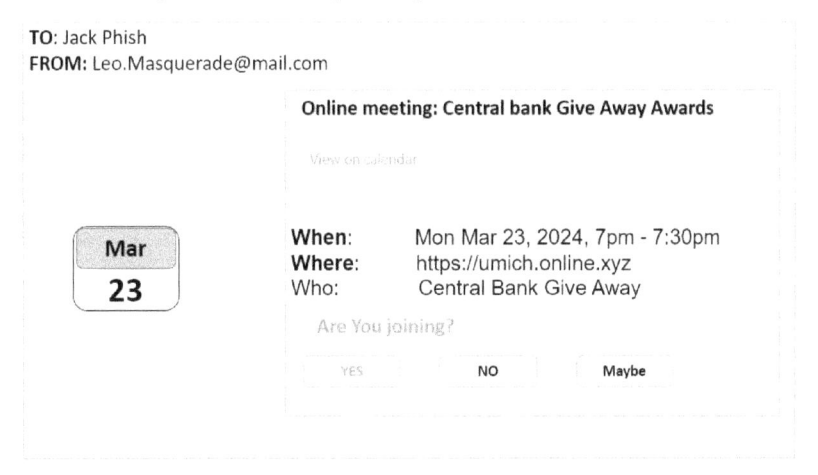

TO: Jack Phish
FROM: Leo.Masquerade@mail.com

Online meeting: Central bank Give Away Awards

View on calendar

Mar
23

When: Mon Mar 23, 2024, 7pm - 7:30pm
Where: https://umich.online.xyz
Who: Central Bank Give Away

Are You joining?

YES   NO   Maybe

Figure 4.9 – Example of a calendar phishing attack

As shown in *Figure 4.9*, the email sender is not the email address of a bank employee. Also, the link to participate in the event is not from a legitimate online meeting platform, which alerts you to be careful before accepting the invitation.

Detecting calendar phishing

To detect and protect from calendar phishing, follow these tips:

- Check the email of the sender
- Carefully check any link without clicking it (by hovering over it with your mouse) so that you can double-check the link
- Check the content of the invitation
- Look for spelling errors
- Check whether the invitation is from a recognized company but the invite came from a free email service (Gmail, Hotmail, and so on)

Protecting yourself from calendar phishing attacks

To protect yourself from calendar phishing, follow these tips:

- Never accept an unexpected invitation
- Check the calendar settings to ensure that you are sharing it only with trusted contacts
- Ensure that meetings are not automatically accepted
- Use anti-phishing software
- Don't accept invitations from unknown senders
- Don't trust invitations to free events or events that promise some type of reward from unknown senders
- Ask yourself whether there is any connection between you and the sender
- Avoid invitations to corporate events that came from a sender using a free email address (Gmail, Hotmail, and so on)

Technical support scam

A **technical support scam** is a type of fraud in which the attacker contacts the victim while impersonating a technical support agent.

In most cases, they will leverage tactics such as fear and lack of technical knowledge to trick the victims into executing an action, such as giving remote access to the attacker, downloading and installing a given app (full of malware), or even disclosing some sensitive information (usernames, passwords, PINs, and so on).

In some cases, the attacker will leverage the lack of technical knowledge of the victim to execute a given action to gain the victim's trust. As seen in *Figure 4.10*, the attacker will leverage some technical knowledge to trick the user:

Figure 4.10 – Example of the technical support scam

In this case, the attacker is asking the victim to check for a process that they know will be running on the computer (such as Windows Explorer).

Protecting yourself from technical support scams

Here are some tips to protect yourself from technical support scams:

- Be wary when receiving unsolicited emails or calls from technical support.
- If you receive an unsolicited call claiming to be from technical support, ask for the name of the analyst and let them know that you will close the call and contact them again using the approved channels.
- Never give remote access to your computer.
- Never share your credentials via email or phone.
- Don't click any links on emails claiming to be from technical support. Always contact your local IT department and validate any emails with them first.
- If you receive a phone call claiming to be from technical support, do not share any information (validate first, talk later).
- Never install any update or software received via email claiming to be from technical support (until you validate the source).
- If the email is from a free email service (`@yahoo`, `@gmail`), immediately delete the message (IT support will always use corporate emails for communications).

With that, we've provided a comprehensive review of the most common phishing attacks. However, while phishing is one of the most famous types of social engineering attacks, many more types of attacks leverage social engineering principles. Let's review them.

Baiting

Baiting is a very interesting type of social engineering attack where attackers offer their victims something of interest but, in exchange, the attacker will gather some sensitive information from the victim, get unauthorized access to systems, or even infect the entire infrastructure of a company.

There are two types of baiting attacks – one can be done physically and the other is a virtual attack. Let's explore them in detail.

Physical baiting

In this type of attack, the attacker uses a physical object to lure the victim into connecting the object to the computer to infect the system and exfiltrate data or cause damage to the system.

In most cases, the physical objects are storage devices such as a CD or a USB storage device. However, more sophisticated attacks may include other devices, such as a USB cable, a phone charger, a keyboard, a mouse, a webcam, and many others. This confirms that companies must restrict the devices connected to their systems, even when those devices are as trivial as a cable.

> Note
> As mentioned previously, many devices can be used to exfiltrate data once they are connected to a computer, such as the **OMG cable** and the **USB Ninja**, while other devices such as the **Bad USB** can destroy a system if it's connected to a computer.

To enhance the effectiveness of these types of attacks, the attacker will label the objects to attract the victim's attention and curiosity, thus enhancing the chance that the victim will plug them into a computer. Some examples of labels are **Confidential information**, **Salary information of staff**, **Private Pictures**, and **Business plan for 2023**.

> Note
> If you want to know more about those USB threats, we highly recommend you check the book: *Mastering Defensive Security* by Cesar Bravo as *Chapter 2* has an entire section explaining those USB vulnerabilities and the most common types of USB attacks.

Then, once the device has been plugged in, it will trigger a range of actions, including the deployment of malware (ransomware), remote injection of code, execution of a command and control system (allowing the attacker to remotely control the system), or even planting a keystroke to steal sensitive information.

Cyber baiting

In **cyber baiting**, the attacker uses digital resources to attract the victim. Let's look at some examples:

- A web page (or email) offering incredible discounts
- A free download for expensive software
- A free download for software to spy on social media accounts
- A free download for software to *mine* crypto
- A link to meet attractive people in your area
- A link to claim some type of award
- Links to scandals related to famous people
- Recipes to easily cure some common illnesses
- A guide with *tricks* to win the lottery
- A page to access paid resources for free (books, movies, and so on)

As in physical baiting, the final goal of the attacker is to inject some malware to harvest some personal information, gain unauthorized access to systems, or obtain credit card information.

Protecting yourself against baiting

Here is a list of tips that you can leverage to reduce the risk of falling victim to baiting:

- Avoid clicking on links or content mentioned previously
- Avoid downloading content from unsecured pages
- Avoid installing software from untrusted sources
- Never connect a device that you find lying around
- Report any unattended and suspicious device to your cybersecurity team

Moving on, let's discuss another type of cyberattack, called dumpster diving, and explore how it can pose a serious threat to an organization's security.

Dumpster diving

You may not be familiar with this attack, but while it is not as common as the other attacks, the **dumpster diving** attack is an interesting type of cyberattack (not a social attack) that is worth understanding.

The assault is simple but effective and is founded on the reality that many companies lack a suitable procedure for disposing of paper, which attackers take advantage of by scouring through ordinary trash to find documents containing sensitive information that was discarded in its original form.

Many companies do not give the proper attention to this type of low-tech attack. However, ignoring this type of threat is what makes this attack effective.

One of the most famous dumpster diving attacks was performed back in 1992 when Kevin Mitnick gained access to sensitive information from the trash of the Pacific Bell data center in Los Angeles. By searching the trash of the office, Kevin found documentation containing users and passwords, user manuals, and other sensitive information that gave him access to their systems.

The attack exposed the vulnerabilities in the company's security and highlighted the importance of properly disposing of sensitive information. As a result, Pacific Bell had to review and strengthen its security measures to prevent similar attacks from happening in the future. The attack also damaged the company's reputation and caused a loss of public trust, which could have harmed their business. Overall, the incident was a wake-up call for the company to take its security seriously and invest in stronger cybersecurity measures to protect against future attacks.

This case shows the importance of having a policy to properly label and dispose of physically sensitive information to avoid this type of attack.

Protecting yourself against dumpster diving

Here is some advice on how to protect yourself against dumpster diving attacks:

- Implement a policy that addresses the appropriate labeling and disposal of physical documents
- Limit the access of unauthorized people in sensitive areas
- Implement shredders across the office and educate users on where to find them
- Implement a policy for properly disposing of digital devices
- Implement a wipeout policy for storage devices
- Implement a document retention policy

Next, we'll talk about another type of cyberattack, called tailgating, which involves gaining unauthorized access to secure areas within an organization.

Tailgating

The **tailgating** attack, also known as **piggybacking**, consists of gaining unauthorized access to a secure or restricted area. Normally, the attack is achieved by following an authorized person and leveraging that person's access to illegally enter the restricted area. Like the rest of the attacks, this is normally done to gather private or sensitive data, steal devices or goods, cause some physical damage, harm employees, or execute some physical cybersecurity attacks (for example, connecting a physical keystroke device).

As illustrated in *Figure 4.6*, attackers will use a range of social engineering techniques to execute this attack, including authority, liking, and reciprocity.

There are many ways in which the attacker executes this attack. The most common are as follows:

- Rushing to enter before the door gets closed
- Using social engineering techniques to get help from another person to gain access
- Placing an object to prevent the door from closing
- Using cloned or stolen credentials

The best way to prevent this attack is by implementing a physical security policy enforced with training and other security controls, such as security guards and cameras.

Also, in this case, the best security guards are your employees, so make sure they are well-trained regarding this attack and motivate them to report any tailgating incidents to security.

Now, let's delve into the topic of quid pro quo attacks and understand how they work.

Quid pro quo

This is a lesser-known type of attack where an attacker offers something of value, such as a gift, discount, trip, or other benefits to the victim, in exchange for sensitive information or personal data. This is why this attack is also called **favor to favor**.

Let's review the most common types of **quid pro quo** attacks and tactics.

Free tech support

Free tech support is a quid pro quo attack where an attacker impersonates a technology support company offering free services. Once the user agrees to the free service, the attackers request remote access to the victim's device. Once it is granted, the attackers will either deploy malware (such as ransomware), exfiltrate sensitive data, or even install a backdoor to gain further access to the corporate network.

Free software to download

Free software to download is a quid pro quo attack where the attackers offer a free software download or a license of common or expensive software. There are several variations of the attack. In some cases, the software will include some malware (for example, a remote control tool) or a keylogger to exfiltrate sensitive information. In another scenario, the user will be requested to make a small payment (for example, $1) to access premium features or activate the software. In that case, the attacker will harvest the credit card data to perform fraudulent transactions.

How to protect yourself against quid pro quo attacks

Here is some advice on how to protect yourself against quid pro quo attacks:

- Think twice if you get a message or offer that appears to be too good to be true
- Always be suspicious of unsolicited offers
- Always verify the identity of the person who is offering you the benefit
- Never share your personal information when you're installing untrusted (cracked) software
- Never enter your personal information in non-secure or unverified web pages
- Never give remote access to your system
- Be careful with the permissions that are requested by apps when installing them.

Another type of social engineering attack that is commonly used to steal sensitive information is pretexting. Let's take a look at what pretexting attacks involve and how they can be prevented.

Pretexting

Pretexting is a type of social engineering attack where the attacker creates false content to trick their victims, such as a job offer or a charity.

Fake job offers

In the **fake job offers** attack, the attacker impersonates a recruiter of a company, offering a job position to the victim. In most cases, the job offer is associated with a super high salary, an executive or leadership role, or incredible benefits. In some cases, the recruiter will even give the candidate the option to select the desired benefits. This is done to make this job offer super attractive to trap the victim in the scam.

One way to prevent this attack is to double-check the identity of the person (for example, using LinkedIn). Also, make sure that the email address matches the corporate emails as, in most cases, the attacker uses a generic email (such as Gmail or Hotmail).

Figure 4.11 shows an example of a fake job offer attack:

> **From**: Jessica Polo
> **To**: Thomas@gmail.com
> **Topic**: Work from home position
>
> Hello,
> My name is Jessica, and I am the recruiter of Work from home Company.
> We are an international company that want to promote and help students to professionally grow offering international growth programs and free certifications and paid work hours.
> The open position is completely remote and is paid 500$ for days.
> If you are interest and want to know more info, please do not hesitate to contact me on:
> jessicapolo779@outlook.com
>
> Do have a good day,
> Thank you

Figure 4.11 – Example of a fake job offer attack

As you can see, in this email, there are signs of alerts – for example, the job offer proposes incredible professional and financial benefits, contains grammatical errors, and the contact is a private email. Remember, always be vigilant of these details that seem small but can save you from a potential attack.

False charities

This is a sad type of attack because it is targeted at kind-hearted people by asking them to donate to **false charities**.

This attack uses several social engineering techniques aimed at emotionally touching the hearts of victims. In general, this type of attack is very common during natural disasters, financial crises, or tragedies.

In other cases, the attacker will ask for charities related to families in need, people with disabilities, immigrants, or abandoned kids. In most cases, they will use real people's photos, but attackers also leverage some AI tools to create photos of people that look just like real people.

> **Note**
> Several pages use AI to create hyperrealistic pictures of fake (non-existent) humans. You can try it yourself at `https://this-person-does-not-exist.com/en`.

To avoid these attacks, people need to verify the charity and the associated accounts to ensure that they are giving the funds to the right people. In some cases, the attackers will impersonate a real charity but will provide a fake account number to get the money routed to their accounts.

Now, let's discuss another type of cyberattack, known as a watering hole attack, which is often used to target specific groups or organizations.

Watering hole

This type of attack begins with identifying a website that is popular for a target audience. Then, the attacker tries to find a vulnerability in the code of the website or uses stolen credentials to manipulate the site to harvest private sensitive information. In other cases, the attacker will add some code to automatically download some malware when the site is visited.

Crypto mining

In this variation of the attack, the attacker adds some **crypto-mining** code to the website to leverage the computing power of the people who visit the page to mine some cryptocurrency. Of course, in this case, all the profits from the mining will be deposited into the wallet of the attacker.

Summary

The very first step to protect against a social engineering attack is being aware of the attack itself; in this chapter, we provided a comprehensive review of the most common types of attacks that you may encounter in your personal and professional life.

Additionally, we explored different strategies that you can leverage to easily identify those threats.

Furthermore, we discovered a number of methods to prevent those types of attacks both in your personal life and also in a corporate environment.

In the next chapter, you will enhance your skills by understanding more technically complex attacks, including social engineering with additional technical skills to create **enhanced social engineering attacks**.

Further reading

As mentioned, if you want to enhance your cybersecurity skills including learning about the latest physical (USB) vulnerabilities, then we highly recommend this book:

```
https://www.packtpub.com/product/mastering-defensive-security/9781800208162
```

Part 2: Enhanced Social Engineering Attacks

In this part, we will explore how attackers leverage technology to enhance their social engineering attacks, including AI driving techniques.

We will focus on the most effective tools and technical components used to augment the impact and effectiveness of these attacks.

This part has the following chapters:

- *Chapter 5, Enhanced Social Engineering Attacks*
- *Chapter 6, Social Engineering and Social Networks Attacks*
- *Chapter 7, AI-Driven Techniques in Enhanced Social Engineering Attacks*
- *Chapter 8, The Social Engineering Toolkit (SET)*

5
Enhanced Social Engineering Attacks

The use of social engineering attacks has been on the rise in recent years and with the help of technology, these attacks have become even more sophisticated and effective.

In this chapter, we will explore how technology is being used to enhance social engineering attacks and the tools that attackers are leveraging to achieve their goals.

We will start by discussing a very important topic: **high-value target attacks**, where attackers target specific individuals with more elaborate schemes that increase the chance of success. Those attacks are normally targeted at wealthy individuals or big corporations where the reward for the attacker is higher.

Additionally, we will look at the role of **open source intelligence** (OSINT) in social engineering attacks, including their methods and the most common tools.

Then we will do a deep dive into the core of the topic by analyzing the most common types of social engineering attacks that leverage web platforms to execute them. This includes fake login pages, forum-based attacks, gaming attacks, and many more.

By studying these topics, you will develop a comprehensive understanding of how technology is used to enhance social engineering attacks and gain valuable knowledge about the tools, methods, and preventive measures associated with these attacks.

That section includes examples of the attacks to help you identify them as well as a section with insights into how to prevent each of those attacks.

In this chapter, we will cover the following main topics:

- Targeted attacks:
  - Identifying high-value targets

- OSINT:
  - OSINT tools
  - OSINT methods
  - OSINT use cases
- Web-based attacks:
  - Fake logins
  - Fake updates
  - Scareware
  - Fake pages
  - Magic-ware
  - Hacking-ware
  - Gaming based attacks
  - Forum-based attacks
  - Adware

Technical requirements

There are no technical requirements for this chapter.

Disclaimer

All characters in this chapter are fictional characters.

Illustrations are inspired by real attacks; therefore, the language used (including spelling and grammatical errors) is intentional.

Targeted attacks

Over time, social engineering attacks have shifted from huge indiscriminate campaigns to highly targeted and sophisticated operations. Attackers now invest more effort in personalized approaches, conducting extensive research and reconnaissance on their intended victims.

In these targeted attacks, the attackers focus on specific individuals or organizations based on factors such as job roles, access to sensitive information, or financial standing. Exploiting trust and authority has become a prominent tactic, as attackers impersonate trusted entities to manipulate targets into divulging sensitive data or performing desired actions. Additionally, attackers strive to blend in with legitimate communication channels, making it harder for targets to distinguish between genuine and malicious content.

These changes reflect the adaptability and resourcefulness of attackers, as they aim to maximize their success while minimizing the risk of detection. This shift toward targeted and sophisticated attacks has made social engineering a more significant threat than ever before.

These enhanced social engineering attacks are designed to bypass or overcome some security measures, making these attacks very difficult to detect and counter. As a result, individuals and organizations must remain vigilant and proactive in their efforts to recognize and mitigate these ever-present threats.

Identifying high-value targets

As mentioned before, social engineering attacks involve manipulating individuals or groups to divulge sensitive information or perform actions that could compromise their security. An attack can be **random** or **personalized**, which means directed to a target person or organization.

In the case of **targeted attacks**, attackers identify **high-value targets** (individuals or groups) that have a significant impact on an organization. Successful attacks on a high-value target can result in significant financial or reputational damage to an organization.

Here are some examples of people that can be considered as high-value targets for an attacker:

- Executives and managers
- IT employees
- Finance employees
- The HR team of an organization
- Celebrities
- Politicians
- Contractors or vendors that have access to organization systems

Profiling potential victims involves gathering personal and professional information that can be used to create a comprehensive profile of the target. Attackers may use a range of sources to gather this information, including social media, public records, online databases, and **open source intelligence** (**OSINT**) techniques.

Personal information such as name, surname, address, phone number, and email address can be used to identify potential targets while professional information such as job title, company size, and industry can help attackers understand the target's role within an organization.

Once the attacker has gathered the necessary information, they can make a customized attack based on the target. This attack may take the form of a phishing email, a phone call, or a fake website designed to steal sensitive information.

Attackers may customize their attack in different ways. Let's see some of the ways:

- **Personalization** – Attackers use personal information of the target such as name and job title to make the attack more credible
- **Emotional appeals** – Attackers use emotional appeals such as fear to manipulate the target into taking action
- **Relevance** – Attackers use language that is relevant to the target's job function or personal life
- **Timing** – Attackers are careful to coincide their attack with an event or deadlines the target has
- **Platforms** – Attackers may use platforms that the target is familiar with and uses in their daily life, such as phone, social media, or email

In conclusion, cyber attackers often use a variety of tactics to make their attacks more effective. By personalizing their approach, using emotional appeals, and using language and platforms that are relevant to the target, attackers can increase the likelihood that the victim will fall for their scam.

Additionally, timing plays a crucial role in these attacks, as attackers often choose to strike when the victim is under pressure or has an urgent deadline. Being aware of these tactics and taking steps to protect oneself can help individuals and organizations avoid falling victim to these types of attacks.

OSINT

As previously noted, one of the sources that attackers use to gather information about their target victims is open source intelligence techniques, known as **OSINT**.

OSINT is a framework used to gather information from public sources such as social media, public records, government websites, academic research, news articles, or other publicly available data.

It enables analysts to gather information from sources that may not be accessible through conventional means. For instance, a social media post could provide valuable information about a person's thoughts or actions that would be impossible to obtain through a background check or conventional searches.

OSINT tools

OSINT tools are software or applications that are used to facilitate the process of collecting, analyzing, and visualizing information from publicly available sources. Here are some examples of OSINT tools:

- **Shodan**: This is used for internet-connected devices to allow users to discover devices, open ports, and vulnerabilities

- **SpiderFoot**: This automates OSINT data collection and analyses from a wide range of sources
- **WayBack Machine**: This is an internet archive used to check historical versions of websites
- **FOCA: Fingerprinting Organizations with Collected Archives** is a tool that's used for metadata analysis and data mining to gather information on an organization's public-facing assets
- **Maltego**: This tool allows analysts to visualize and analyze relationships between people, organizations, and other entities

OSINT methods

OSINT methods are techniques used to collect information from publicly available sources. These methods are not mutually exclusive and can be combined and customized to suit specific OSINT goals and requirements.

Here are some examples of OSINT methods:

- **Google Dorking** – This method is based on leveraging Google's advanced search options to harvest specific data from websites.
- **Public records** – Another common method used is to harvest information from public records – records the victim may not even be aware of.
- **Web Scraping** – A well-known method in cybersecurity used to harvest data from websites.
- **Image and video analysis** – OSINT analysts rely on specialized tools to extract valuable information from images and videos. These tools may use techniques such as facial recognition, object recognition, or geolocation analysis to reveal hidden details that could aid in their investigations. By leveraging this method of extraction, OSINT analysts can gather a wealth of information from visual media sources that might otherwise have gone unnoticed.
- **Website analysis** – In this method, analysts examine both the design and metadata of website content in order to obtain insights into an organization's operations.

In conclusion, OSINT methods involve a variety of techniques that OSINT analysts use to gather information from a range of sources. From Google Dorking to public records, OSINT methods provide a powerful toolkit for cybersecurity professionals to identify vulnerabilities and threats to people and organizations.

By leveraging these techniques, cybersecurity analysts can gather valuable information that might otherwise go unnoticed, providing an essential line of defense against cyber-attacks.

OSINT use cases

Let's now see some examples of when OSINT techniques can be used:

- **Cybersecurity** – OSINT plays a significant role in cybersecurity as it enables the identification of vulnerabilities and potential threats to computer systems and networks. By gathering and analyzing information from open sources, such as social media and public databases, OSINT analysts can identify potential risks and help organizations take proactive measures to mitigate them. This can include measures such as software patching, access control, and other security protocols to safeguard against cyber-attacks.
- **Investigative journalism** – In the field of investigative journalism, journalists use OSINT techniques to find and verify information before writing an article.
- **Reputation management** – OSINT helps to monitor mentions of brands, organizations, or people and to detect potential threads or opportunities for engagement.
- **Academic research** – Researchers use OSINT techniques to gather data for their projects.
- **Law enforcement** – OSINT helps to gather information about suspects or criminal activities.

Now that we have discussed OSINT tools and methods, let's shift our focus to web-based attacks.

Web-based attacks

Web-based attacks have a long history dating back to the early days of the internet, and their prevalence has only increased over time. As the internet became more widely used in the 1990s, web-based attacks became more sophisticated and frequent.

Web-based attacks are malicious actions that take advantage of vulnerabilities in web-based applications, servers, and web browsers to gain unauthorized access or steal sensitive information. These attacks can come in many different forms. In the following sections, we are going to see the most common types of web-based attacks.

Fake logins

In *Chapter 4*, we discussed the AOL attack which was one of the first major attacks and happened in 1995, when attackers used a **fake login** page to steal victims' data. This was only the beginning of this kind of attack and they have evolved over time and become more sophisticated and difficult to detect.

This type of attack is executed in two phases:

- In the first phase, the attackers impersonate a trustworthy entity and send a phishing email to the victim asking them to update their information by clicking on a link, as shown in *Figure 5.1*:

Web-based attacks   85

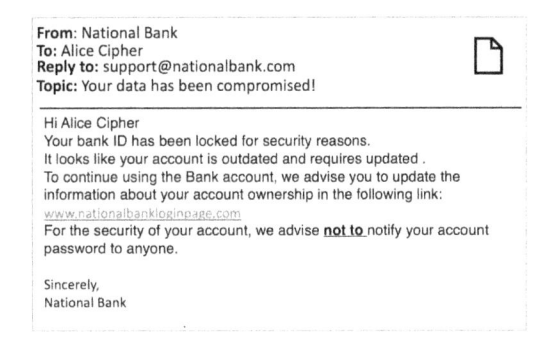

> **From**: National Bank
> **To**: Alice Cipher
> **Reply to**: support@nationalbank.com
> **Topic**: Your data has been compromised!
>
> Hi Alice Cipher
> Your bank ID has been locked for security reasons.
> It looks like your account is outdated and requires updated .
> To continue using the Bank account, we advise you to update the
> information about your account ownership in the following link:
> www.nationalbankloginpage.com
> For the security of your account, we advise **not to** notify your account
> password to anyone.
>
> Sincerely,
> National Bank

Figure 5.1 – Example phishing email

- In the second phase, once the user clicks on the link, they will be redirected to a cloned page of the bank that will ask the user to enter their credentials to update their account. As you may have guessed, that fake page will harvest the victim's credentials and send them to the attacker.

Figure 5.2 shows an example of a fake login page:

Figure 5.2 – Example of a fake login page

A fake login page can be a powerful tool for cybercriminals to steal personal information and credentials from unsuspecting victims so it is important to know how to be protected from this type of attack.

How to prevent this type of attack

It's important to be cautious and vigilant when it comes to protecting your login credentials. Here are some tips on how to protect against this type of attack:

- Always double-check the website's URL and make sure it's legitimate before entering your login information.
- Be wary of any unsolicited emails, messages, or links that ask you to enter your login credentials.
- Never use the same password for two or more accounts.
- Avoid the use of public Wi-Fi connections as attackers can present you with fake logins in an attempt to capture your credentials.
- Always enable **multi-factor authentication** (**MFA**) to better secure your account.
- Change your passwords regularly.
- Use a password manager to easily manage your passwords. It will ensure all passwords are different, that they are strong, and are changed frequently.

By following these simple tips, you can greatly reduce the risk of falling victim to a fake login page attack. Always remember to be cautious and attentive when entering your login credentials, and never share your personal information with unknown or suspicious sources. With the use of multi-factor authentication and password managers, you can enhance the security of your accounts and ensure your online safety.

Fake updates

Fake update attacks have been present in the cybersecurity landscape for many years and have undergone changes as technology has advanced. The earliest known instance of such an attack occurred in 2011 when the Duqu malware employed fake Microsoft Windows updates to gain access to computers in Iran. Subsequently, fake update attacks have become more prevalent and have been used in several other high-profile cyber-attacks, such as the NotPetya ransomware attack in 2017.

To carry out fake update attacks, attackers conduct extensive research into the software they want to target and exploit any vulnerabilities they discover. Then, they create fake updates that are designed to appear as if they are legitimate and trustworthy, using tactics such as mimicking the logo and branding of the software vendor. Attackers also use social engineering techniques, such as sending convincing-looking emails or creating fake websites, to convince victims to download and install the fake updates.

Figure 5.3 shows an example of a fake update:

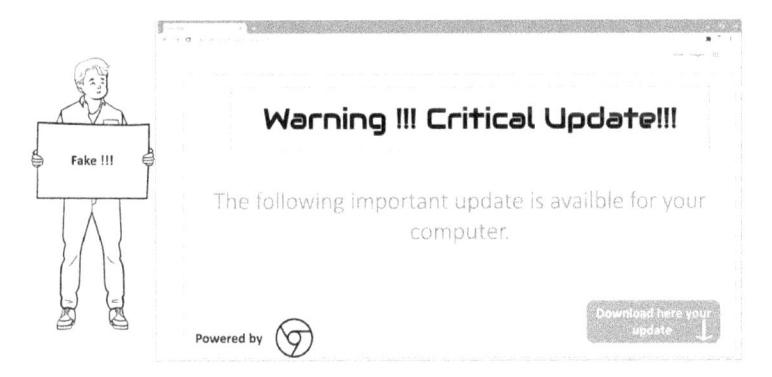

Figure 5.3 – Example of a fake update attack

To avoid falling prey to fake update attacks, it is crucial to always verify the legitimacy of any update notifications before downloading and installing any updates. Now let's see more details on how to protect from this type of attack.

How to prevent this type of attack

To prevent fake update attacks, it is essential for individuals and organizations to take proactive measures. Here are some tips on how to be protected:

- Avoid downloading updates from the internet. Instead, use the embedded update option within the tool to keep the software up to date.
- Download software updates only from trusted sources or channels.
- Verify the authenticity of updates by checking for the vendor's digital signature or certificate.
- Be wary of unexpected updates that appear urgent.
- Confirm the legitimacy and necessity of software updates before installing.
- Always back up important data to avoid data loss in case of a fake update attack.

Now that we have discussed the risks of fake update attacks, let's shift our focus to another potential threat: scareware.

Scareware

Scareware attacks have been around for over a decade, evolving from pop-up windows to more sophisticated social engineering tactics. In this type of attack, a web page displays pop-up windows that falsely claim that the user's computer has a virus. When the user clicks on a link to fix the issue, they are directed to a page that conducts a fake scan of their computer, which shows multiple viruses detected. *Figure 5.4* shows an example:

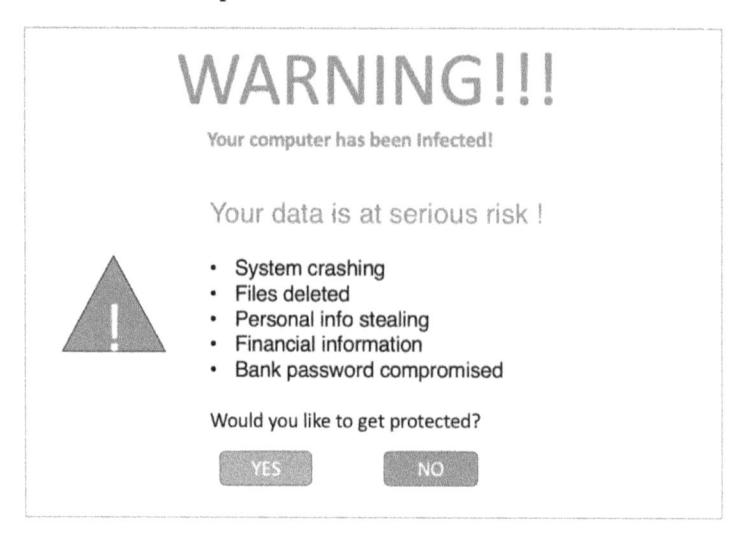

Figure 5.4 – Scareware attack example

The objective of the attacker is to make the victim scared that their data is in real danger. Additionally, the attacker may use other social engineering tactics such as a false sense of urgency by telling you that you have only a few minutes to buy antivirus software at a crazily high discount (normally between 80% and 90% off). This is done to trick the victim into buying the antivirus now (before checking further and eventually discovering the scam).

How to prevent this type of attack

It is important to note that scareware attacks can take many different forms, and attackers are always coming up with new ways to attack their victims. Therefore, it is important to remain vigilant and help others to avoid falling into those traps. Now, let's review some tips on how to stay protected against such attacks:

- Install anti-virus software and keep it up to date
- Don't trust any message claiming that your computer is infected (unless the message comes directly from your installed antivirus software)
- Enable the pop-up blockers in your browser
- Be wary of popups or alerts claiming your computer is infected and avoid clicking on them
- Do not trust unsolicited offers for software or services, especially when they come via emails or social media

- Avoid downloading or installing software from untrusted sources
- Use pop-up blockers or ad blockers
- Ensure you have an updated backup to protect in case you fall victim to an attack

Moving on from scareware attacks, let's now discuss another type of attack that cybercriminals commonly use to trick users into downloading malware or giving away sensitive information: fake pages.

Fake pages

A **fake page attack** refers to a technique used by hackers to create a website that is designed to mimic a legitimate website, such as those of banks or social media platforms. The objective is to deceive unsuspecting individuals into divulging their confidential information, such as login credentials and credit card numbers. Although these attacks have been around for a while, they have evolved in complexity over time as hackers discover new ways to ensnare their victims.

In the past, it was easy to spot fake pages, but with the advancements in technology, hackers can now create pages that are much more convincing.

Additionally, attackers leverage social engineering techniques to enhance the effectiveness of an attack by sending emails that appear to be from a trusted source and requesting that you click on a link to verify your account details. However, clicking on the link will direct you to the hacker's fake page, which they use to collect your sensitive information. Furthermore, attackers will also use other social engineering tactics such as a sense of urgency to increase the possibility that the victim will fall into the trap. In some cases, the sense of urgency can be expressed with something like **Check your account before it gets disabled, This offer expires in 1 Hour**, or similar.

Let's review interesting examples of a fake page attack:

- People usually leverage booking platforms such as Booking.com or Airbnb to reserve their vacations and their popularity is one of the reasons why attackers target the users of those sites. Now, let's explore the following link:

    ```
    https://airbnb-com.rooms-923481903.com/676f/charming-spacious-apartment-in-bristol/464643
    ```

    At first sight, it seems to be the site of Airbnb, but if you look closely, you will realize that the real domain is `rooms-923481903.com`.

    In this example, the attacker created a subdomain called `airbnb-com` to trick the victim into thinking that they were accessing the real site, while in reality, they were accessing the `rooms-923481903.com` domain, which contains a cloned version of the real page, which in this case was designed by the attacker to harvest credit card information.

- In other cases, the attack came in the form of an advertisement that offered a big discount on any of those accommodation platforms, as shown in the following screenshot:

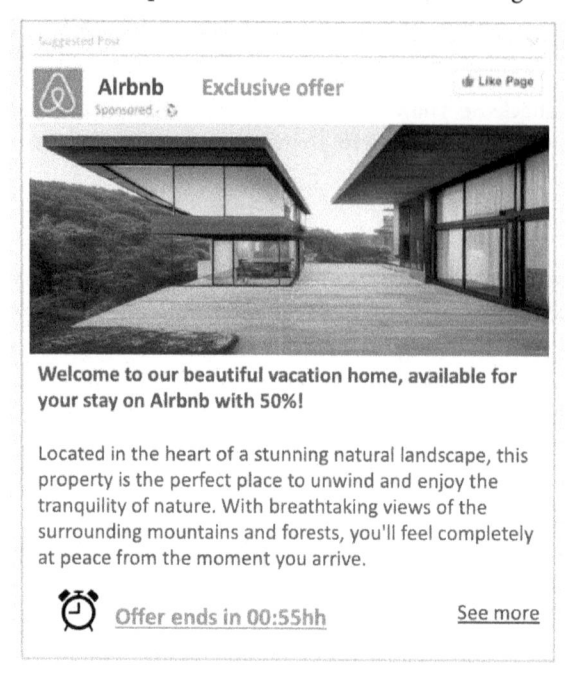

Figure 5.5 – Example of a fake Airbnb advertisement

Figure 5.6 shows another interesting type of attack where the attacker impersonates a real page by changing one letter of the name. The attacker substituted the letter "l" for "i," which enabled them to access the fraudulent web page by using a different name ("ALrbnb" ≠ "Airbnb"). This name variation allowed them to create a counterfeit social media page to mislead unsuspecting individuals.

Then, once the user clicks on the fake advertisement, the user will be routed to the fake page where the attacker is expecting to harvest the victim's credit card information. This fake page is similar to the previous example where the attackers used a subdomain to confuse the victim.

An example of a fake page is shown in *Figure 5.6*:

Figure 5.6 – Example of a fake page attack

Given the level of sophistication of fake pages, it is crucial to exercise caution when sharing sensitive information online. In the following section, we will discuss several measures that can be taken to safeguard oneself against these types of attacks.

How to prevent this type of attack

Is important to stay safe and always be vigilant when we navigate the web. Therefore, here are some tips to help you stay protected from fake page attacks:

- It is highly recommended to verify the legitimacy of a website's URL before entering any personal information to avoid falling victim to fraudulent attacks. Check the website's URL for spelling or grammatical errors.
- Check the entire URL to ensure they are not using a subdomain to trick you (`www.page.com` is not the same as `www.page.com.abc345.net/fake`)
- Be wary of any unsolicited emails, messages, or links that ask you to enter your personal information.
- Never access a page that requires your financial information (such as an accommodation page) through a link on the internet.

- Never put your credit card information on pages that you accessed through a link on social media.
- Use strong and unique passwords for accounts. Avoid using easily guessable passwords such as `password123` or `12345678`.
- Never use the same password for two or more accounts.
- Enable MFA to better secure your accounts.

Moving on to another type of attack, let's now discuss the concept of magic-ware.

Magic-ware

In the realm of cybersecurity, it is not uncommon to encounter software that claims to provide an effortless and convenient means of accessing data from other individuals' social media accounts. These software solutions, called magic-ware, often present themselves as attractive tools that offer an easy way to bypass privacy settings or security protocols and access confidential information from other user's accounts.

However, it is important to understand that such software is not only illegal but also potentially harmful. In many cases, the use of such software constitutes a violation of ethical and legal standards, as it entails accessing other people's private information without their consent or authorization. Furthermore, this type of software is often a guise for malicious actors seeking to steal personal information, install malware on the user's device, or engage in other malicious activities.

As such, it is vital to exercise caution and refrain from using any software that promises unauthorized access to social media accounts or personal data. Instead, users should rely on legitimate and ethical means of accessing information, such as requesting permission from the account owner or following established legal procedures. This approach not only safeguards personal privacy and security but also upholds the highest ethical standards and legal practices in the cybersecurity domain:

Figure 5.7 – Example of magic-ware attacks

In conclusion, magic-ware attacks can be highly dangerous as they can allow hackers to gain complete control over a victim's device without their knowledge or consent. It is important to take precautions and to be protected.

How to prevent this type of attack

Here are some tips on how to protect from magic-ware attacks:

- Only install apps using the official app store of the mobile device
- Never install apps on mobile devices using the installer (`apk` or `IPA`)
- Never jailbreak your device
- Be suspicious if the app requires you to disable your antivirus before installing
- Only install apps from trusted providers
- Always verify the name of the company before installing the software
- Always check the permissions required by the app and uninstall any app that requires excessive permissions
- Avoid installing apps that *spy* on social media accounts

After discussing magic-ware attacks, let's move on to the next topic: hacking-ware.

Hacking-ware

In the context of cybersecurity, it is not uncommon for malicious actors to create web pages that advertise software or tools for hacking into a computer system. This kind of web page is called hacking-ware and often employ manipulative tactics to lure unsuspecting individuals into downloading and installing the malicious software onto their computers.

Typically, the advertised software will offer a range of attractive and tempting features, such as the ability to access a friend's camera, sensitive pictures, email accounts, and other confidential information. However, this software is designed to exploit vulnerabilities in the target system and provide unauthorized access to its data.

It is important to note that using such software to hack into a computer system without authorization is illegal and can result in severe consequences, including fines, legal penalties, and even imprisonment. Therefore, it is crucial to be vigilant and avoid downloading or using any software that is advertised as a hacking tool or that promises access to sensitive information without proper authorization:

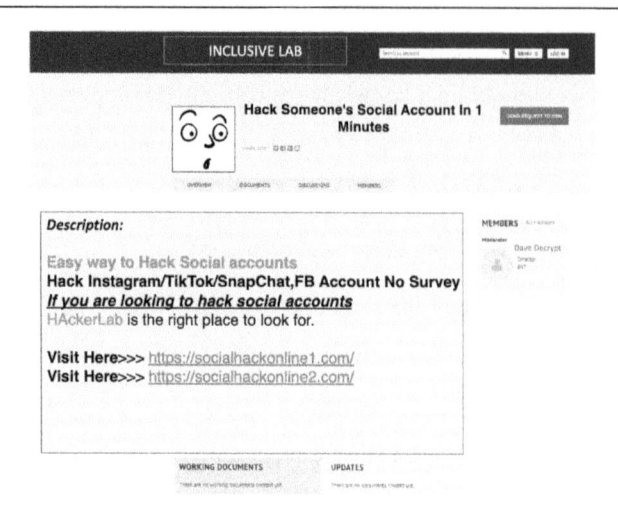

Figure 5.8 – Example of a hacking-ware attack

Hacking-ware attacks can be very sophisticated and difficult to detect, making it essential to take appropriate measures to protect your devices and data.

How to prevent this type of attack

Here are some tips on how to protect against this type of attack:

- Avoid installing *easy-hacking tools*
- Distrust any app that requires excessive permissions
- Avoid *one-click* hacking tools, as most of them are fake
- Avoid opening any email, link, or advertisement related to hacking-ware as they may infect your computer
- Never install apps from unknown sources
- Never disable antivirus software (or any other security system) to install an app

Moving on from discussing hacking-ware attacks, let's now turn our attention to gaming-based attacks.

Gaming-based attacks

Gaming-based attacks can take different forms, but one of the most common tactics used by attackers is to offer free mods, cheats, or codes that can give gamers an unfair advantage or unlock exclusive content. These offers often sound too good to be true and can be found on websites, forums, or social media platforms. Once gamers download these files or provide their login credentials, cybercriminals can gain access to their devices, steal personal information, or use their accounts for malicious purposes.

Another common tactic used by attackers is to offer gamers the ability to modify their avatars and obtain free in-game currency/gold or premium skins. These offers can be particularly appealing to gamers who want to customize their gaming experience or show off their progress to other players. However, these offers often involve the installation of third-party software or the provision of sensitive information, which can result in malware infection or data theft.

How to prevent this type of attack

By observing the following tips, you can enjoy your favorite games without worrying about cyber threats:

- Never disable antivirus software to *improve system performance*. Instead, use the gaming mode option that is available on most antivirus software to keep your system secure while avoiding interruptions in the game.
- Always distrust links offering free *premium* goods or accounts as they are likely to be a scam.
- Play games on trusted platforms and avoid using third-party cheats or mods as these can contain malware or other malicious components that can infect your system or steal your personal information.
- Be wary of unknown users asking for personal information. Cybercriminals often use social engineering tactics to trick you into revealing sensitive information or downloading malware.
- Use reputable anti-DDoS services to protect against DDoS attacks. These attacks can disrupt the normal functioning of gaming servers or websites, causing them to crash or become unavailable.
- Keep your gaming system and accessories updated with the latest security patches. This will help ensure that your system is protected against known security vulnerabilities.
- Only update your games using the in-game update tool and never download and install updates or patches from third-party sites as they may contain malware.
- Never install a patch or update that requests you to disable your antivirus or other security system.

As we wrap up the section on gaming-based attacks, let's now turn our attention to another type of cyber threat – forum-based attacks.

Forum-based attacks

Forum-based attacks are a type of cyber-attack that specifically target the users of online forums. These platforms provide a space for users to post messages and engage in discussions. The objective of these attacks is typically to persuade forum users to open a malicious link, download malware, or to provide personal information.

These types of attacks can take place in different ways. A common approach used in forum-based attacks involves the posting of malicious links or attachments in forum messages. This means that attackers may post links to fake websites or files that contain malware, disguised as legitimate content, and as soon as the user clicks on these links or downloads these files, their computer becomes infected with malware, which could compromise their personal information or give the attacker control of the victim's device.

Another approach involves attackers creating fake user profiles to gain the trust of other forum members. Once they have gained the trust of a victim, they may ask for personal information such as passwords or financial details.

Figure 5.9 shows another example of a forum-based attack wherein the attacker advertised access to some sensitive information for a low cost:

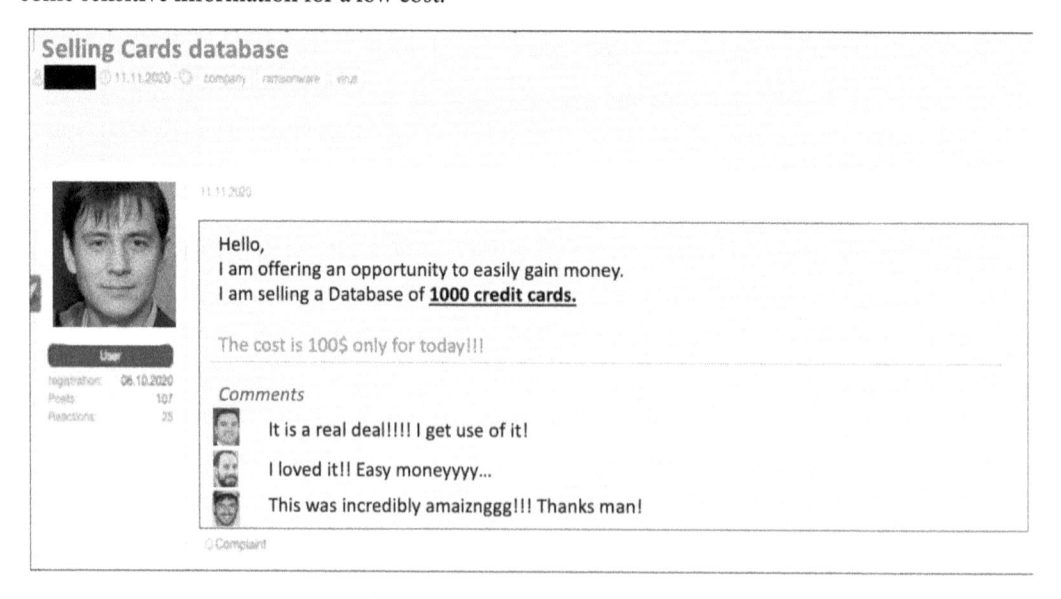

Figure 5.9 – Example of a forum-based attack

Referral scams are a common variation of forum-based attacks and typically involve multiple scammers working together. In this type of scam, the attacker has *trusted clients* – other scammers who confirm that the software is legitimate and convince people to pay for it. *Figure 5.10* is an example of this type of attack:

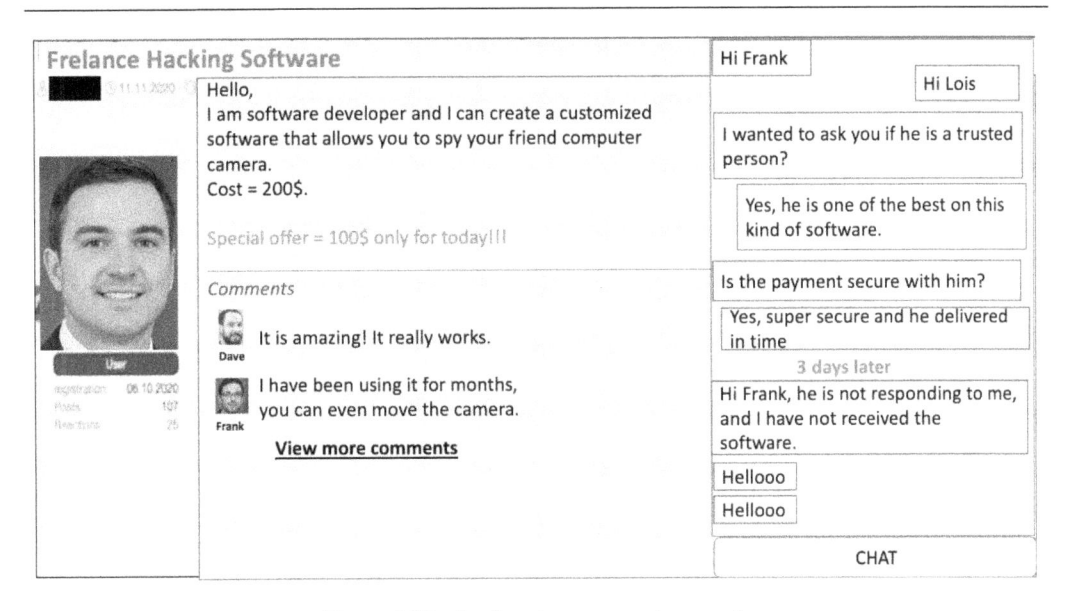

Figure 5.10 – A referral scam report example

Despite having doubts about the trustworthiness of the second scammer, the victim was convinced to give money to them due to the reassurances of the first scammer.

How to prevent this type of attack

To protect against forum-based attacks, users should practice the following:

- Never transfer any money to people that you have only met in a forum
- Distrust any service provided by forum users where you need to pay a fee in advance
- Avoid hiring any freelancer found in a forum; instead, use a recognized platform such as Fiverr
- Don't trust an unknown person in a forum just because another unknown user is backing that person
- Avoid forums related to illegal activities as those are normally full of scammers who know that people are less likely to report scams related to an illegal activity
- Be wary when clicking on links or downloading attachments from unknown sources
- Be wary of sharing personal information with anyone
- Use a forum platform that has a good reputation and is known to implement security measures such as *captcha verification* and *content filtering*
- It is important to monitor your forum activity regularly to detect any unusual or suspicious behavior or posts

Now, let's shift our focus to another type of cyber-attack, known as adware, which can infect your device through various online activities.

Adware

An **adware attack** involves the use of software that claims to improve the performance of your electronic device (smartphone, laptop, tablet, etc.). Typically, a pop-up window will appear automatically while you are navigating a web page, displaying a message that suggests your computer's performance is slow. The popup presents a unique solution to address this issue.

In some cases, the web page is aware of the attack and leverages it to gain some profit, while in other cases the page has been infected by malware that displays this popup without the consent of the owner of the page. *Figure 5.12* is an example of an adware attack:

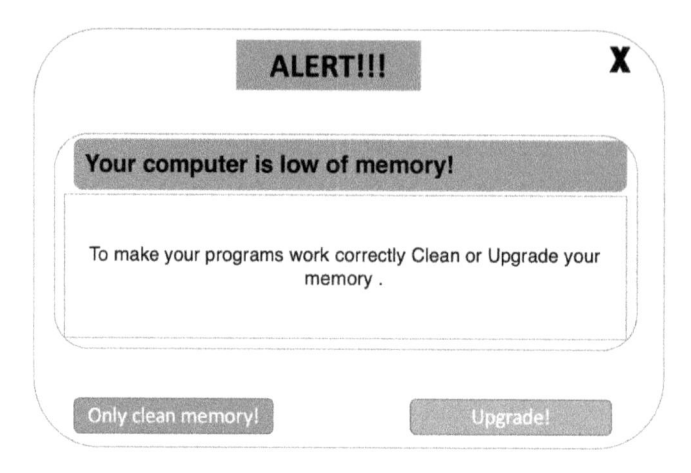

Figure 5.12 – Example of an adware attack

In the pop-up window, the attacker only put two options: **Only clean memory!** and **Upgrade!**. Both options are dangerous as one could infect your computer with malware while the other would request that you make payment, which would result in the attacker stealing your money and credit card information. In this case, the best option is to completely close the browser, as even clicking the **X** may download some malware.

It is important to highlight that, in this case, the attacker may have several goals, including the following:

- Selling software to enhance the performance of the computer
- Capturing credit card information
- Downloading malware to the victim's device
- All of the above

It's crucial to be cautious and vigilant when browsing the internet and downloading software. Let's see some tips on how to stay protected.

How to prevent this type of attack

Here are some tips for protecting yourself against adware attacks:

- Keep your antivirus up to date
- Keep your operating system and all applications current, with the latest security updates
- Be careful when downloading software or clicking on links from unknown or shady sources
- Customize your browser settings to prevent popups and automatic downloads
- Be cautious of offers that seem too good to be true (such as free software that claims to make your device faster)
- Distrust any message claiming that your computer is slow and offering you *free* software to fix it
- Trust your instincts; if something seems off, don't download it or click on it

By following these simple tips, you can reduce the risk of falling victim to adware attacks and keep your system secure. It is always better to be cautious and avoid clicking on suspicious links or downloading software from unknown sources, rather than dealing with the consequences of a potentially harmful adware attack.

Summary

This chapter explored the various ways in which technology is leveraged by attackers to enhance social engineering attacks. It covered tools that can be used by attackers to conduct high-value target attacks, such as OSINT.

Additionally, we did a deep dive into the most common types of attacks in which attackers leverage web-based tools to enhance their social engineering attacks. This included fake logins, fake updates, scareware, fake pages, magic-ware, hacking-ware, and many others.

The chapter also delved into gaming-based attacks, forum-based attacks, and adware, which can be used to target individuals or organizations.

Overall, the chapter highlighted the various techniques and tools that attackers use to exploit human vulnerabilities and gain access to sensitive information or systems. This chapter equipped you with skills in technology-enhanced social engineering attacks. You've learned about tools used in high-value target attacks and explored various web-based attack types, such as fake logins, gaming-based attacks, and adware. You've gained an understanding of human vulnerabilities exploited by attackers and how to identify and prevent such attacks.

In the following chapter, we will delve deeper into the further evolution of these attacks, looking at attacks specifically designed to target social media users and accounts. Additionally, we will learn how to identify and prevent these attacks.

6
Social Engineering and Social Network Attacks

This chapter delves into the realm of social engineering, exploring its manifestations through mobile applications and social network attacks. It examines the various tactics employed by malicious actors to manipulate individuals and exploit their vulnerabilities. It further explores the growing threat of social engineering via social networks, shedding light on the techniques used to deceive users and compromise their personal information.

Additionally, the chapter delves into WhatsApp- and Instagram-based attacks that have gained widespread attention. This section shows how attackers leverage these social networks to execute a variety of social engineering attacks. Furthermore, the chapter delves into dangerous clickbait attacks, emphasizing their ability to mislead users and drive them to malicious websites or distribute malware.

The chapter also addresses the role of social engineering in the perpetration of extortion, fake news, and forex attacks. It sheds light on how malicious actors utilize social engineering techniques to extort individuals or organizations, leveraging personal information obtained through mobile applications and social networks.

Then, we will discover the pervasive issue of fake news attacks, highlighting the spread of misinformation through social media and the detrimental consequences it poses for individuals and society. Lastly, the chapter touches upon forex attacks, exploring the fraudulent schemes related to the forex market and how social engineering tactics are utilized to deceive traders and users.

Throughout the chapter, we emphasize the importance of awareness, education, and proactive measures in combating social engineering attacks. We provide insights into the challenges of identifying and mitigating these attacks and offer strategies to protect you from falling victim to social engineering through mobile applications, social networks, and related tactics, such as clickbait, extortion, fake news, and forex attacks.

In this chapter, we will cover the following main topics:

- Social engineering through mobile applications:
  - Malicious apps and app-based attacks
  - Exploiting app permissions for data access
  - The challenges in identifying and mitigating such attacks
- Social engineering via social networks:
  - Clickbait attacks
  - WhatsApp-based attacks
  - Instagram-based attacks
- Other attacks:
  - Sextortion
  - Fake news attacks
  - Forex scams

Disclaimer

All characters in the examples are fictional characters.

The examples are inspired by real attacks; therefore, the language used (including spelling and grammatical errors) has been used on purpose.

Social engineering through mobile applications

The rise of smartphones and app-based technologies has led to significant transformations in social engineering through mobile applications. In the pre-smartphone era, limited functionality and connectivity minimized social engineering attacks. However, the introduction of app stores provided a platform for malicious actors to exploit the popularity of apps, tricking users into downloading fake or malicious applications.

An important development in this evolution was the emergence of app permissions and data access. Users often granted *excessive* permissions without fully understanding the associated risks, granting attackers access to personal information.

As smartphone apps grew, cybercriminals became more sophisticated, distributing malware-infected apps and employing phishing tactics. Social networking platforms and dating apps also became targets for manipulation through fake profiles, romance scams, and clickbait attacks.

Moreover, attackers began tailoring targeted attacks, such as spear-phishing campaigns, to exploit personal interests, affiliations, or professional relationships through mobile applications.

Overall, the evolution of mobile app-based social engineering attacks reflects the changing landscape of technology and the increasing ingenuity of cybercriminals.

In response to these threats, organizations and individuals have taken steps to mitigate the risks associated with social engineering through mobile applications. App store security measures have been strengthened, and app developers have focused on enhancing security and privacy features. Concurrently, security awareness campaigns aimed at educating users about app permissions, recognizing suspicious app behavior, and adopting general best practices have gained prominence.

> **Note**
> Social engineering through mobile applications continues to evolve alongside technological advancements. As new features, platforms, and technologies emerge, attackers find innovative ways to exploit them. Consequently, ongoing efforts in security research, technology development, and user education are crucial in staying ahead of these evolving threats.

By staying informed and adopting security best practices, both users and app developers can better protect themselves and their data from social engineering attacks in the mobile app ecosystem.

Malicious apps and app-based attacks

Malicious apps and **app-based attacks** refer to the exploitation of mobile applications to gather sensitive information or disrupt a device. These attacks involve the distribution of malicious software or the misuse of legitimate applications to compromise user devices, steal sensitive information, or perform unauthorized activities.

Types of malicious apps

The following are some of the most known types of malicious apps:

- **Malware-infected apps**: Attackers create and distribute apps that contain malware, including viruses, worms, trojans, or ransomware. These apps exploit vulnerabilities or deceive users to gain unauthorized access or control over devices. It is important to highlight that most of these apps are not in official marketplaces of apps such as **Google Play Store** or **Apple's App Store**; therefore, attackers use several social engineering tactics to deceive users to download and install these malicious apps manually – for example, by downloading and installing an APK on Android devices.

- **Fake apps**: Attackers create fake versions of popular apps, mimicking their appearance and functionality. Users unknowingly download and install these fake apps, which can lead to data theft, financial fraud, or other malicious activities. In other cases, attackers may leverage the popularity of a given TV show or a very popular system to create a fake app. One recent and famous case is **ChatGPT**. As of the writing of this book, OpenAI (the company behind ChatGPT) does not have a mobile app for ChatGPT (it is only accessible through a web-based interface), and the attackers are leveraging that to create hundreds of fake ChatGPT apps and distribute them through social media channels. Sadly, with over 100 million active users, many have fallen into this trap and installed a bogus application that, while it may have ChatGPT functionality, could be also downloading all your data (passwords, pictures, chats, and so on) into the hands of the attackers.
- **Grayware**: Grayware refers to apps that exhibit unwanted or intrusive behavior without being explicitly malicious. These apps may display excessive advertisements, track user behavior without consent, or execute unwanted functions.

Now, let's see which channels are used for the distribution of malicious apps and app-based attacks.

Distribution channels

Distribution channels for malicious apps and app-based attacks play a crucial role in the proliferation of such threats. Attackers employ various methods to distribute and spread malicious apps, targeting unsuspecting users. Here are some common distribution channels for malicious apps and app-based attacks:

- **Official app stores**: Despite rigorous security measures, malicious apps occasionally find their way onto official app stores such as Apple's App Store or Google Play Store. Attackers may exploit vulnerabilities in the app review process or use sophisticated techniques to bypass security checks. These malicious apps often masquerade as legitimate or popular apps, deceiving users into downloading and installing them.
- **Third-party app stores**: Unofficial or third-party app stores are common sources of malicious apps. These app stores operate outside the control and regulation of official channels, making it easier for attackers to distribute malicious apps. Users who download apps from such sources expose themselves to a higher risk of encountering malware-infected or counterfeit apps.
- **File-sharing platforms and websites**: Attackers may distribute malicious apps through file-sharing platforms, torrents, or websites that offer free or pirated app downloads. Users who obtain apps from these sources bypass traditional security checks and unknowingly expose themselves to the risk of installing malicious software.
- **Phishing and malicious websites**: Phishing websites and malicious websites serve as avenues for the distribution of malicious apps. Attackers may create websites that mimic legitimate app download pages or utilize social engineering techniques to trick users into downloading and installing malicious apps.

- **Social engineering and messaging platforms**: Attackers leverage social engineering techniques to distribute malicious apps through messaging platforms, social media, or email. They may send enticing messages or fraudulent links that lead users to download and install malicious apps.

- **Pre-installed apps**: Some devices come with pre-installed apps that contain malware or have vulnerabilities that can be exploited by attackers. These apps may be included in the device's firmware or added by untrusted manufacturers or distributors. This attack vector is mostly related to untrusted or unknown brands.

- **Drive-by downloads**: Drive-by downloads occur when users visit compromised websites that automatically trigger the download and installation of malicious apps or malware onto their devices without their knowledge or consent.

- **App update mechanisms**: Attackers may compromise app update mechanisms to deliver malicious updates to legitimate apps. Users who update their apps through compromised channels may inadvertently download and install malicious versions of the apps.

It is crucial for users to exercise caution and follow best practices to minimize the risk of encountering malicious apps. This includes downloading apps only from reputable sources, being wary of suspicious links or messages, keeping devices and apps updated with the latest security patches, and avoiding navigating untrusted pages.

Prevention and mitigation

Preventing and mitigating the risks associated with malicious apps and app-based attacks requires a proactive, multi-layered approach. Here are some preventive measures and mitigation strategies to safeguard against these threats:

- **User education and awareness**: Promote user education and awareness of the risks associated with downloading apps from untrusted sources, granting excessive permissions, and falling victim to social engineering tactics.

- **Official app store**: Make sure to only use official app stores as they have robust security measures and strict app review processes.

- **App permissions and privacy**: Review and understand the permissions requested by apps before granting access. Limit permissions to only what is necessary for the app's functionality and avoid installing apps requesting excessive permissions.

- **Device and app updates**: Keep mobile devices and apps updated with the latest security patches and bug fixes. Enable automatic updates whenever possible to ensure the timely installation of security updates. Remember, only install updates from within the app and never through an external web page.

- **Mobile security software**: Install reputable mobile security software that provides real-time threat detection and prevention. Make sure you only install reputable security software as there is a lot of malware disguised as security software.

- **User reviews and ratings**: Read user reviews and ratings before downloading an app. Pay attention to negative reviews or reports of suspicious activities associated with the app.

- **User-enabled security settings**: Leverage security settings provided by the operating system, such as app sandboxing, encryption, and app validation, to enhance the overall security of the device.

- **Collaboration and reporting**: Collaboration between users, app developers, and security researchers is key to identifying and reporting suspicious apps or potential vulnerabilities.

By implementing these preventive measures and mitigation strategies, users and app developers can significantly reduce the risks associated with malicious apps and app-based attacks.

Exploiting app permissions for data access

Exploiting app permissions for data access refers to the misuse or abuse of the permissions granted to mobile applications to gain unauthorized access to sensitive user data.

App permissions are the privileges that users grant to apps, allowing them to access specific features, functions, or personal information on their devices. Here are the most important things you need to know about exploiting app permissions for data access:

- **App permissions and user consent**:

  - App permissions are typically requested during installation or when a specific feature is accessed for the first time.

  - Common app permissions include access to contacts, the camera, the microphone, location, storage, messages, call logs, and device sensors.

  - Users should grant access only to necessary data to provide the intended functionality. For example, if you want to install a calculator app, then access to the camera or photos should not be granted.

- **Risks and concerns**:

  - App permissions can potentially grant access to sensitive information that, if misused, can lead to privacy breaches, identity theft, or other undesired attacks.

  - Some app developers may request unnecessary or excessive permissions, either intentionally or unintentionally, which can increase the risk of data misuse or abuse. Therefore, even if that excessive request was unintentional, users should avoid those apps.

  - Users may inadvertently grant permissions without fully understanding the implications or reviewing the requested access. Therefore, always *think before you click*.

- **Exploitation techniques**:

    - **Over-reaching permissions**: Malicious apps may request permissions that exceed their legitimate requirements – for example, a flashlight app requesting access to contacts or messages.

    - **Permission collusion**: Multiple apps working together may share data obtained through different permissions to gather more comprehensive user profiles or engage in targeted advertising.

    - **Permission re-delegation**: Some apps, particularly those pre-installed on devices, may exploit permissions to access data from other apps without explicit user consent.

    - **Permission escalation**: Malware-infected apps may exploit vulnerabilities in the operating system or app platforms to gain unauthorized access to additional permissions or sensitive data.

- **Consequences of exploitation**:

    - **Personal data exposure**: Exploiting app permissions can result in the unauthorized access and exfiltration of personal information, including contacts, messages, photos, location data, and browsing history.

    - **Privacy violations**: Misuse of permissions can lead to violations of user privacy, as sensitive data may be collected and shared with third parties, or used for targeted advertising without proper consent.

    - **Identity theft and fraud**: Access to personal data obtained through app permissions can be exploited for identity theft, financial fraud, or other malicious activities.

    - **Surveillance and tracking**: Unauthorized access to device sensors, location data, or the microphone can enable surveillance and tracking of users without their knowledge or consent.

Understanding the risks associated with app permissions and being cautious while granting them can help mitigate the potential misuse or abuse of personal data. Users should exercise vigilance and make informed decisions to protect their privacy and ensure their data remains secure while using mobile applications.

The challenges in identifying and mitigating such attacks

Identifying and mitigating malicious apps and app-based attacks is a complex task that involves various challenges due to the ever-changing nature of these threats. One of the primary challenges is the presence of polymorphic malware, which alters its code and behavior to evade traditional detection methods.

Additionally, while app stores implement security measures, some malicious apps manage to slip through the review process, exploiting vulnerabilities or using social engineering techniques. Third-party app sources further increase the risk of encountering malicious apps, as they often lack robust security measures.

Furthermore, malicious actors continuously adapt their techniques, incorporating social engineering and encryption to make detection and mitigation more difficult. Balancing user experience and security is another challenge, as stringent security measures may impact app functionality and user satisfaction.

> **Note**
> The global nature of app-based attacks raises legal and jurisdictional complexities, making it challenging to track down and prosecute attackers effectively.

But remember, user *awareness and education* are one of the best defense mechanisms as many users are not fully aware of the risks associated with untrusted app sources or excessive permissions.

Social engineering via social networks

In *Chapter 2*, we mentioned social media attacks and their impact but, here, we will dig deeper into the topic. Social engineering via social networks is a pervasive and concerning threat in the digital age where attackers exploit the vast user base and easily accessible personal information to perform several social engineering attacks.

They create convincing profiles and manipulate unsuspecting users through psychological tactics, persuasive techniques, and emotional triggers. By posing as trusted individuals, they deceive people into sharing confidential data, clicking malicious links, or downloading harmful files.

The consequences of social engineering on social networks include identity theft, financial fraud, and unauthorized account access. To counter this threat, users should exercise caution, use privacy settings, be mindful of shared information, and verify requests or messages before responding.

Social network platforms also play a crucial role in implementing security measures, raising user awareness, and promptly addressing reported incidents to protect their users from falling victim to social engineering attacks. However, the ultimate responsibility will always fall on the user.

Clickbait attack

A **clickbait attack** is a deceptive technique that entices users to click on a link through sensational or misleading content. Its primary goals include driving web traffic, increasing advertising revenue, or delivering malicious payloads. Clickbait content utilizes catchy headlines, provocative statements, or captivating images to grab users' attention and trigger curiosity or emotional responses.

These attacks can occur on various platforms such as social media, email, search engines, and news websites. Clicking on clickbait links poses risks such as malware infection, phishing attempts, and financial or identity theft.

Figure 6.1 shows an example of a clickbait attack on social media in which the user is presented with ads that use clickbait to get the user's attention to visit those sites:

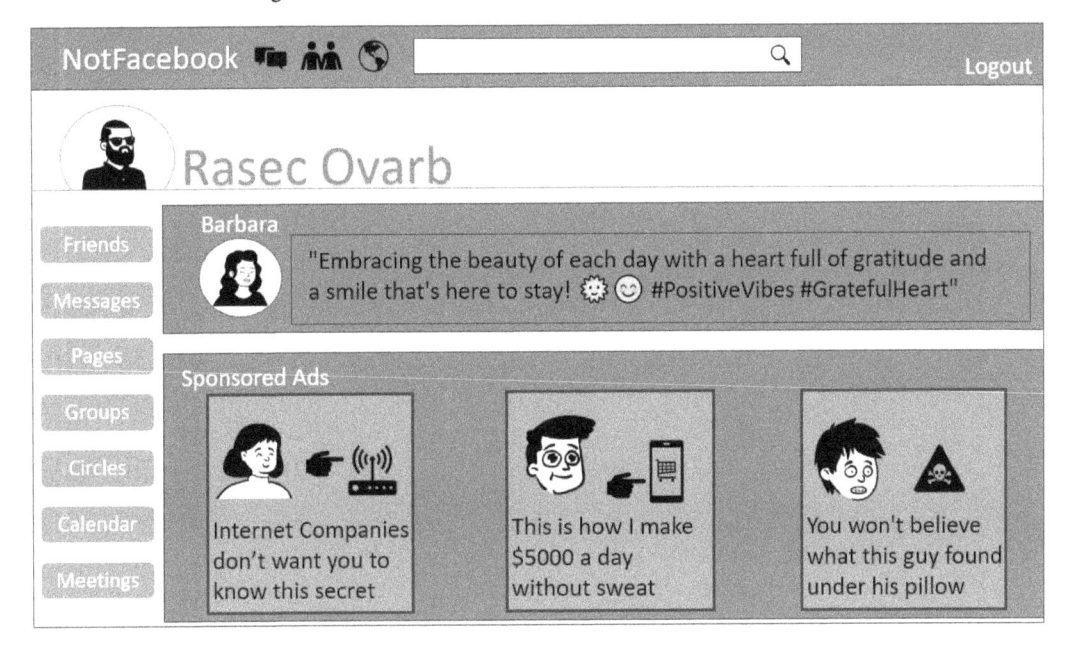

Figure 6.1 – Example of a clickbait attack

One of the most famous clickbait attacks in recent years was the *Miley Cyrus Dead* hoax that circulated on social media platforms. In 2013, numerous clickbait headlines and posts claimed that the popular singer and actress Miley Cyrus had died.

These posts attracted a significant amount of attention and sparked widespread concern among fans and the general public. The clickbait content employed sensational language, alarming headlines, and manipulated images to create a sense of urgency and shock. Users were enticed to click on the links to find out more details about the alleged incident. However, upon clicking, they were redirected to websites that aimed to generate web traffic, increase ad revenue, or distribute malware.

The *Miley Cyrus Dead* clickbait attack demonstrated the power of sensationalized content to attract users' attention and exploit their curiosity. It also highlighted the potential risks associated with clicking on such misleading links, including exposure to malicious websites and the spread of false information.

This incident served as a reminder of the importance of critically evaluating online content and being cautious of clickbait tactics. It also underscored the need for users to rely on trusted sources for news and information to avoid falling victim to such deceptive practices.

How to protect against clickbait attacks

Protecting yourself from clickbait attacks requires a combination of awareness, caution, and preventive measures. Here are some effective steps to help safeguard against clickbait attacks:

- **Be skeptical and exercising critical thinking**: Approach sensationalized headlines, provocative claims, or alarming content with caution.
- **Verify information from trusted sources**: Rely on reputable news outlets, official websites, or established sources for accurate and verified information.
- **Hover over links without clicking**: Before clicking on a link, hover your mouse pointer over it to preview the URL. This allows you to see the actual destination address and verify whether it matches the expected website or source.
- **Keep software up to date**: Ensure that your operating system, web browser, and security software are regularly updated.
- **Utilize ad-blockers and browser extensions**: Install reputable ad-blockers or browser extensions that can filter out clickbait advertisements and block malicious content.
- **Exercise caution with email and social media**: Be cautious when opening emails or messages from unknown or suspicious sources. Avoid clicking on links or attachments unless you can verify their authenticity and refrain from interacting with them.
- **Develop digital literacy and awareness**: Stay informed about common clickbait tactics, trends, and the potential risks they pose. Educate yourself on identifying clickbait content, understanding its motivations, and recognizing the red flags associated with deceptive tactics.
- **Report clickbait content**: If you come across clickbait content on social media or other platforms, report it to prevent the spread of that content.

By adopting these preventive measures and developing a cautious online approach, you can significantly reduce the likelihood of falling victim to clickbait attacks. Remember, staying informed, verifying information, and exercising critical thinking are key elements in protecting yourself from the deceptive tactics of clickbait.

WhatsApp-based attacks

WhatsApp has more than two billion active users around the world. That makes it one of the most used apps globally and this popularity also got criminals' attention to use it to execute social engineering attacks.

These attacks can take various forms, such as the distribution of malware, phishing attempts, account takeovers, or even the request for security codes to take over the account.

Again, the popularity of WhatsApp makes this app one of the favorite forms of media for attackers to execute social engineering attacks. Here, attackers may try to impersonate a famous person, a family member, a friend, or even your boss.

One common attack is based on the attacker sending a message to a victim while personating one of the victim's friends. As seen in *Figure 6.2*, the attacker will say that they are out and need some help from you. Here, several social engineering tactics such as a sense of urgency will be used by the attacker.

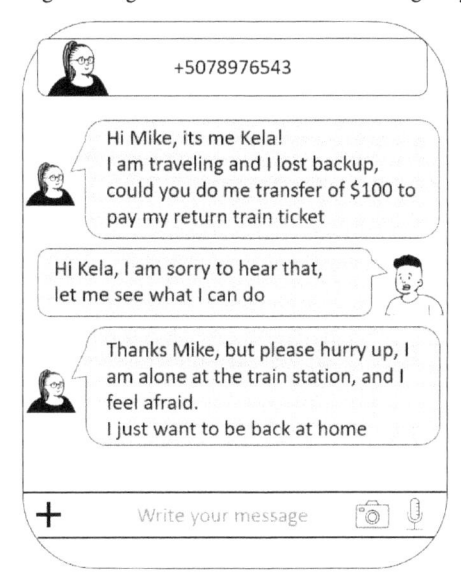

Figure 6.2 – Example of a WhatsApp attack

How to protect against WhatsApp attacks

To protect yourself from WhatsApp attacks, consider the following preventive measures:

- **Keep your app updated**: Ensure that you have the latest version of WhatsApp installed on your device.
- **Be wary of suspicious messages**: Exercise caution when receiving messages from unknown or suspicious contacts. Be particularly vigilant if the message contains unexpected links, attachments, or requests for personal information.
- **Verify the authenticity of messages**: If you receive a message from a familiar contact that seems unusual or out of character, verify its authenticity through a separate communication channel before taking any action.
- **Avoid clicking on suspicious links**: Refrain from clicking on links received through WhatsApp, especially from unknown sources or those that appear suspicious.

- **Be cautious of phishing attempts**: Be wary of phishing attempts that aim to trick you into revealing sensitive information. Be skeptical of messages requesting login credentials, financial details, or other personal information.

- **Enable two-step verification:** Take advantage of WhatsApp's two-step verification feature. This adds an extra layer of security by requiring a passcode in addition to your phone number when verifying your account.

- **Use official app sources**: Download WhatsApp only from official app stores, such as Google Play Store for Android or the Apple App Store for iOS.

- **Secure your device**: Implement robust security measures on your device, such as setting a strong lock screen passcode, using biometric authentication, and regularly updating your device's operating system and security software.

- **Report suspicious activity**: If you encounter any suspicious or malicious activity on WhatsApp, such as phishing attempts or spam messages, block the user and report it on WhatsApp.

By following these precautions and staying vigilant, you can significantly reduce the risk of falling victim to WhatsApp attacks and protect your personal information and privacy while using the app.

Instagram-based attacks

Instagram, one of the most popular social media platforms, is also a target for cyber-attacks. These attacks can take various forms, including phishing, account hijacking, malware distribution, and social engineering.

One common attack method is **phishing**, where attackers create fake Instagram login pages or send messages that appear to come from Instagram asking users to click on a link and enter their login credentials. Once the attacker has obtained the user's login information, they can take over the account and use it to spread spam, scam links, or malware. Another type of attack is **account hijacking**, where attackers use various methods to gain unauthorized access to an Instagram account, such as guessing passwords, exploiting vulnerabilities, or stealing login credentials. Once the account is compromised, the attacker can lock the user out, change the account's settings, or post inappropriate or malicious content.

Malware distribution is another threat to Instagram users, where attackers use social engineering tactics to trick users into downloading and installing malware-infected apps or clicking on malicious links that lead to the installation of malware on their devices. This malware can then steal sensitive information, spy on user activity, or control the device. Social engineering attacks, such as fake giveaways, impersonation scams, or phishing messages, are also common on Instagram. Attackers use these tactics to trick users into disclosing personal information, downloading malware, or following links that lead to malicious websites.

Figure 6.3 shows an example of an Instagram attack where an unknown person sends an SMS to say that they have seen your photos on another profile. The SMS contains the tag of another profile, which is a fake profile:

Figure 6.3 – Example of an Instagram attack

One of the most famous Instagram attacks occurred in 2017 and involved the manipulation of Instagram's email recovery system. Hackers exploited a vulnerability to gain unauthorized access to high-profile accounts, including celebrities and influencers. By changing an account's associated email address, the attackers took control and could post malicious content or blackmail the account owners. Instagram took immediate action to address the issue and enhance security measures. The incident highlighted the importance of strong authentication protocols and continuous security monitoring to prevent similar attacks.

How to protect against Instagram attacks

To protect yourself from Instagram attacks, consider the following preventive measures:

- **Use strong, unique passwords**: Use a strong, unique password for your Instagram account.
- **Enable two-factor authentication**: Activate **two-factor authentication (2FA)** for your Instagram account.
- **Be cautious of suspicious links and messages**: Avoid clicking on suspicious links or messages received through Instagram. Be wary of messages from unknown users, especially those containing requests for personal information or enticing offers.
- **Be wary of phishing attempts**: Verify the authenticity of any requests for personal information or login credentials before providing them.

- **Keep your app updated**: Developers release updates to patch security vulnerabilities and enhance the overall security of applications.

- **Be mindful of third-party apps**: Exercise caution when granting permissions to third-party apps linked to your Instagram account.

- **Review privacy settings**: Regularly review and adjust your privacy settings on Instagram. Limit the visibility of your posts, control who can tag you, and review the permissions you have granted to third-party apps.

- **Report suspicious activity**: If you notice any suspicious activity on your account, such as unauthorized login attempts or unfamiliar posts, report it to Instagram immediately.

- **Educate yourself**: Stay informed about the latest Instagram security features, best practices, and common attack techniques. Familiarize yourself with Instagram's official guidelines and recommended security measures.

- **Be wary of public Wi-Fi**: Avoid logging into your Instagram account on public Wi-Fi networks.

By implementing these preventive measures, you can significantly reduce the risk of falling victim to Instagram attacks and better protect your account and personal information.

Other attacks

Now, we will explore the dark underbelly of the digital landscape as we delve into the realms of extortion, the pervasive spread of fake news, and the deceptive allure of forex scams.

Sextortion

Sextortion is a form of cybercrime where malicious individuals or groups threaten to reveal sensitive or damaging information about a person or organization unless a demand is met. The primary goal of these attacks is to exploit fear, embarrassment, or financial repercussions to coerce victims into complying with the attackers' demands.

In email sextortion attacks, the attacker sends threatening messages to the victim, often claiming to have compromising or confidential information. They demand a payment, usually in cryptocurrency, in exchange for keeping the information secret. The attacker may threaten to leak sensitive data, publish damaging content, or disrupt the victim's online presence.

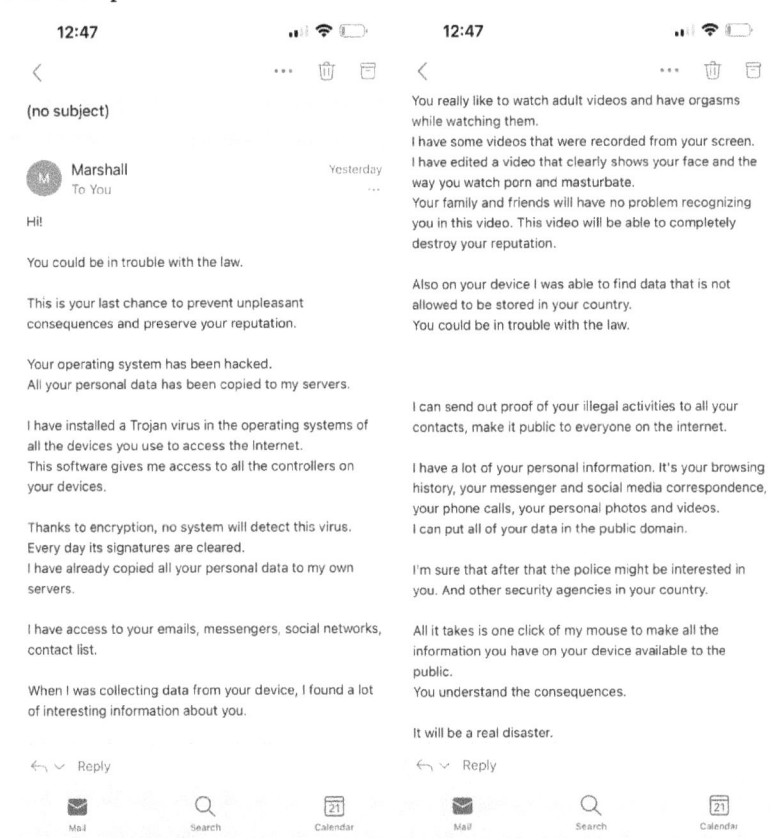

Figure 6.4 is an example of what a sextortion attack can look like:

Figure 6.4 – Example of a sextortion attack

Now let's see some tips on how to protect against this kind of attack.

How to protect against sextortion attacks

Protecting against extortion attacks requires a multi-layered approach:

- **Regularly back up data**: Maintain up-to-date backups of your important files and systems to mitigate the impact of a ransomware attack. Ensure the backups are stored securely and offline to prevent them from being compromised.

- **Use strong security measures**: Implement robust security measures, including firewalls, antivirus software, and intrusion detection systems, to detect and prevent malware infections and unauthorized access.

- **Be cautious with personal information**: Be mindful of sharing personal information online and on social media platforms. Limit the information publicly available about yourself or your organization to minimize the risk of being targeted.

- **Stay vigilant**: Be wary of suspicious emails, messages, or requests for personal information. Avoid clicking on links or opening attachments from unknown sources, as they may contain malware or be part of phishing campaigns.

- **Maintain up-to-date software**: Keep your operating system, applications, and security software updated with the latest patches and security fixes. This helps protect against known vulnerabilities that attackers may exploit.

- **Educate yourself and employees**: Stay informed about the latest attack techniques and educate yourself and your employees about the risks of extortion attacks. Provide training on how to recognize and respond to suspicious emails, phishing attempts, or other social engineering tactics.

- **Develop an incident response plan**: Establish an incident response plan that outlines the steps to take in the event of an extortion attack. This includes reporting the incident to law enforcement and engaging with cybersecurity professionals to assist with investigation and recovery.

By following these preventive measures and maintaining a proactive approach to cybersecurity, individuals and organizations can reduce their vulnerability to extortion attacks and better protect themselves from potential harm or financial loss.

Fake news attacks

Fake news attacks refer to deliberate efforts to spread false or misleading information with the aim of deceiving and manipulating audiences. These attacks occur through various channels, such as social media, websites, blogs, and online news platforms. The goal is to create confusion, shape public opinion, and achieve specific agendas.

One of the most famous fake news attacks in recent history was the **Pizzagate** conspiracy theory. In 2016, false claims began circulating on social media and fringe websites that a pizzeria in Washington, D.C. was involved in a child sex trafficking ring led by high-ranking officials connected to the Democratic Party. The conspiracy theory gained traction, fueled by misleading articles and social media posts.

In December 2016, an individual influenced by the conspiracy theory entered the pizzeria with a firearm, firing shots but not injuring anyone. The incident highlighted the real-world consequences of fake news and the potential for harm that can arise from the spread of false information.

The Pizzagate incident serves as a stark reminder of the power of fake news to manipulate public opinion, incite violence, and disrupt lives. It also underscored the importance of critical thinking, fact-checking, and media literacy in the digital age.

Fake news attacks work through several mechanisms:

- **Fabrication and dissemination**: Attackers create fictional stories or manipulate existing news to fabricate false information. They often mimic the style and appearance of legitimate news sources, making it difficult for users to distinguish between real and fake news.
- **Social media amplification**: Fake news spreads rapidly through social media platforms due to their wide reach and fast information dissemination. Users share and engage with content, and algorithms prioritize popular or engaging posts, amplifying their visibility.
- **Emotional manipulation**: Fake news often targets people's emotions to provoke strong reactions. By exploiting biases, fears, or hopes, attackers aim to generate intense emotional responses that can cloud judgment and lead to the rapid spread of misinformation.
- **Confirmation bias and echo chambers**: Fake news often confirms pre-existing beliefs or aligns with a specific worldview, making it more likely for individuals to accept and share it without verifying its accuracy. People tend to be drawn to information that reinforces their existing opinions, leading to the formation of echo chambers where false information thrives.
- **Impersonation and parody**: Attackers may impersonate reputable news organizations or public figures to lend credibility to fake news. They create fake websites or social media accounts that closely resemble legitimate sources, making it challenging for users to distinguish between real and fake content.
- **Clickbait and ad revenue**: Fake news articles or headlines designed to be sensational or controversial attract users' attention and generate high click-through rates. This increases ad impressions and revenue for the attackers, who profit from increased traffic to their websites.
- **Disinformation campaigns**: Fake news attacks can be part of broader disinformation campaigns with political, social, or economic motives. These campaigns often involve well-coordinated efforts to spread false narratives, manipulate public opinion, and influence events such as elections or geopolitical conflicts.

Fake news attacks exploit the vulnerabilities of the digital information landscape, where information spreads quickly and often without proper verification. They can have serious consequences, including the erosion of trust in media, the polarization of societies, and the undermining of democratic processes.

Countering fake news attacks requires a multi-faceted approach, including media literacy education, critical thinking, fact-checking initiatives, responsible information sharing, and algorithmic transparency. Collaboration among technology platforms, governments, journalists, and civil society organizations is crucial in combating the spread of fake news and promoting a more informed and resilient society.

How to protect against fake news attacks

Protecting yourself from fake news attacks requires critical thinking, media literacy, and responsible information consumption. Here are some strategies to help protect against fake news:

- **Verify sources**: Before accepting information as true, verify the credibility and reputation of the sources. Look for well-established and reputable news organizations known for their journalistic standards and fact-checking practices.
- **Cross-check information**: Cross-reference information across multiple reliable sources to ensure accuracy. If a story or claim seems sensational or too good to be true, it's important to investigate further before accepting it as fact.
- **Fact-check**: Utilize fact-checking websites or tools that specialize in debunking false information. These resources can provide objective assessments of the accuracy of news stories and claims.
- **Read beyond the headlines**: Avoid sharing news based solely on headlines. Often, misleading or exaggerated headlines don't accurately reflect the content of the article. Read the full article to gain a comprehensive understanding before drawing conclusions.
- **Be skeptical of viral content**: Viral content doesn't always equate to reliable or accurate information. Popular or widely shared posts should be scrutinized even more carefully to ensure they are not part of a misinformation campaign.
- **Develop critical thinking skills**: Enhance your critical thinking abilities to evaluate information critically. Consider the source's credibility, assess the evidence provided, look for biases or propaganda techniques, and consider alternative perspectives before accepting news as factual.
- **Media literacy education**: Promote media literacy education in schools, workplaces, and communities. Equip individuals with the skills to discern reliable information from fake news. This includes understanding journalistic standards, recognizing bias and manipulation tactics, and learning how to evaluate sources.
- **Share responsibly**: Take responsibility for the information you share. Before reposting or sharing news articles, verify their accuracy, and consider the potential consequences of spreading false information. Be cautious about sharing unverified or sensationalized content that may contribute to the proliferation of fake news.
- **Report fake news**: Report instances of fake news to relevant platforms or authorities. Many social media platforms have mechanisms to flag or report false content, which helps in identifying and taking down misleading information.
- **Support quality journalism**: Support reputable and trustworthy news sources by subscribing to their services or donating. Quality journalism plays a crucial role in providing accurate and balanced information to the public.

By adopting these strategies and fostering a critical mindset, individuals can protect themselves from falling victim to fake news attacks and contribute to the promotion of accurate and reliable information in the digital landscape.

Forex scams

Forex scams refer to fraudulent schemes and manipulative practices in the **foreign exchange** (**forex**) market. These attacks aim to deceive traders, investors, or individuals interested in participating in forex trading. Here's an overview of important aspects of forex attacks:

- **Forex fraud schemes**: Forex fraud schemes come in various forms, including Ponzi schemes, fake investment opportunities, signal services, and trading robots. These schemes often promise high returns with minimal risk, attracting unsuspecting individuals to invest their money.

- **Fake forex brokers**: Fraudulent individuals or entities may pose as legitimate forex brokers to lure investors. They may create professional-looking websites, offer attractive trading conditions, and claim to be regulated. However, their intention is to deceive and defraud investors by misappropriating funds or manipulating trades.

- **Pump and dump schemes**: Pump and dump schemes involve artificially inflating the price of a particular currency pair through false information or manipulation. Fraudsters will spread positive news or recommendations about a currency, enticing unsuspecting traders to buy in. Once the price rises, they sell their holdings, causing the price to collapse, and leaving other traders with significant losses.

- **Manipulation of forex prices**: In some cases, individuals or groups may attempt to manipulate forex prices for their benefit. This can involve spreading false rumors or using illegal trading strategies to create artificial price movements, exploiting market volatility, and profiting from the resulting trades.

- **Pyramid schemes**: Some forex attacks take the form of pyramid schemes, where participants are encouraged to recruit others into a trading network. These schemes promise substantial profits from recruiting new members rather than from actual trading activities. As the scheme grows, it eventually collapses, leaving many participants with losses.

- **Fake trading signals and analysis**: Fraudsters may offer paid trading signals or analysis services claiming to provide accurate predictions for profitable trades. However, these signals may be fabricated or manipulated to deceive traders into making losing trades, benefiting the fraudsters who receive commissions or fees.

- **Unauthorized trading**: Unauthorized trading occurs when a broker or individual engages in trades without the investor's consent. This can lead to substantial losses for the investor while benefiting the unauthorized trader.

In conclusion, forex fraud schemes involve various deceptive practices, such as fake brokers, pump and dump schemes, price manipulation, pyramid schemes, fake trading signals, and unauthorized trading. These schemes exploit unsuspecting investors, leading to significant financial losses. Investors must exercise caution and verify the legitimacy of brokers and investment opportunities to protect themselves from forex fraud.

How to protect against forex scams

Protecting yourself from forex attacks involves taking precautions and conducting thorough research:

- **Choose regulated brokers**: Trade with regulated brokers that are authorized and overseen by reputable financial regulatory authorities. Check their licensing status and verify their credibility before depositing funds.
- **Conduct due diligence**: Research brokers or investment firms thoroughly before engaging with them. Look for reviews, testimonials, and independent assessments of their reputation and track record.
- **Be wary of unrealistic promises**: Exercise caution when confronted with forex opportunities that promise guaranteed high returns with little or no risk. Forex trading involves inherent risks, and no legitimate broker or trader can guarantee consistent profits.
- **Verify trading signals and analysis**: If relying on trading signals or analysis services, verify their track record and authenticity. Look for transparency, including clear explanations of trading strategies and risk management practices.
- **Educate yourself**: Acquire a solid understanding of forex trading principles, market dynamics, and risk management strategies. This knowledge will help you identify suspicious activities or offers that deviate from legitimate trading practices.
- **Monitor your account**: Regularly review your trading account statements, trade confirmations, and activity to ensure there are no unauthorized transactions or suspicious activities.
- **Report suspected fraud**: If you encounter fraudulent activities or suspect forex attacks, report them to the relevant financial authorities or regulatory bodies in your jurisdiction. This helps protect others and contributes to the investigation and prevention of future fraud.

By being vigilant, conducting proper research, and staying informed, individuals can reduce the risk of falling victim to forex attacks and safeguard their investments in the forex market.

Summary

In this chapter, we have highlighted several key skills that are important for navigating the digital landscape safely. These skills include the following:

- **App permissions awareness**: Understanding the permissions requested by apps and being cautious about granting excessive access to personal information can help mitigate the risk of unauthorized data access

- **Privacy and security measures**: Implementing robust measures such as strong passwords, 2FA, and regularly updating security settings can enhance privacy and protect against malicious attacks

- **Clickbait recognition**: Developing the ability to identify and avoid enticing yet potentially harmful links can help protect against clickbait attacks and the associated risks

- **Critical thinking and skepticism**: Cultivating a healthy level of skepticism toward information encountered on social media can help in identifying and mitigating the spread of fake news and misinformation

- **Personal content protection**: Being mindful of sharing sensitive or compromising content online can reduce the vulnerability to sextortion and other forms of blackmail

- **Financial literacy**: Developing a good understanding of financial scams and being cautious about promises of quick financial gains can help guard against falling victim to forex scams or other fraudulent schemes

By acquiring and honing these skills, individuals can empower themselves to navigate the digital world with increased awareness, protect their personal information, and mitigate the risks associated with social engineering attacks through mobile applications.

Also, we have highlighted the numerous challenges faced in identifying and mitigating social engineering attacks. The ever-evolving nature of these tactics, combined with the complexity of technological systems, requires continuous vigilance and proactive measures. As we move forward, it is crucial to foster awareness, educate users, and develop robust security mechanisms to safeguard against the multifaceted threats posed by social engineering in today's interconnected world.

7
AI-Driven Techniques in Enhanced Social Engineering Attacks

In the rapidly evolving landscape of cybersecurity, one of the most concerning developments is integrating **artificial intelligence** (**AI**) into social engineering attacks. Social engineering, which is the practice of exploiting human psychology to manipulate individuals into divulging sensitive information or performing certain actions, has long been a favored tactic of malicious actors. However, the advent of AI has taken social engineering to new heights, empowering attackers with enhanced capabilities and sophistication.

This chapter will explore the intersection of AI and social engineering, delving into the growing role of AI in facilitating these attacks and the techniques employed by AI-driven social engineers. We will also delve into strategies for combating AI-enhanced social engineering attacks, acknowledging the need for a multi-faceted approach to defend against this evolving threat landscape.

Furthermore, we will emerge into the field of deepfakes, a powerful AI-driven technology that enables the creation of fabricated content, such as videos and audio, that is indistinguishable from reality. We will explore the implications of deepfakes for social engineering attacks, highlighting the potential for deception and manipulation on an unprecedented scale.

Lastly, we will shed light on other AI-powered attacks, specifically focusing on AI-powered phishing attacks and AI-assisted social media manipulation attacks. Understanding these distinct forms of AI-driven attacks is crucial to comprehending the breadth of the threat landscape and developing comprehensive defense strategies.

By exploring the techniques employed, strategies for defense, and the emerging landscape of deepfakes, we aim to equip you with the knowledge necessary to navigate this ever-evolving realm of cybersecurity. Together, we can strengthen our defenses, mitigate the risks posed by AI-enhanced social engineering attacks, and preserve the trust and security of our digital ecosystems.

In this chapter, we will cover the following main topics:

- Artificial intelligence in social engineering attacks:
  - The growing role of AI in social engineering
  - AI-driven social engineering techniques
- Strategies for combating AI-enhanced social engineering attacks:
  - Understanding the threat landscape
  - Implementing effective security measures
  - Fostering a culture of security and awareness
  - Strengthening collaboration and information sharing
- Understanding deepfakes:
  - Deepfake videos
  - Deepfake audio
  - Implications for social engineering attacks
- Other AI attacks:
  - AI-powered phishing attacks
  - AI-assisted social media manipulation attacks

Technical requirements

There are no technical requirements for this chapter.

Artificial intelligence in social engineering attacks

As AI continues to advance, its influence on social engineering attacks has grown significantly. As you now know, social engineering attacks involve exploiting human vulnerabilities, trust, and manipulation techniques to deceive individuals or organizations into revealing sensitive information, performing actions, or compromising security measures. The integration of AI techniques in social engineering has introduced a new level of sophistication and effectiveness to these malicious activities.

The growing role of AI in social engineering

With the increasing availability and power of AI technologies, threat actors have begun leveraging AI in social engineering attacks to achieve higher success rates and more significant impact. AI brings several advantages to social engineering:

- **Personalization and targeting**: AI enables threat actors to analyze vast amounts of data, such as social media profiles, online activity, and public records, to gather information about their targets. This information allows them to craft highly personalized social engineering attacks that exploit the specific characteristics, interests, and vulnerabilities of individuals or organizations.
- **Automated campaigns**: AI automates various aspects of social engineering attacks, such as message generation, response analysis, and follow-up interactions. This automation allows threat actors to scale their attacks, targeting a larger number of individuals or organizations simultaneously with minimal effort.
- **Behavioral analysis**: AI algorithms can analyze patterns of human behavior, including language use, response patterns, and decision-making processes. By understanding these behavioral patterns, AI can mimic human interactions more convincingly, increasing the success rate of social engineering attacks.

AI-driven social engineering techniques

AI has enabled the development of sophisticated techniques that enhance the deception and manipulation capabilities of social engineering attacks. Some notable AI-driven social engineering techniques include the following:

- **Natural language processing** (**NLP**): AI-powered chatbots and conversational agents can simulate human-like conversations by processing and generating natural language. This enables threat actors to engage with targets in a realistic manner, building trust and extracting sensitive information.
- **Voice cloning**: AI algorithms can clone and mimic voices with high accuracy. This allows threat actors to impersonate trusted individuals over phone calls or voice-based communication channels, making their social engineering attempts more credible and convincing.
- **Deepfake technology**: AI-powered deepfake technology can manipulate audio, video, or images to create deceptive content that appears genuine. Threat actors can use deepfakes to fabricate evidence, impersonate individuals, or create misleading scenarios, further enhancing the effectiveness of social engineering attacks. A lot of free AI tools exist such as NVIDIA, My Heritage, Lensa AI, and many more that can be used to adjust life video streams, audio, or images in both malicious and benign ways.

Now, let's look at some strategies for combating AI-enhanced social engineering attacks.

Strategies for combating AI-enhanced social engineering attacks

The rise of AI has introduced new complexities and challenges in combating social engineering attacks. With AI-driven techniques becoming increasingly sophisticated, it is crucial to develop effective strategies to mitigate the risks posed by AI-enhanced social engineering attacks.

Understanding the threat landscape

To effectively combat AI-enhanced social engineering attacks, it is crucial to have a deep understanding of the threat landscape. The threat landscape encompasses the evolving tactics, techniques, and motivations of threat actors who exploit AI technologies for social engineering purposes. We are going to explore the various aspects of the threat landscape and provide insights into the factors that contribute to the success and prevalence of AI-driven social engineering attacks:

- **Evolving tactics and techniques**:

  - **AI-driven deception**: Threat actors leverage AI technologies, such as NLP and deepfake technology, to create sophisticated and convincing social engineering attacks. They employ techniques such as spear phishing, impersonation, and manipulation of multimedia content to deceive targets and elicit the desired response.

  - **Automation and scalability**: AI enables threat actors to automate various stages of social engineering attacks, from initial reconnaissance to follow-up interactions. This automation allows them to target a larger number of individuals or organizations simultaneously, increasing their chances of success.

  - **Social engineering blends**: Threat actors combine AI techniques with traditional social engineering tactics to create hybrid attacks. By leveraging AI to personalize and refine their approaches, they can overcome the skepticism and defenses that individuals and organizations have developed against traditional social engineering techniques.

- **Motivations of threat actors**:

  - **Financial gain**: Many social engineering attacks driven by AI have a financial motive. Threat actors may seek to gain access to financial accounts, steal sensitive information for monetary value, or exploit vulnerabilities to conduct fraudulent activities.

  - **Espionage and information gathering**: State-sponsored threat actors may employ AI-enhanced social engineering attacks to gather intelligence, access classified information, or compromise critical infrastructure. They may target government agencies, research institutions, or organizations that have valuable intellectual property.

  - **Disinformation and influence**: Threat actors may utilize AI-driven social engineering attacks to spread disinformation, manipulate public opinion, or influence social and political discourse. This can have far-reaching consequences, including destabilizing governments, undermining trust in institutions, or manipulating election outcomes.

- **Vulnerabilities and exploitation**:

  - **Human factors**: AI-enhanced social engineering attacks exploit innate human vulnerabilities, such as trust, curiosity, and the desire to help others. Threat actors capitalize on these traits to deceive individuals into disclosing sensitive information, clicking on malicious links, or taking unauthorized actions.

  - **Technological weaknesses**: AI-driven social engineering attacks may exploit vulnerabilities in software, systems, or infrastructure. Outdated software, misconfigurations, and lack of robust security measures can provide entry points for threat actors to launch their attacks.

  - **Emerging AI technologies**: The rapid advancement of AI technologies presents new challenges in defending against social engineering attacks. As AI becomes more accessible, threat actors have access to powerful tools that can generate convincing content, imitate human behavior, and adapt their approaches based on evolving defense mechanisms.

Understanding the threat landscape is essential for developing effective countermeasures and defense strategies against AI-enhanced social engineering attacks. By staying informed about evolving tactics, motivations, and vulnerabilities, organizations and individuals can proactively identify potential risks, implement appropriate security measures, and respond effectively to mitigate the impact of these sophisticated attacks. Continual monitoring, threat intelligence gathering, and collaboration with security professionals are vital for keeping up with the dynamic threat landscape and maintaining robust defenses.

Implementing effective security measures

Implementing effective security measures is crucial in safeguarding against AI-enhanced social engineering attacks. These measures help organizations and individuals mitigate the risks associated with social engineering tactics driven by AI and enhance their overall security posture. In this section, we'll explore key security measures that can be implemented to protect against AI-enhanced social engineering attacks:

- **Strong authentication mechanisms**:

  - Implement **multi-factor authentication** (**MFA**) to add an extra layer of security beyond passwords

  - Promote the use of strong, complex passwords and enforce regular password changes

  - Encourage the adoption of password managers to securely store and manage passwords, reducing the risk of password-related vulnerabilities

- **Employee training and awareness**:

  - Conduct regular security awareness training sessions to educate employees about the risks and tactics associated with social engineering attacks

- Conduct phishing simulation exercises to assess employees' susceptibility to phishing attacks and enhance their ability to identify and report suspicious emails or messages

- **Robust incident response**:
  - Develop an incident response plan that outlines the steps to be taken in the event of a social engineering attack.
  - Implement systems and processes to monitor and detect potential social engineering attacks. Establish reporting channels that allow employees to easily report suspicious activities, ensuring prompt investigation and mitigation.

- **Access controls and least privilege**:
  - Implement **role-based access control (RBAC)** to restrict access to sensitive information and critical systems based on individuals' roles and responsibilities
  - Follow the principle of least privilege, granting users the minimum access necessary to perform their job functions

- **Security assessments and vulnerability management**:
  - Conduct periodic security assessments, including vulnerability scanning, penetration testing, and security audits
  - Establish a robust patch management process to ensure that software, operating systems, and applications are up to date with the latest security patches

- **Ongoing monitoring and threat intelligence**:
  - Deploy monitoring tools that provide visibility into network traffic, user activities, and system logs to monitor for suspicious behavior, anomalous patterns, or indicators of compromise that may signal an AI-enhanced social engineering attack
  - Stay updated on emerging threats, AI-driven attack techniques, and evolving social engineering tactics

By implementing these security measures, organizations can significantly enhance their resilience against AI-enhanced social engineering attacks. However, it is important to recognize that security is an ongoing process and requires regular reassessment, adaptation, and collaboration between security teams and users. Constant monitoring, continuous education, and staying up to date with emerging threats and best practices are essential to maintaining effective security.

Fostering a culture of security and awareness

Fostering a culture of security and awareness is essential in protecting against AI-enhanced social engineering attacks. It involves creating an environment where individuals prioritize security, remain vigilant, and actively contribute to protecting sensitive information and systems. By instilling a culture of security and awareness, organizations can build a strong line of defense against social engineering attacks driven by AI. This can be achieved through several strategies:

- First, leadership and management support are crucial in setting a security-conscious tone. Leaders should emphasize the importance of security and promote a culture that values information protection and adherence to security policies. Allocating resources, such as budget and personnel, demonstrates a commitment to security.

- Comprehensive security policies and procedures are vital for establishing clear expectations and guidelines. Organizations should develop robust security policies that cover areas such as data handling, password management, and reporting procedures for security incidents. Regular policy reviews ensure policies remain up to date with emerging threats.

- Continuous security awareness and training programs are essential for educating employees about social engineering techniques, AI-driven threats, and best practices for safeguarding sensitive information. Conducting phishing simulations helps employees recognize and respond to phishing attempts, while security training sessions provide practical knowledge to enhance their security awareness.

- Open communication channels encourage employees to report suspicious activities, potential social engineering incidents, or security concerns. Establishing reporting mechanisms and providing feedback and recognition for proactive security practices contribute to a reporting culture.

- Regular communication and updates keep employees informed about emerging threats, recent security incidents, and best practices. Security bulletins or newsletters disseminate valuable information and serve as reminders to reinforce key security messages.

- Collaboration and engagement across departments foster a holistic approach to security. A cross-functional collaboration involving IT teams, security teams, HR, and other departments promotes information sharing and the exchange of expertise. External partnerships with industry associations, security vendors, and security communities facilitate knowledge sharing and staying informed about emerging threats.

By fostering a culture of security and awareness, organizations empower individuals to become the first line of defense against social engineering attacks. Continuous education, open communication, and leadership support are fundamental elements in building a resilient security culture that effectively combats AI-enhanced social engineering attacks.

Strengthening collaboration and information sharing

Strengthening collaboration and information sharing plays a critical role in combating AI-enhanced social engineering attacks. In an ever-evolving threat landscape, organizations, security professionals, and individuals need to work together, exchanging knowledge and insights to effectively identify and respond to these sophisticated threats. By establishing information-sharing networks within industries and fostering public-private partnerships, organizations can share information on emerging threats, attack patterns, and defense strategies. Utilizing threat intelligence platforms and collaborative incident response platforms enables real-time sharing of intelligence and incident details, facilitating a timely response and proactive defense. Responsible vulnerability disclosure practices and publicly sharing threat intelligence further contribute to collective defense capabilities. Collaborative threat-hunting exercises, joint red team engagements, and participation in industry conferences and training programs enhance knowledge sharing and skill development. Coordinated incident response protocols and real-time information exchange during incidents enable a unified and efficient response across affected organizations. Through strengthened collaboration and information sharing, the cybersecurity community can enhance its ability to detect, prevent, and respond to AI-enhanced social engineering attacks, bolstering the overall defense posture.

Understanding deepfakes

Deepfakes refer to synthetic media that have been altered or created using AI techniques, particularly deep learning algorithms. These sophisticated AI techniques enable the analysis and manipulation of existing data, such as images, videos, or audio, to create highly realistic and often deceptive content that closely mimics the appearance and sound of real individuals.

Deepfakes exhibit a remarkable level of realism, striving to replicate intricate visual and auditory qualities, including facial expressions, gestures, and voice patterns. By leveraging deep learning algorithms, deepfakes possess the ability to manipulate and transform original material, allowing for face swapping, modification of facial expressions, lip-syncing, and even voice synthesis.

The accessibility of deepfake creation tools and software has significantly increased, empowering individuals with basic technical skills to produce their own deepfakes. However, this accessibility also amplifies the potential for misuse, as deepfakes can be exploited for malicious purposes, such as spreading misinformation, defaming individuals, perpetrating harassment, engaging in fraud, or manipulating public opinion.

The technologies and techniques behind deepfakes involve sophisticated AI algorithms and various data processing methods. Here are the key components:

- **Deep learning algorithms**: Deepfakes rely on neural networks, particularly **generative adversarial networks** (**GANs**) and autoencoders. GANs consist of two components: a generator network and a discriminator network. The generator creates the synthetic content, while the discriminator tries to distinguish between real and fake content. Through an iterative process, the generator learns to create increasingly realistic deepfakes, while the discriminator improves its ability to detect them.

- **Facial recognition and mapping**: *Face swapping* is a common deepfake technique. Facial recognition algorithms analyze the source and target videos or images to identify key facial landmarks, such as the position of the eyes, nose, and mouth. These landmarks are then mapped onto the target face, aligning the two faces and enabling seamless face swapping.

- **Image and video processing**: Deepfake algorithms manipulate and transform images or videos to create realistic alterations. They can adjust facial expressions, change lip movements to match altered speech, or even generate entirely new frames that maintain visual coherence with the original material. Techniques such as **convolutional neural networks** (**CNNs**) are commonly used for image processing in deepfakes.

- **Voice synthesis**: Deepfakes are not limited to visual manipulation; they can also generate synthetic voices. By analyzing audio samples of a person's voice, deep learning models can learn to replicate the voice's characteristics, intonation, and speech patterns. Techniques such as text-to-speech synthesis and vocoders are employed to generate speech that sounds similar to the target person.

- **Data collection and training**: Deepfakes require large amounts of data to train the AI models. This data includes diverse samples of the target person's face or voice from different angles, lighting conditions, or audio variations. Collecting and curating this training data is essential for achieving more accurate and realistic deepfake results.

- **Hardware and computing power**: Deepfake creation often requires substantial computing power, particularly for training complex neural networks. **Graphics processing units** (**GPUs**) are commonly used due to their ability to handle parallel computations. High-performance computing infrastructure is leveraged to accelerate the training and generation process.

The continuous advancement of deepfake technologies and techniques poses challenges in terms of detecting and mitigating the impact of deepfakes. Researchers and technology experts are actively working on developing robust detection methods to identify deepfakes and raise awareness about the risks associated with their misuse.

Deepfake videos

Deepfake videos are a concerning application of deepfake technology, where existing videos are manipulated or fabricated using AI algorithms. These videos often involve face swapping, altering facial expressions, or generating entirely new content that appears deceptively authentic. *Figure 7.1* shows an example of how deepfake videos work:

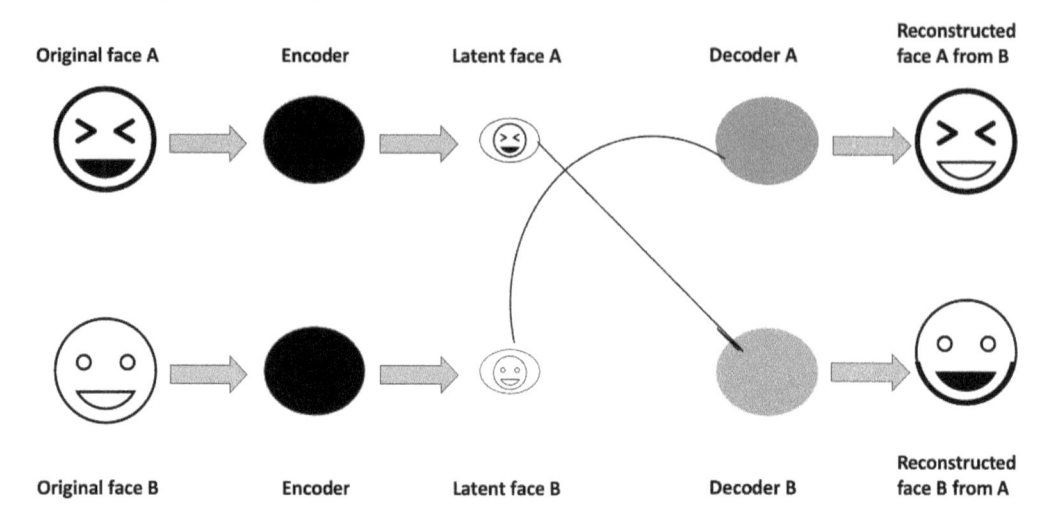

Figure 7.1 – An example of how deepfake videos work

Examples of deepfake videos include *celebrity face swaps*, where the faces of famous individuals are superimposed onto other people's bodies, political manipulation videos that spread misinformation or falsely depict politicians engaging in inappropriate behavior, parody videos that use deepfakes for comedic or satirical purposes, and the creation of non-consensual explicit content that violates privacy rights.

One of the most famous examples of a deepfake video is the viral deepfake featuring former president Barack Obama. Released in 2018 by a team at the University of Washington, the video showcased Obama delivering a fabricated public service announcement that addressed the potential dangers of deepfakes themselves.

The impact of this deepfake video was significant as it sparked widespread discussions and raised awareness about the potential for deepfake technology to manipulate and deceive. It served as a wake-up call for both the general public and policymakers regarding the urgency to understand and address the risks associated with the proliferation of deepfakes. This high-profile example helped bring the issue of deepfakes to the forefront of public consciousness and led to increased attention and research into developing detection and mitigation techniques.

How to detect deepfake videos

Detecting deepfakes can be challenging as the technology behind them continues to evolve. However, several techniques and indicators can help you identify potential deepfakes. Here are some steps you can take to detect a deepfake:

- **Pay attention to inconsistencies**: Look for any inconsistencies or abnormalities in the video or image. This could include unnatural movements, glitches, or mismatches between facial expressions and emotions. Deepfakes often have subtle errors or artifacts that might give them away.

- **Check for visual artifacts**: Deepfakes can sometimes introduce visual artifacts, such as strange shadows, blurriness, or inconsistent lighting. Pay close attention to details and look for any signs of manipulation that don't align with the rest of the scene.

- **Analyze facial and body movements**: Deepfakes may exhibit unnatural or exaggerated facial movements, especially around the eyes and mouth. Look for any odd or robotic behavior in the person's gestures or expressions. Also, pay attention to the synchronization between facial expressions, speech, and body movements, as deepfakes may struggle to match these accurately.

- **Compare with authentic sources**: If the video or image is of a public figure or someone known to have a significant online presence, compare it with other authentic videos or images of that person. Look for consistencies in their appearance, voice, and behavior across different sources. Inconsistencies between the deepfake and genuine content can be a strong indicator.

- **Conduct a reverse image search**: If you suspect an image is a deepfake, you can perform a reverse image search using platforms such as *Google Images* or *TinEye*. This can help you identify whether the image has been manipulated or is a modified version of an existing image.

- **Seek expert opinion**: If you have strong suspicions but are uncertain, consider consulting experts in the field of deepfake detection. Organizations and researchers actively work on developing techniques to identify deepfakes and may offer specialized tools or services.

Remember that these techniques are not foolproof as deepfake technology continues to advance. It's important to stay informed about the latest developments in deepfake detection and rely on a combination of techniques to increase your chances of detecting them accurately.

Deepfake audio

Deepfake audio refers to the manipulation or synthesis of audio content using AI techniques. Like deepfake videos, deepfake audio leverages deep learning algorithms to create or modify audio recordings to sound like someone else or to produce entirely fabricated audio clips. *Figure 7.2* shows how deepfake audio works:

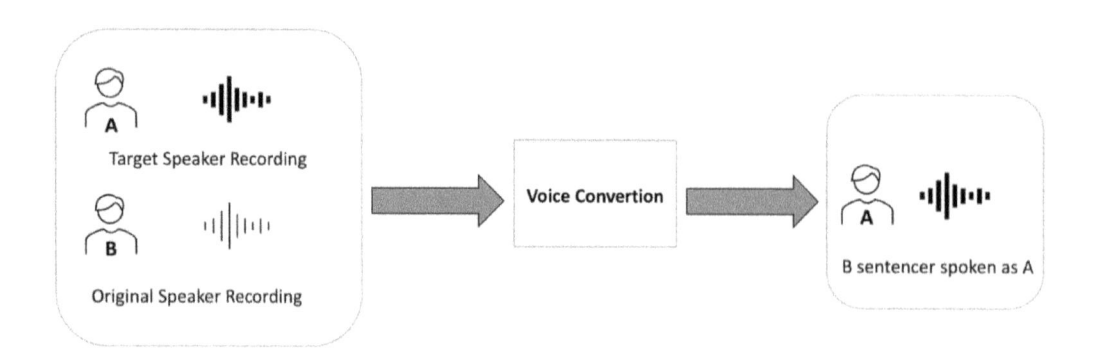

Figure 7.2 – An example of how deepfake audio works

Here are some key aspects to understand about deepfake audio:

- **Voice synthesis**: Deepfake audio can synthesize speech that closely mimics the characteristics, intonation, and speech patterns of a specific individual. By analyzing large amounts of audio samples of the target person's voice, deep learning models can learn and generate speech that sounds convincingly similar.

- **Voice conversion**: Deepfake audio techniques can convert one person's voice into another person's voice while preserving the linguistic content. This can involve altering the pitch, tone, and other vocal characteristics to make the converted voice sound like the target person.

- **Impersonation and misuse**: Deepfake audio can be misused for impersonation purposes, enabling someone to generate audio clips that sound like another person speaking words they never actually said. This has implications for identity fraud, spreading false information, or manipulating audio evidence.

- **Dubbing and localization**: Deepfake audio has applications in dubbing and localization, where it can be used to synchronize speech in different languages or match the lip movements of actors in movies or television shows.

- **Fraud and social engineering**: Deepfake audio can be used in fraudulent activities, such as **voice phishing** (**vishing**) or scam calls, where the perpetrator impersonates someone to gain access to personal information or manipulate individuals into performing certain actions.

- **Detection challenges**: Detecting deepfake audio presents significant challenges as the technology continues to advance and create increasingly convincing audio forgeries. Researchers are actively working on developing methods to detect and identify manipulated or synthetic audio.

- **Ethical considerations**: The use of deepfake audio raises ethical concerns regarding consent, privacy, and the potential harm caused by the misuse of someone's voice or creating false audio recordings that could damage reputations or incite conflict.

One example of deepfake audio is the **Voice Conversation** (**VoCo**) demonstration showcased by Adobe in 2016. VoCo presented a prototype technology that could synthesize speech based on a small sample of someone's voice. During the demonstration, the audience heard a manipulated audio clip of a fictional speech by former president Barack Obama, which was generated using just 20 minutes of his recorded speech. The deepfake audio was remarkably convincing, capturing the nuances and speech patterns of Obama's voice. This demonstration sparked significant attention and raised concerns about the potential for deepfake audio to deceive and manipulate, as it showcased how easily someone's voice could be replicated and used to create false audio recordings. The *VoCo* demonstration by Adobe served as a wake-up call, emphasizing the need for heightened awareness and research into deepfake audio detection and mitigation methods.

Understanding the capabilities and risks associated with deepfake audio is essential for individuals, organizations, and society. It underscores the importance of promoting media literacy, responsible use of technology, and the development of robust detection mechanisms to mitigate the potential harm caused by deepfake audio.

How to detect deepfake audio

Detecting deepfake audio poses considerable challenges due to the perpetual advancements in the underlying technology. However, here are some methods and considerations that can help you identify potential deepfake audio:

- **Analyze speech patterns**: Pay attention to the speaker's tone, pacing, and pronunciation. Deepfake audio may have subtle anomalies, such as unusual pauses, inconsistent speech patterns, or unnatural intonations. Compare the audio with other recordings of the same person to identify any significant differences.

- **Listen for background noise**: Deepfake audio may lack appropriate background noise or contain inconsistencies in ambient sounds. Authentic recordings typically capture the environmental sounds that would naturally occur during the recording, so discrepancies in background noise could be a red flag.

- **Check for audio artifacts**: Deepfake audio might exhibit audio artifacts or glitches. Listen for any distortions, clicks, or unusual echoes that are not typically present in high-quality recordings. These artifacts can indicate that the audio has been manipulated.

- **Analyze the context and content**: Consider the context of the audio and evaluate whether the content aligns with what you would expect from the speaker. Deepfake audio may contain improbable or out-of-character statements, so be skeptical of any audio that seems unusually controversial, inflammatory, or inconsistent with the person's known beliefs or behavior.

- **Investigate the source**: Determine the origin and credibility of the audio. Deepfake audio is more likely to be found in unofficial or unverified sources. If the audio comes from a suspicious or unknown origin, be cautious and seek corroborating evidence.

- **Consult experts**: Deepfake audio detection is a complex task, and there are organizations and researchers actively working on developing techniques to detect it. Consider reaching out to experts in the field or utilizing specialized tools or services designed to detect deepfake audio.

It's important to note that deepfake audio detection is an evolving field, and new techniques and countermeasures may emerge over time. Staying informed about the latest advancements in audio forensics and relying on a combination of methods will increase your chances of identifying deepfake audio accurately.

Implications for social engineering attacks

Deepfake technology has significant implications for social engineering attacks as it enables perpetrators to manipulate audio and visual content with high accuracy and realism.

One implication is identity deception, where deepfakes can convincingly impersonate individuals, such as high-profile figures or trusted contacts, to gain the trust of unsuspecting victims. This technology also manipulates trust and credibility by creating false evidence or spreading misinformation, potentially compromising reputations and manipulating decision-making processes.

Deepfakes can exploit emotional manipulation techniques by creating content that elicits strong emotional responses, prompting victims to take immediate action or divulge sensitive information. They can facilitate various social engineering scams, including vishing, where attackers use deepfake audio to impersonate trusted entities and trick victims into revealing sensitive information or performing financial transactions. Deepfake technology can amplify spear phishing attacks by combining deepfake audio with other techniques to craft highly tailored and convincing messages.

Successful deepfake social engineering attacks can cause severe reputational damage and erode trust. To mitigate these risks, it is important to prioritize education and awareness, implement robust security measures, and utilize MFA. Ongoing research and development of detection tools are crucial for identifying and combating deepfake content used in social engineering attacks.

How to prevent deepfakes

Preventing the complete proliferation of deepfakes proves to be an arduous undertaking, given the persistent advancements in their underlying technology. Nonetheless, various measures can be implemented to mitigate the risks associated with deepfakes. The following strategies should be considered:

- **Raise awareness**: Understanding how deepfakes are created and the impact they can have helps people become more skeptical and cautious when encountering suspicious content.
- **Develop and improve detection techniques**: Invest in research and the development of robust deepfake detection methods.

- **Promote media literacy**: Teach individuals how to evaluate the authenticity of information sources, identify signs of manipulation, and question the credibility of media content.
- **Strengthen digital security**: Enhance cybersecurity measures to protect personal data, including biometric information, voice recordings, and images.
- **Watermark and track content**: Content creators and platforms can consider incorporating visible or invisible watermarks into their media files.
- **Promote transparency and accountability**: Encourage platforms, social media networks, and content creators to be transparent about their content policies and verification processes. Establish clear guidelines for content sharing and implement mechanisms to report and address deepfake content promptly.
- **Develop regulations and legal frameworks**: Governments and policymakers can work toward developing regulations and legal frameworks that address the risks posed by deepfakes.
- **Support ongoing research**: Support academic and industry research initiatives focused on developing deepfake detection methods, countermeasures, and ethical guidelines for the responsible use of AI technologies.

While prevention is challenging, a combination of technological advancements, user awareness, and regulatory efforts can help mitigate the impact of deepfakes and reduce their potential harm. Continued collaboration and proactive measures across various sectors are crucial in addressing this evolving threat.

Other AI attacks

Now, let's consider some other types of AI attacks.

AI-powered phishing attacks

AI-powered phishing attacks leverage AI technologies to enhance the effectiveness, sophistication, and scale of phishing campaigns. As we now know, phishing attacks are a form of cyberattack where malicious actors impersonate trusted individuals or organizations to deceive targets into revealing sensitive information, such as login credentials or financial data. AI-powered techniques enable attackers to create highly convincing and personalized phishing attempts, increasing the success rate of their campaigns.

Several types of AI-powered phishing attacks exploit AI technologies to enhance their effectiveness and sophistication. Here are some common types:

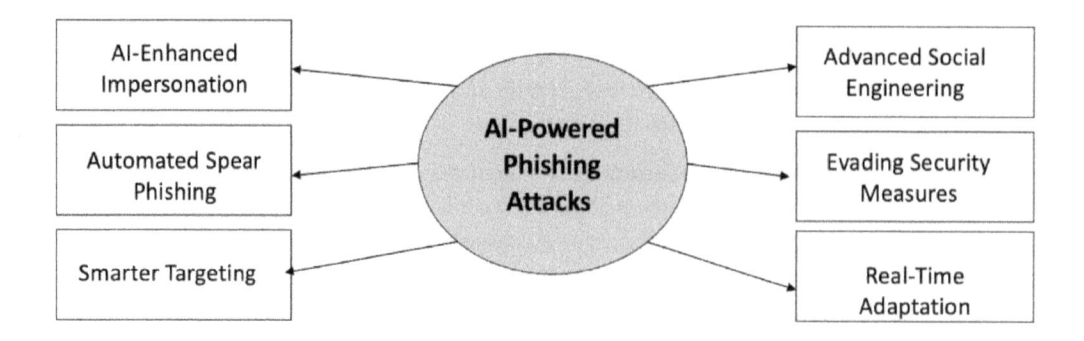

Figure 7.3 – Types of AI-powered phishing attacks

These common AI-powered phishing attacks are described in detail here:

- **AI-enhanced impersonation**: By harnessing the capabilities of AI algorithms, attackers can delve into vast amounts of data from diverse sources, such as social media platforms, public databases, and leaked information. This trove of data serves as the foundation for crafting remarkably authentic and persuasive phishing emails or messages. Leveraging AI, attackers can replicate the writing style, tone, and language patterns of trusted individuals or organizations, making it incredibly challenging for recipients to discern the fraudulent nature of the communication.

- **Automated spear phishing**: AI-powered phishing attacks take personalization to new heights through the automation of tailored spear phishing emails. Machine learning algorithms meticulously analyze the gathered data, extracting relevant information such as personal details, interests, or recent activities. This wealth of insights empowers attackers to create highly personalized messages that appear genuinely legitimate, significantly amplifying the probability of success.

- **Smarter targeting**: Through the intelligent application of AI algorithms, attackers can scrutinize vast datasets to identify potential targets based on their online behavior, interests, or demographics. By harnessing machine learning techniques, attackers can pinpoint individuals who are particularly susceptible to phishing attempts. This laser-focused targeting enables them to concentrate their efforts on vulnerable individuals, thereby maximizing their chances of achieving their malicious objectives.

- **Advanced social engineering**: AI-powered phishing attacks leverage the power of NLP to comprehend and exploit human language patterns and emotional cues. Deep analysis of linguistic and behavioral data empowers AI algorithms to generate phishing messages that are remarkably persuasive and emotionally resonant. These carefully crafted messages play on the target's emotions, curiosity, or sense of urgency, significantly increasing the likelihood of the target falling victim to the desired action, such as clicking on a malicious link or divulging sensitive information.

- **Evading security measures**: To circumvent traditional security measures, AI-powered phishing attacks employ a plethora of evasion techniques. For instance, attackers can harness the capabilities of AI algorithms to generate polymorphic malware, constantly altering its signature with each iteration. This makes it exceedingly difficult for antivirus software to detect and neutralize the threat. Furthermore, AI can automate the creation of deceptive domain names that strikingly resemble legitimate ones, creating significant challenges for users in identifying phishing websites. These evasion tactics enable attackers to bypass security defenses, escalating the probability of infiltrating their targets successfully.

- **Real-time adaptation**: AI-powered phishing attacks possess the ability to adapt and evolve in real time based on the responses received. Through careful analysis of user interactions and feedback, attackers can swiftly modify their strategies mid-attack. This adaptability empowers them to fine-tune their phishing attempts, enhancing their authenticity and tailoring them to exploit specific vulnerabilities or outmaneuver countermeasures.

In conclusion, AI-powered phishing attacks represent a formidable advancement in the realm of cyber threats. The integration of AI technologies allows attackers to execute highly convincing, personalized, and adaptable campaigns. Understanding the intricacies of these attacks is crucial for individuals and organizations to develop effective defense strategies and safeguard against the evolving sophistication of malicious actors.

How to protect against AI phishing attacks

To defend against AI-powered phishing attacks, it is crucial to stay vigilant and follow best practices:

- **Be cautious of AI-generated content**: Attackers can leverage AI technologies to create highly convincing phishing emails, messages, or even voice recordings. Stay vigilant and carefully scrutinize the content, even if it appears to be from a familiar source.

- **Watch out for AI chatbots**: Phishing attacks can employ AI chatbots that simulate human-like conversations. These chatbots may attempt to trick you into revealing sensitive information or clicking on malicious links. Exercise caution when interacting with unknown chatbots, especially those requesting personal or financial details.

- **Analyze URLs and hyperlinks**: AI-powered phishing attacks can generate deceptive URLs and hyperlinks that closely resemble legitimate websites. Hover over hyperlinks to reveal the actual destination URL and verify its legitimacy before clicking it.

- **Leverage AI-powered security tools**: As attackers use AI to enhance their phishing techniques, you can also utilize AI-powered security tools for defense. Some advanced security solutions employ machine learning algorithms to detect and block phishing attempts in real time. Consider utilizing these tools to enhance your protection.

- **Enable AI-based threat detection**: Many cybersecurity platforms and email services use AI algorithms to identify and flag potential phishing emails. Enable these AI-based threat detection features to add an extra layer of defense against AI phishing attacks.

- **Stay informed about AI-driven threats**: Regularly educate yourself about the latest AI-driven phishing techniques. Keep up to date with news and security advisories that highlight emerging trends and attack vectors. By staying informed, you can adapt your security practices and recognize evolving AI-driven threats.
- **Implement AI-based anomaly detection**: AI technology can be utilized to identify anomalous patterns in communication and behavior. Implement AI-based anomaly detection systems that can identify unusual email requests or suspicious activities.

It's worth noting that as AI technology advances, both attackers and defenders will continue to incorporate AI into their strategies, creating a perpetual cycle of innovation and adaptation in the realm of cybersecurity.

AI-assisted social media manipulation attacks

AI-assisted social media manipulation attacks have emerged as a significant concern in the digital age, leveraging AI technologies to deceive and manipulate users on social media platforms. This form of manipulation involves the strategic use of AI algorithms and techniques to spread misinformation, shape public opinion, and influence social media users.

AI-assisted social media manipulation can come in different ways. Let's see some of them:

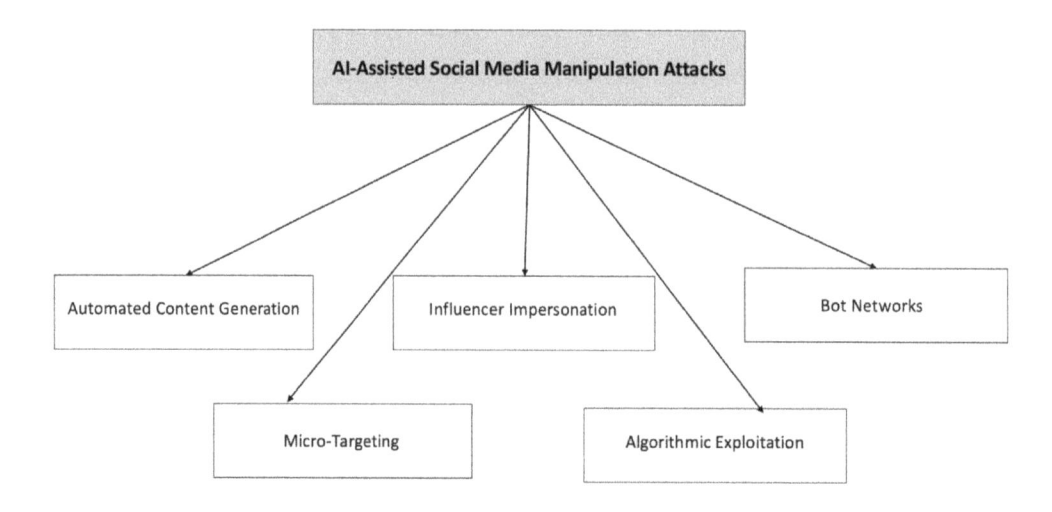

Figure 7.4 – Types of AI-assisted social media manipulation attacks

These AI-assisted social media manipulation attacks are described in detail here:

- **Automated content generation**: AI algorithms can generate vast amounts of content, including text, images, and videos, which can be tailored to specific target audiences. This content is designed to propagate certain narratives, manipulate emotions, or deceive users into accepting false information.

- **Influencer impersonation**: AI algorithms can mimic the online behavior, communication style, and characteristics of influential individuals. By impersonating these individuals, manipulators can establish credibility and trust, thereby enhancing the impact of their manipulated content.

- **Bot networks**: AI-powered bots, programmed to mimic human behavior, can amplify manipulated content through likes, shares, comments, and retweets. These bot networks create an illusion of widespread support, making manipulated messages appear more credible and influential.

- **Micro-targeting**: AI algorithms analyze user data and behavior patterns to identify specific target groups susceptible to manipulation. By tailoring content to resonate with the interests, beliefs, and biases of these groups, manipulators can effectively influence their opinions and behaviors.

- **Algorithmic exploitation**: Manipulators leverage AI algorithms to understand and exploit the algorithms used by social media platforms to curate content. This allows them to maximize the visibility and reach of manipulated content by capitalizing on the platforms' recommendation systems.

Is important to know that AI-assisted social media manipulation carries profound implications for society. Firstly, it contributes to the widespread dissemination of misinformation, eroding trust in online content and giving rise to conspiracy theories, societal polarization, and a threat to democratic processes.

Secondly, by strategically manipulating social media content using AI, it has the power to shape public opinion on a range of issues, including politics, society, and culture, influencing public discourse and impacting decision-making processes.

Additionally, collecting and analyzing user data for manipulation purposes raises significant privacy and security concerns, with AI-powered manipulators able to access personal information and potentially engage in identity theft or cybercrimes. Furthermore, AI-assisted manipulation fosters the creation of echo chambers and filter bubbles, reinforcing existing beliefs and exacerbating societal divisions, hindering constructive dialogue, compromising societal cohesion, and impeding the resolution of critical issues. These implications highlight the pressing need for awareness, countermeasures, and responsible use of AI in social media environments.

How to protect ourselves against AI-assisted social media manipulation attacks

To safeguard against AI-assisted social media manipulation attacks, it is crucial to employ a range of proactive measures and develop a strong awareness of potential risks. Here are some key strategies to consider:

- **Cultivate media literacy skills**: Enhance your ability to critically assess information and identify manipulation techniques. Educate yourself about prevalent tactics employed in AI-assisted social media manipulation, such as misinformation dissemination, influencer impersonation, and bot networks.

- **Verify sources and information**: Prioritize the verification of sources before accepting information as credible. Engage in fact-checking by cross-referencing multiple sources and consulting reputable news outlets or fact-checking organizations to ensure accuracy.

- **Strengthen privacy and security settings**: Take control of your online privacy by reviewing and adjusting the privacy settings of your social media platforms. Limit the public sharing of personal information and regularly update passwords to enhance security.

- **Exercise caution with emotional manipulation**: Remain vigilant regarding emotional triggers and attempts to exploit them. Manipulators often employ emotional appeals to influence opinions and actions. Exercise critical thinking before reacting to emotionally charged content.

- **Analyze content**: Conduct thorough scrutiny of social media content by considering the source, context, and supporting evidence. Exercise caution when engaging with unfamiliar accounts or suspicious content to avoid becoming a victim of manipulation.

- **Utilize reliable security software**: Install reputable security software and ensure it remains up to date. This can aid in detecting and blocking malicious activities, such as bot networks or malware, that may be associated with AI-assisted social media manipulation.

- **Report suspicious activity**: Report any instances of suspicious or manipulative content to the respective social media platform. Such reports play a vital role in enabling platforms to identify and address instances of manipulation, contributing to a safer online environment.

- **Stay informed and educate others**: Stay abreast of emerging trends and techniques in AI-assisted social media manipulation. Share your knowledge with friends, family, and colleagues to raise awareness and collectively combat manipulation.

It is important to recognize that protection against AI-assisted social media manipulation necessitates ongoing effort. By remaining well-informed, exercising vigilance, and applying critical thinking skills, individuals can mitigate the risk of falling victim to manipulation and contribute to fostering a healthier online environment.

Summary

To sum up, this chapter highlighted the evolving landscape of AI in social engineering attacks. It provided strategies to combat AI-enhanced attacks, explored the implications of deepfakes, and shed light on other AI-driven attack vectors, emphasizing the importance of vigilance, education, and collaboration in mitigating these emerging threats.

We delved into the role of AI in social engineering attacks, highlighting the growing influence of AI and the techniques employed by attackers. We also explored strategies for combating AI-enhanced social engineering attacks and discussed the implications of deepfakes. Remember that understanding the threat landscape is crucial as it helps us identify risks and vulnerabilities. Implementing effective security measures, including AI-based detection systems, is vital for detecting and preventing attacks in real time. Fostering a culture of security and awareness among individuals plays a significant role in mitigating these threats. Furthermore, strengthening collaboration and information sharing within the cybersecurity community improves collective defense against evolving AI-driven attacks.

Now, we will jump into a new interesting chapter that talks about the **Social-Engineer Toolkit (SET)** and its importance in the field of social engineering.

8

The Social Engineering Toolkit (SET)

Welcome to this exciting chapter where we dive deep into the **Social Engineering Toolkit (SET)** and explore its pivotal role in the realm of cybersecurity.

In this chapter, we will explore the importance of understanding the SET framework; here, we will guide you through its installation, configuration, components, and modules.

Moreover, we'll equip you with invaluable insights into mitigating and defending against SET attacks, making this knowledge an indispensable asset in safeguarding the digital world against malicious social engineering exploits.

Join us on this journey to strengthen your cyber defenses and unravel the mysteries of SET. In this chapter, we will cover the following main topics:

- SET
  - Importance of understanding SET in cybersecurity
- Installing and setting up SET:
  - System requirements for SET installation
  - Downloading and installing SET
  - Executing SET
- Understanding the main components and modules of SET:
  - Social-Engineering Attacks
  - Penetration Testing (Fast-Track)
  - Other options

- Mitigation and defense against SET attacks:
  - Technical controls and vulnerability management
  - User awareness and training
  - Email and web filtering
  - **Incident response (IR)** and **threat intelligence (TI)**
  - Access controls and privilege management
  - Continuous monitoring and response

Technical requirements

This chapter requires basic knowledge of **virtual machines (VMs)** and Linux environments.

SET

SET is a powerful open source penetration testing framework developed by Dave Kennedy for social engineering.

It serves as a powerful framework for assessing the vulnerabilities present in the human element of security systems, emphasizing the vital role that humans play in safeguarding sensitive information.

SET combines an array of social engineering attacks that are easy to execute and deploy, which makes it an indispensable asset for cybersecurity professionals. However, we cannot deny the fact this these powerful tools are also used by malicious actors to perform their social engineering attacks.

At its core, SET is designed to replicate real-world social engineering attacks. This enables cybersecurity professionals to test how vulnerable their users are against various social engineering techniques.

This assessment of the organization's susceptibility to social engineering attacks allows organizations to identify vulnerable employees who can be educated to prevent them from falling into a real social engineering attack.

This enables organizations to proactively develop strategies that mitigate the risk posed by social engineering attacks, bolstering their resilience against the ever-evolving landscape of cyber threats.

> **Note**
> It is crucial to recognize that SET requires responsible usage. Its usage must be governed by ethical considerations to ensure that it is employed exclusively for legitimate and authorized purposes. Remember this: *"With great power comes great responsibility."*

Additionally, it is important to highlight that SET provides an immersive and dynamic training ground that provides realistic attack scenarios to enhance employee awareness and training, making this framework a mandatory tool for cybersecurity professionals.

Importance of understanding SET in cybersecurity

While technical measures are essential, hackers often exploit human vulnerabilities through social engineering to execute their attacks. Therefore, it is of the utmost importance that cybersecurity professionals understand the SET framework and its tools to leverage them to support a successful defensive strategy.

Now, let's see some additional benefits of understanding and using SET:

- **Awareness campaigns**: The SET framework includes a plurality of tools used by attackers to perform social engineering attacks. Therefore, you can leverage SET as a tool to demonstrate how easy it is for an attacker to deploy a social engineering attack.

- **Readiness assessments**: Cybersecurity professionals can also leverage SET to assess the employee's readiness to identify a social engineering attack.

- **Developing effective countermeasures**: SET serves as a valuable tool that provides useful insights about how attackers may execute these types of attacks. These insights will enable cybersecurity teams to design proactive strategies and controls to reduce the probability and impact of social engineering attacks.

- **IR enhancement**: Cybersecurity teams can leverage the SET framework to create realistic scenarios and conduct simulated drills that will enable the execution of effective IR procedures related to social engineering attacks.

- **Mitigating insider threats**: SET is instrumental in addressing insider threats, which often involve individuals within an organization exploiting their access privileges for malicious purposes. By understanding the techniques employed by attackers, security professionals can monitor and detect suspicious behavior, implement robust access controls, and enforce strict authentication mechanisms.

- **Ethical hacking and red teaming**: The understanding of SET is invaluable for ethical hackers and red teamers engaged in testing an organization's security defenses. By using SET responsibly (and ethically), these professionals can simulate real-world social engineering attacks to identify vulnerabilities that would otherwise remain undetected.

In essence, SET is a must-have framework for cybersecurity professionals. By comprehending the techniques, vulnerabilities, and countermeasures associated with social engineering attacks, organizations can enhance their overall security posture, mitigate risks, and foster a culture of cybersecurity awareness.

Installing and setting up SET

Now that the value of SET in cybersecurity is clear, it is time to understand how to install and set up SET in your own environment.

System requirements for SET installation

Currently, the SET framework is only supported on Linux platforms. However, you can also use it on a Windows machine using any of the following methods:

- **Install Kali using a VM**: In this scenario, you need to install a hypervisor (VMware or VirtualBox) and then load a pre-built VM with Kali Linux. The official pre-built VM can be downloaded directly from the Kali Linux site using this link: https://www.kali.org/get-kali/#kali-virtual-machines.
- **Install Kali using Windows Subsystem for Linux (WSL)/WSL2**: You can also run Kali Linux on a Windows machine using WSL/WSL2 (this is only supported on Windows 10 and 11). You can follow this guide to install Kali Linux using WSL/WSL2: https://www.kali.org/docs/wsl/.

Downloading and installing SET

As mentioned, the SET framework is currently only supported on Linux platforms. Now, it is important to highlight that SET is already pre-installed on Kali Linux, so if you have Kali Linux, then *congratulations!* You already have SET installed on your machine.

> **Note**
> Kali Linux on Windows 10 is a minimal installation, which means that it doesn't have any tools installed. Therefore, if you are using Kali Linux on WSL/WSL2, the SET framework is not pre-installed.

But don't worry—installation of SET on Kali Linux (WSL/WSL2) is fairly simple; you just need to run the following command:

```
$ sudo apt install set -y
```

However, if you are using any other version of Linux, you will have to execute the following command to have the SET framework installed:

```
$ git clone https://github.com/trustedsec/social-engineer-toolkit/setoolkit/
$ cd setoolkit
$ pip3 install -r requirements.txt
$ python setup.py
```

Now that you have SET successfully installed, it's time to take a look at the tools included in this social engineering framework.

Executing SET

Once SET is installed, you then just need to execute the following command to open it:

```
$ setoolkit
```

Oh, wait—SET needs to be executed as root, so if you are not logged in as root, then you may get an error such as the one illustrated in *Figure 8.1*:

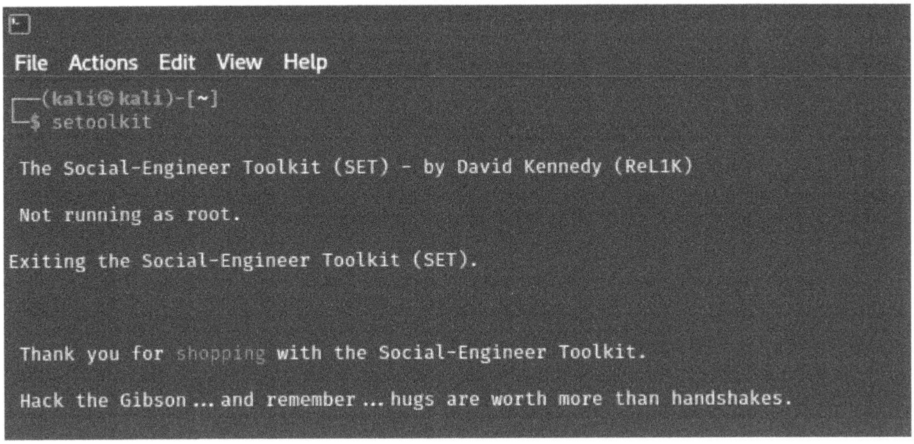

Figure 8.1 – SET error

One option to overcome that error would be to run the following command:

```
$ sudo su
```

As illustrated in *Figure 8.2*, the system will ask for your user password to grant you root access:

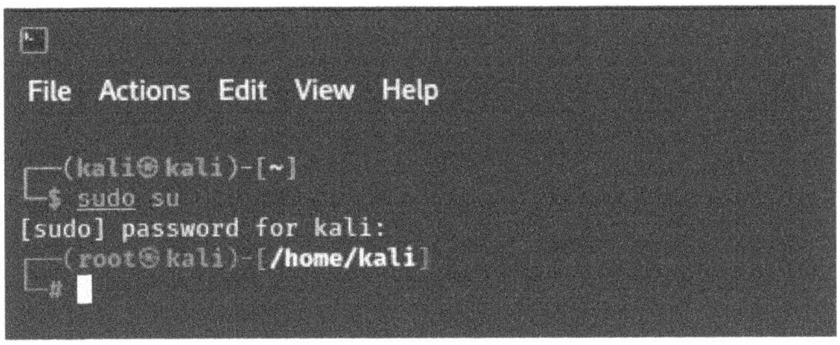

Figure 8.2 – Obtaining root access

> **Note**
>
> To know more about elevating permissions and `root` access on Kali Linux, visit their site: https://www.kali.org/docs/general-use/enabling-root/.

On the other hand, if you are logged in as `root`, you should then be able to execute SET. The first time you open SET, the system will ask you to accept its terms and conditions before executing SET, as illustrated in *Figure 8.3*:

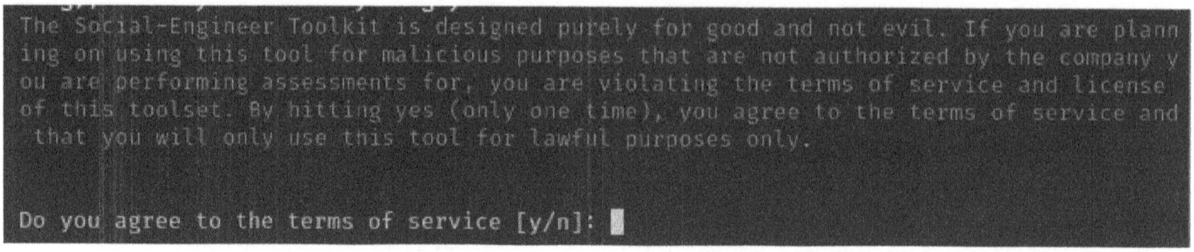

```
The Social-Engineer Toolkit is designed purely for good and not evil. If you are plann
ing on using this tool for malicious purposes that are not authorized by the company y
ou are performing assessments for, you are violating the terms of service and license
of this toolset. By hitting yes (only one time), you agree to the terms of service and
 that you will only use this tool for lawful purposes only.

Do you agree to the terms of service [y/n]:
```

Figure 8.3 – SET terms and conditions

Understanding the main components and modules of SET

In this section, we are going to do a walkthrough to help you familiarize yourself with the interface of the SET framework. Additionally, we are also going to show you the main components and modules within SET, so let's get started!

After you accept the terms and conditions, you should be able to see SET's main page, which includes the main menu, as illustrated in *Figure 8.4*:

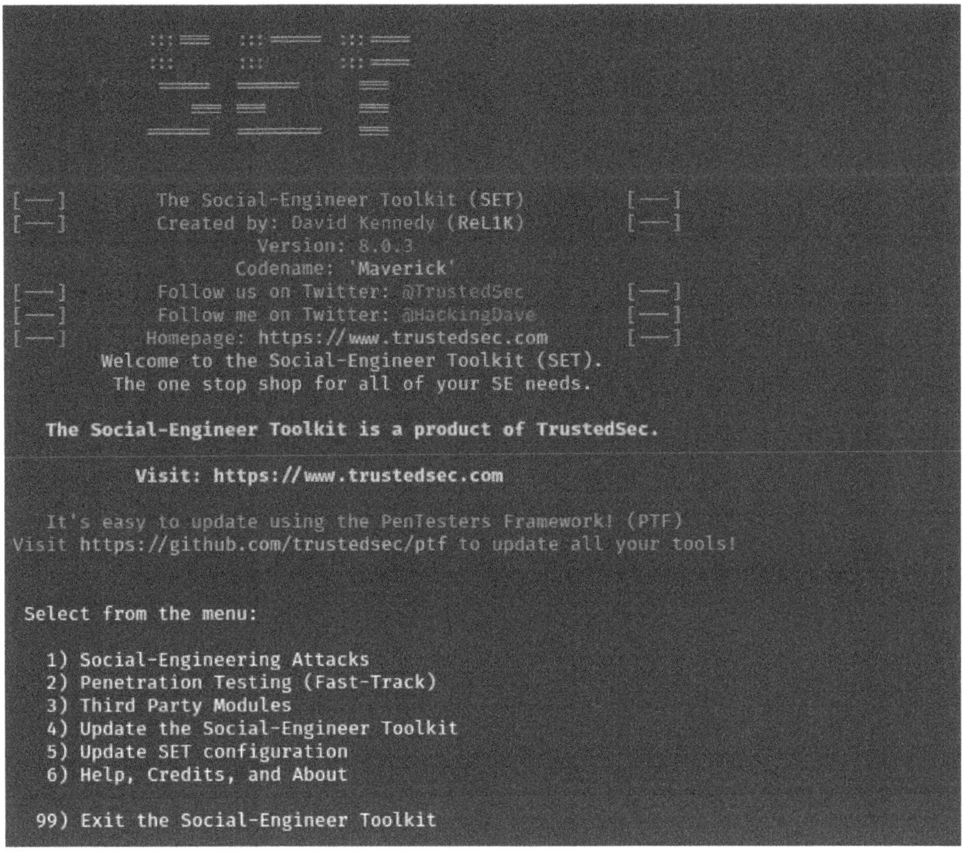

```
[---]          The Social-Engineer Toolkit (SET)         [---]
[---]          Created by: David Kennedy (ReL1K)         [---]
                        Version: 8.0.3
                       Codename: 'Maverick'
[---]          Follow us on Twitter: @TrustedSec         [---]
[---]          Follow me on Twitter: @HackingDave        [---]
[---]          Homepage: https://www.trustedsec.com      [---]
          Welcome to the Social-Engineer Toolkit (SET).
          The one stop shop for all of your SE needs.

    The Social-Engineer Toolkit is a product of TrustedSec.

           Visit: https://www.trustedsec.com

      It's easy to update using the PenTesters Framework! (PTF)
  Visit https://github.com/trustedsec/ptf to update all your tools!


  Select from the menu:

     1) Social-Engineering Attacks
     2) Penetration Testing (Fast-Track)
     3) Third Party Modules
     4) Update the Social-Engineer Toolkit
     5) Update SET configuration
     6) Help, Credits, and About

    99) Exit the Social-Engineer Toolkit
```

Figure 8.4 – SET main menu

Next, let's look at the six options available on SET's main menu.

Social-Engineering Attacks

This is the core of SET. To access it, just type 1 and hit *Enter* to see the **Social-Engineering Attacks** menu. The menu has 10 options, including **Spear-Phishing Attack Vectors**, **Website Attack Vectors**, **Mass Mailer Attack**, as illustrated in *Figure 8.5*:

```
Select from the menu:

   1) Spear-Phishing Attack Vectors
   2) Website Attack Vectors
   3) Infectious Media Generator
   4) Create a Payload and Listener
   5) Mass Mailer Attack
   6) Arduino-Based Attack Vector
   7) Wireless Access Point Attack Vector
   8) QRCode Generator Attack Vector
   9) Powershell Attack Vectors
  10) Third Party Modules

  99) Return back to the main menu.
```

Figure 8.5 – SET Social-Engineering Attacks menu

Now, let's explore each of the options, and remember that to access each option, you just need to type the number of the option and hit *Enter*.

Spear-Phishing Attack Vectors

As you can see in *Figure 8.6*, one of the cool things about SET is that its interface is very user-friendly, and once you access a module, it provides you with an introduction to the module plus some additional configuration tips:

```
set> 1

The Spearphishing module allows you to specially craft email messages and send
them to a large (or small) number of people with attached fileformat malicious
payloads. If you want to spoof your email address, be sure "Sendmail" is in-
stalled (apt-get install sendmail) and change the config/set_config SENDMAIL=OFF
flag to SENDMAIL=ON.

There are two options, one is getting your feet wet and letting SET do
everything for you (option 1), the second is to create your own FileFormat
payload and use it in your own attack. Either way, good luck and enjoy!

   1) Perform a Mass Email Attack
   2) Create a FileFormat Payload
   3) Create a Social-Engineering Template

  99) Return to Main Menu
```

Figure 8.6 – Spear-Phishing Attack Vectors

This module is designed to distribute emails that include a malicious payload. As with most SET modules, this one allows a plurality of options, including the option to spoof an email address and even to create your own file format payload.

As seen in *Figure 8.6*, there are three options available for the spear-phishing attack: **Perform a Mass Email Attack**, **Create a FileFormat Payload**, and **Create a Social-Engineering Template**.

> **Note**
> While most Linux-based applications are command-based, the SET framework was designed to be menu-based, which makes it easier to use.

Let's do a quick overview of each of those three options:

- **Perform a Mass Email Attack**: As seen in *Figure 8.7*, once you enter this option, the system will provide you with a vast list of options to execute the attack:

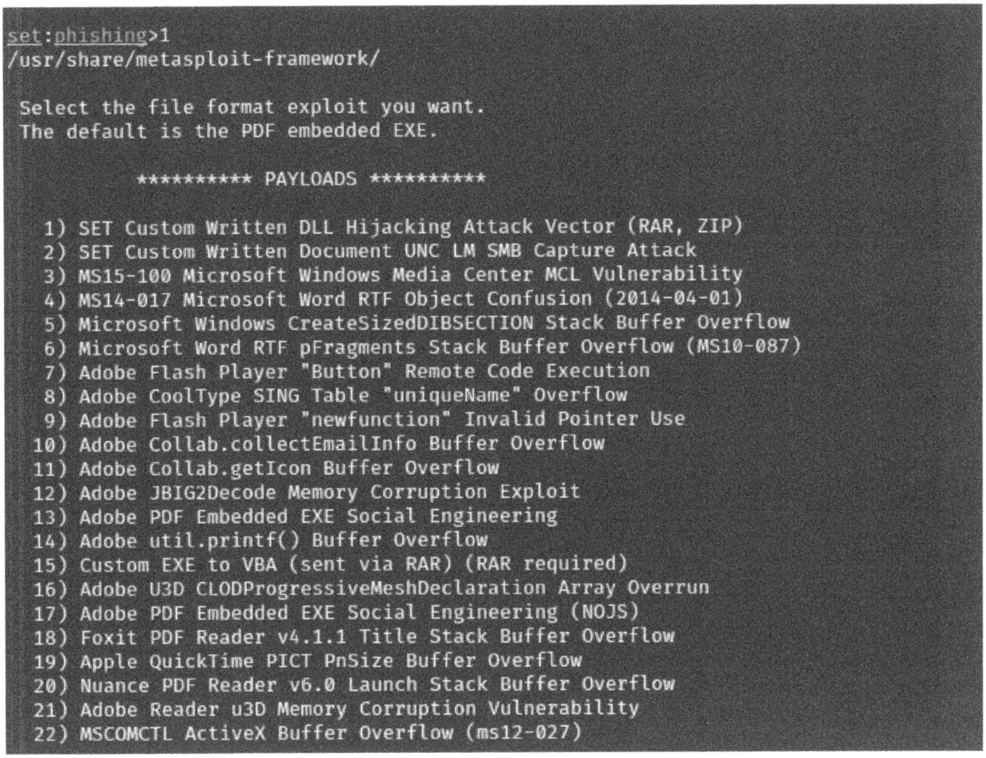

```
set:phishing>1
/usr/share/metasploit-framework/

Select the file format exploit you want.
The default is the PDF embedded EXE.

          ********** PAYLOADS **********

   1) SET Custom Written DLL Hijacking Attack Vector (RAR, ZIP)
   2) SET Custom Written Document UNC LM SMB Capture Attack
   3) MS15-100 Microsoft Windows Media Center MCL Vulnerability
   4) MS14-017 Microsoft Word RTF Object Confusion (2014-04-01)
   5) Microsoft Windows CreateSizedDIBSECTION Stack Buffer Overflow
   6) Microsoft Word RTF pFragments Stack Buffer Overflow (MS10-087)
   7) Adobe Flash Player "Button" Remote Code Execution
   8) Adobe CoolType SING Table "uniqueName" Overflow
   9) Adobe Flash Player "newfunction" Invalid Pointer Use
  10) Adobe Collab.collectEmailInfo Buffer Overflow
  11) Adobe Collab.getIcon Buffer Overflow
  12) Adobe JBIG2Decode Memory Corruption Exploit
  13) Adobe PDF Embedded EXE Social Engineering
  14) Adobe util.printf() Buffer Overflow
  15) Custom EXE to VBA (sent via RAR) (RAR required)
  16) Adobe U3D CLODProgressiveMeshDeclaration Array Overrun
  17) Adobe PDF Embedded EXE Social Engineering (NOJS)
  18) Foxit PDF Reader v4.1.1 Title Stack Buffer Overflow
  19) Apple QuickTime PICT PnSize Buffer Overflow
  20) Nuance PDF Reader v6.0 Launch Stack Buffer Overflow
  21) Adobe Reader u3D Memory Corruption Vulnerability
  22) MSCOMCTL ActiveX Buffer Overflow (ms12-027)
```

Figure 8.7 – Perform a Mass Email Attack menu

- **Create a FileFormat Payload**: This option is for advanced users who want to create their own file format payload and use it to craft their own attack.

- **Create a Social-Engineering Template**: Here, you can create your own template. As seen in *Figure 8.8*, the template generator is very simple to use:

```
set:phishing>3
        [****]   Custom Template Generator   [****]
Always looking for new templates! In the set/src/templates directory send an email
to info@trustedsec.com if you got a good template!
set> Enter the name of the author: Cesar Bravo
set> Enter the subject of the email: You Won!
set> Enter the body of the message, hit return for a new line. Control+c when finished:
:
```

Figure 8.8 – SET template generator

Now, let's explore the next module, **Website Attack Vectors**.

Website Attack Vectors

This module leverages a plurality of web-based attacks to compromise the intended victim. As shown in *Figure 8.9*, several methods can be used:

```
   1) Java Applet Attack Method
   2) Metasploit Browser Exploit Method
   3) Credential Harvester Attack Method
   4) Tabnabbing Attack Method
   5) Web Jacking Attack Method
   6) Multi-Attack Web Method
   7) HTA Attack Method

  99) Return to Main Menu
```

Figure 8.9 – Website Attack Vectors menu

Let's take a quick look at each of these methods:

- **Java Applet Attack Method**: This method will spoof a Java certificate to deliver a Metasploit-based payload using a customized Java applet.
- **Metasploit Browser Exploit Method**: This method uses a Metasploit browser exploit through an **inline frame (iframe)** to deliver a Metasploit payload.
- **Credential Harvester Attack Method**: This method will clone a website that requests user credentials to harvest all the user information entered on the website.
- **Tabnabbing Attack Method**: This is a very interesting attack—when the user moves to a different tab, it will refresh the page to something different.

- **Web Jacking Attack Method**: This method uses iframe replacements to make a highlighted URL link seem legitimate. However, when clicked, a window pops up and the link is replaced with a malicious link.
- **Multi-Attack Web Method**: This module uses a combination of attacks through the web attack menu. For example, you can use **Java Applet Attack Method**, **Metasploit Browser Exploit Method**, **Credential Harvester Attack Method**, or **Tabnabbing Attack Method**.
- **HTA Attack Method**: This new module is aimed to clone a site and perform PowerShell injection through **HTML Application (HTA)** files, which can be used for Windows-based PowerShell exploitation through the web browser.

As you can see, the **Website Attack Vectors** module is very powerful and robust. Now, let's see the next module—the **Infectious Media Generator** module.

Infectious Media Generator

As seen in *Figure 8.10*, the **Infectious Media Generator** module will develop a Metasploit-based payload that creates an `autorun.inf` file that can be placed on an external drive (USB/DVD):

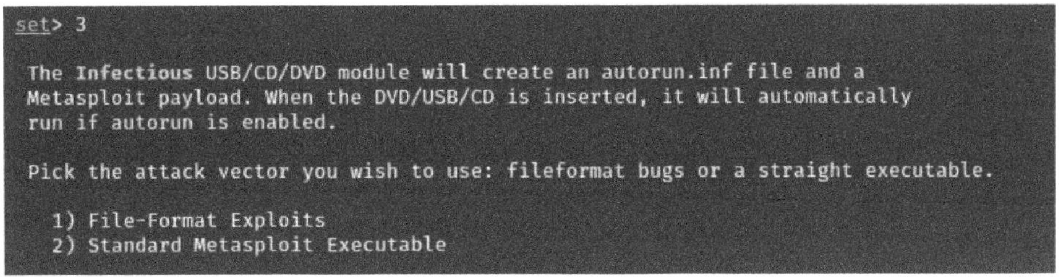

```
set> 3
The Infectious USB/CD/DVD module will create an autorun.inf file and a
Metasploit payload. When the DVD/USB/CD is inserted, it will automatically
run if autorun is enabled.

Pick the attack vector you wish to use: fileformat bugs or a straight executable.

   1) File-Format Exploits
   2) Standard Metasploit Executable
```

Figure 8.10 – Infectious Media Generator

Once **AutoRun** is executed, the system will execute the payload to compromise the target system.

> **Note**
> This highlights the importance of having a plurality of policies and technical controls to disable the **AutoRun** feature.

It is also important to highlight that this is a physical attack that requires a plurality of extra social engineering techniques to be successfully executed, and thus it is important to understand this attack to recognize it at an early stage of the attack (before the devices are connected to the target system).

Create a Payload and Listener

The **Create a Payload and Listener** module is a wrapper around Metasploit to create a payload, export it as an executable file (`.exe`), and generate a listener.

Then, the attacker will have to use some social engineering techniques to transfer and execute the executable file (`.exe`) in the victim's machine.

As seen in *Figure 8.11*, there are several payloads available to execute this attack:

```
set> 4

    1) Windows Shell Reverse_TCP              Spawn a command shell on victim and send back to attacker
    2) Windows Reverse_TCP Meterpreter        Spawn a meterpreter shell on victim and send back to attacker
    3) Windows Reverse_TCP VNC DLL            Spawn a VNC server on victim and send back to attacker
    4) Windows Shell Reverse_TCP X64          Windows X64 Command Shell, Reverse TCP Inline
    5) Windows Meterpreter Reverse_TCP X64    Connect back to the attacker (Windows x64), Meterpreter
    6) Windows Meterpreter Egress Buster      Spawn a meterpreter shell and find a port home via multiple ports
    7) Windows Meterpreter Reverse HTTPS      Tunnel communication over HTTP using SSL and use Meterpreter
    8) Windows Meterpreter Reverse DNS        Use a hostname instead of an IP address and use Reverse Meterpreter
    9) Download/Run your Own Executable       Downloads an executable and runs it
```

Figure 8.11 – Create a Payload and Listener module

Mass Mailer Attack

This module is designed to create, customize, and send multiple emails to a plurality of email addresses.

In contrast to *module 1* (**Spear-Phishing Attack Vectors**), the **Mass Mailer Attack** module does not allow you to create payloads; therefore, this module is generally used to perform mass phishing attacks that rely heavily on the social engineering side.

As seen in *Figure 8.12*, this module has two options—to either attack a single target or to send an email to a massive group of email addresses:

```
set> 5

    Social Engineer Toolkit Mass E-Mailer

    There are two options on the mass e-mailer, the first would
    be to send an email to one individual person. The second option
    will allow you to import a list and send it to as many people as
    you want within that list.

    What do you want to do:

    1.  E-Mail Attack Single Email Address
    2.  E-Mail Attack Mass Mailer

    99. Return to main menu.
```

Figure 8.12 – Mass Mailer Attack

Arduino-Based Attack Vector

Arduino-based attacks are based on a vulnerability related to how machines trust (by default) all **USB human interface devices (USB HIDs)** (such as a USB keyboard or a USB mouse), which makes devices vulnerable to USB HID-injecting devices such as the *USB Rubber Ducky* or the *USB Teensy*.

In this case, the malicious USB device presents itself as a keyboard (which the system will trust), and then it will start injecting data, code, or a payload to compromise or disrupt the targeted system.

As highlighted in *Chapter 2* of the book, *Mastering Defensive Security*, these types of attacks are extremely dangerous because they bypass the most common cybersecurity controls such as antiviruses, **AutoRun** controls, USB controls, and so on.

Going back to this module, it will create the necessary files to import into the Arduino IDE, which is the IDE used to load the code into these USB devices.

As seen in *Figure 8.13*, there are several payloads available to import into the malicious USB HID:

```
Select a payload to create the pde file to import into Arduino:

 1) Powershell HTTP GET MSF Payload
 2) WSCRIPT HTTP GET MSF Payload
 3) Powershell based Reverse Shell Payload
 4) Internet Explorer/FireFox Beef Jack Payload
 5) Go to malicious java site and accept applet Payload
 6) Gnome wget Download Payload
 7) Binary 2 Teensy Attack (Deploy MSF payloads)
 8) SDCard 2 Teensy Attack (Deploy Any EXE)
 9) SDCard 2 Teensy Attack (Deploy on OSX)
10) X10 Arduino Sniffer PDE and Libraries
11) X10 Arduino Jammer PDE and Libraries
12) Powershell Direct ShellCode Teensy Attack
13) Peensy Multi Attack Dip Switch + SDCard Attack
14) HID Msbuild compile to memory Shellcode Attack

99) Return to Main Menu
```

Figure 8.13 – Arduino-Based Attack Vector

Wireless Access Point Attack Vector

This module will create a wireless access point (leveraging your wireless card) to redirect all DNS queries to the attacker.

Then, the attacker can leverage any SET attack (for example, the Java Applet attack) so that when a victim tries to open a website, they will be redirected to a malicious server.

This attack vector leverages several tools, including `Airbase-ng`, `Airmon-ng`, `dnsspoof`, and `dhcpd3`.

QRCode Generator Attack Vector

When scanned, it will redirect to the SET attack vector. What's great about this attack is the ability to redirect victims to any of the built-in attack vectors SET has available to them.

This module will create a QR code to a malicious URL that will redirect the victim to a malicious site to either harvest some user data or execute a payload on the victim's machine. This attack is especially dangerous as it obfuscates the malicious link from the user.

As seen in *Figure 8.14*, this is a very simple module, yet if used by a skilled attacker, it could become a very dangerous attack:

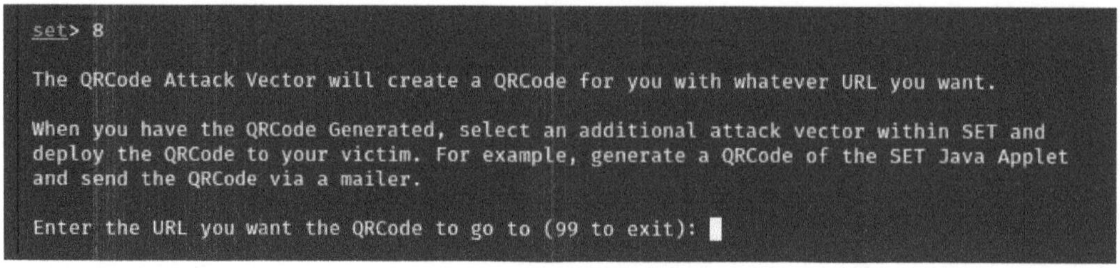

```
set> 8

The QRCode Attack Vector will create a QRCode for you with whatever URL you want.

When you have the QRCode Generated, select an additional attack vector within SET and
deploy the QRCode to your victim. For example, generate a QRCode of the SET Java Applet
and send the QRCode via a mailer.

Enter the URL you want the QRCode to go to (99 to exit):
```

Figure 8.14 – QRCode Generator Attack Vector

Powershell Attack Vectors

The **Powershell Attack Vectors** module was created to craft specific PowerShell attacks.

These attacks will allow a potential attacker to leverage PowerShell, which is available by default in most Windows-based operating systems, starting with Windows Vista and above.

As seen in *Figure 8.15*, an attacker can choose from a variety of options within the **Powershell Attack Vectors** module:

```
set> 9
The Powershell Attack Vector module allows you to create PowerShell specific attacks. These attacks will allow you to
use PowerShell which is available by default in all operating systems Windows Vista and above. PowerShell provides a f
ruitful  landscape for deploying payloads and performing functions that  do not get triggered by preventative technolo
gies.

   1) Powershell Alphanumeric Shellcode Injector
   2) Powershell Reverse Shell
   3) Powershell Bind Shell
   4) Powershell Dump SAM Database

  99) Return to Main Menu
```

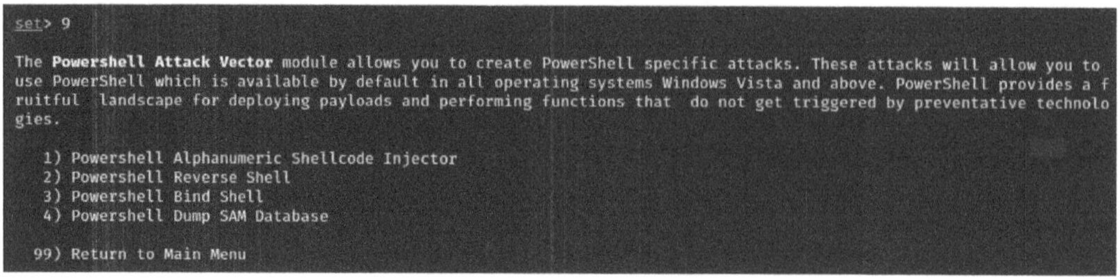

Figure 8.15 – Powershell Attack Vectors

Third Party Modules

This module was designed to allow additions or enhancements to the SET framework by allowing the community to add their contributions to the toolkit.

As seen in *Figure 8.16*, the system shows a few examples of modules developed by the community. Additionally, you can also check the information in the README file to develop your own module:

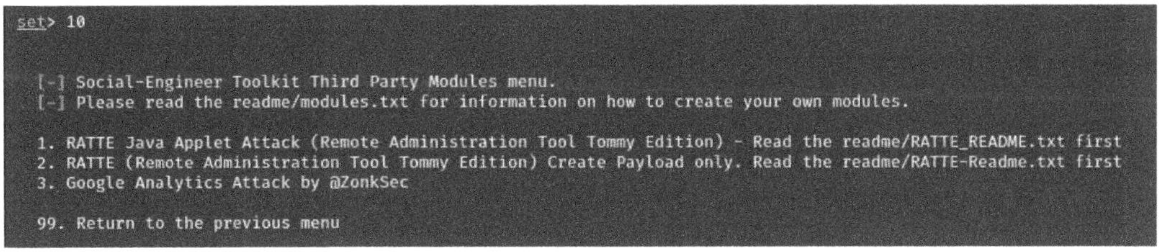

```
set> 10

 [-] Social-Engineer Toolkit Third Party Modules menu.
 [-] Please read the readme/modules.txt for information on how to create your own modules.

  1. RATTE Java Applet Attack (Remote Administration Tool Tommy Edition) - Read the readme/RATTE_README.txt first
  2. RATTE (Remote Administration Tool Tommy Edition) Create Payload only. Read the readme/RATTE-Readme.txt first
  3. Google Analytics Attack by @ZonkSec

 99. Return to the previous menu
```

Figure 8.16 – Third Party Modules

This ends our look at the **Social-Engineering Attacks** menu. Now, let's take a look at the second main option within SET—**Penetration Testing (Fast-Track)**.

Penetration Testing (Fast-Track)

This section includes a series of exploits and automation aspects to assist in the art of penetration testing. As seen in *Figure 8.17*, this section includes a plurality of known attack vectors, including SQL attacks, custom exploits, and PsExec PowerShell injection:

```
set> 2
Welcome to the Social-Engineer Toolkit - Fast-Track Penetration Testing platform. These attack vectors
have a series of exploits and automation aspects to assist in the art of penetration testing. SET
now incorporates the attack vectors leveraged in Fast-Track. All of these attack vectors have been
completely rewritten and customized from scratch as to improve functionality and capabilities.

   1) Microsoft SQL Bruter
   2) Custom Exploits
   3) SCCM Attack Vector
   4) Dell DRAC/Chassis Default Checker
   5) RID_ENUM - User Enumeration Attack
   6) PSEXEC Powershell Injection

  99) Return to Main Menu
```

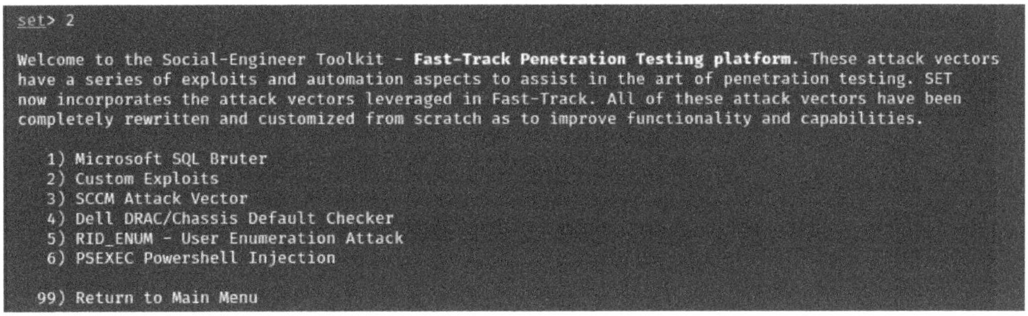

Figure 8.17 – Penetration Testing (Fast-Track) menu

Let's now see some other available options.

Other options

The rest of the options in the SET menu are quite simple and self-explanatory, so we will cover them only briefly.

Third Party Modules

This option will send us to the same **Third Party Modules** module that we just covered for the usage and creation of third-party modules for SET.

Update the Social-Engineer Toolkit

This is a very nice option to keep SET up to date with a single click.

Update SET configuration

This is a simple option to access the SET configuration without navigating manually to the config files.

Help, Credits, and About

This is where you will find the credits of the contributors to the SET framework.

This covers our walk-through of the SET framework, its menus, modules, and tools. Now, it's time to see how we can protect ourselves, our companies, and our employees against social engineering attacks executed with the SET framework.

Mitigation and defense against SET attacks

Mitigation and defense against SET attacks require a comprehensive approach that encompasses technical controls, user awareness, and proactive security measures. By implementing a robust defense strategy, organizations can effectively mitigate the risks associated with SET attacks and protect against the exploitation of human vulnerabilities.

It is good to highlight that while we are talking about the SET framework, these best practices also apply to most social engineering attacks executed with any other technical methods and tools.

Now, let's review those best practices to mitigate and defend against SET attacks.

Technical controls and vulnerability management

Regularly patching and updating software and systems is critical to address known vulnerabilities that attackers may exploit using SET. This includes maintaining up-to-date operating systems, applications, and security software.

Implementing **intrusion detection and prevention systems** (**IDPSs**), firewalls, and antivirus solutions also helps in detecting and blocking suspicious activities associated with SET attacks.

Additionally, conducting regular vulnerability assessments and penetration testing also helps in identifying potential vulnerabilities.

User awareness and training

Educating users about the techniques used in SET attacks is of the *utmost importance* in any cybersecurity strategy. Regular security awareness training should not only cover social engineering concepts, such as phishing, pretexting, and baiting, but should also cover the systems, methods, and tools used by attackers to execute attacks.

Therefore, *training sessions* and *awareness campaigns* should emphasize the importance of verifying sources, scrutinizing email and website authenticity, and adopting secure practices such as strong passwords, **multi-factor authentication** (**MFA**), and safe browsing habits.

Additionally, you should encourage users to report any suspicious activities to create and promote a cybersecurity culture.

Email and web filtering

Implementing robust email and web filtering solutions can help detect and block phishing emails, malicious attachments, and deceptive websites created with technical tools such as the SET framework.

These filters utilize various techniques such as content analysis, reputation-based filtering, and URL blacklisting to identify and block suspicious or malicious content.

Continuous monitoring and the use of up-to-date filtering rules are essential to stay ahead of evolving social engineering threats such as the SET framework.

IR and TI

Developing an IR plan specifically tailored to handle SET attacks is crucial. This plan should outline clear steps for detecting, containing, and mitigating the impact of such incidents.

It should also include procedures for communication, forensics, and reporting if an attack is detected.

Incorporating TI feeds and **security information and event management** (**SIEM**) systems helps organizations stay informed about emerging attack vectors, which will enable them to adapt their defenses accordingly.

Access controls and privilege management

Implementing strong access controls and least-privilege principles helps limit the potential damage caused by social engineering attacks.

Regularly reviewing and enforcing access privileges (including ensuring that users have the minimum required permissions) is also a best practice.

Additionally, the use and enforcement of strong authentication mechanisms (including MFA) to protect against unauthorized access attempts is also considered a best practice.

Continuous monitoring and response

Deploying security monitoring tools and even having a **security operations center** (**SOC**) enables organizations to detect and respond to social engineering attacks faster.

Continuous monitoring of network traffic, system logs, and user activities can help identify suspicious patterns or **indicators of compromise** (**IoCs**). An effective response strategy includes incident triage, containment, eradication, and post-incident analysis to prevent future incidents.

In conclusion, mitigating and defending against social engineering attacks using technical tools (such as the SET framework) requires a multi-faceted approach that combines technical controls, user awareness, and proactive security measures.

By implementing robust technical defenses, educating users, and establishing proactive security practices, organizations can significantly reduce the risk of advanced social engineering attacks and stay protected against the exploitation of human vulnerabilities.

Summary

In this chapter, we learned a lot about the SET framework, from its importance to all cybersecurity experts to its importance in developing and maintaining a strong cybersecurity strategy.

Then, we started getting deeper into the framework itself by learning how to install it, configure it, and execute it.

Once we learned the basics of the installation, we did a deep dive into the framework and all its modules to learn the plurality of tools offered in this framework.

After that, we also covered how to navigate through the tool and how to access its different modules, including a module to execute a spear-phishing attack that includes a malicious payload and a module to craft several web-based social engineering attacks.

In the end, we closed the chapter by explaining a set of best practices aimed at preventing advanced social engineering attacks performed with technical tools such as the SET framework.

In the upcoming chapter, we will take a deep dive into the social engineering life cycle, meticulously unveiling its distinct stages while equipping you with indispensable knowledge and tools to fortify your defenses.

Further reading

If you want to know more about Arduino-based attacks, the book *Mastering Defensive Security* by Cesar Bravo has an entire chapter that covers everything you need to know about these advanced (and clever) physical attacks: https://www.packtpub.com/product/mastering-defensive-security/9781800208162.

Part 3: Protecting against Social Engineering Attacks

This part covers the life cycle of complex social engineering attacks as well as a number of tips and best practices to secure your company on each of the stages of elaborate social engineering attacks. Additionally, we will review some applicable laws and international regulations applicable to social engineering.

This part has the following chapters:

- *Chapter 9, Understanding the Social Engineering Life Cycle*
- *Chapter 10, Defensive Strategies for Social Engineering*
- *Chapter 11, Applicable Laws and Regulations for Social Engineering*

9
Understanding the Social Engineering Life Cycle

In our increasingly interconnected world, social engineering has become a fearsome weapon, exploiting human psychology to gain unauthorized access to information and resources. This chapter aims to give you in-depth knowledge about the social engineering life cycle and each of the stages that attackers follow to execute a social engineering attack, as well as provide essential knowledge and tools for protection.

The chapter includes a deep dive into each of the stages of the social engineering life cycle, including an explanation of the steps, their main characteristics, and even some screenshots to help you identify an attack.

We will also provide several tips and techniques not only to identify but also to protect you and your organization against such attacks.

Also, remember that by understanding the social engineering life cycle, you'll be equipped to defend yourself against these manipulative tactics and keep your company and data safe.

So, join us on this enlightening journey to discover the secrets behind the social engineering life cycle and how attackers could use this against you and your organization.

Here are the main topics that we will cover in this chapter:

- The history of the social engineering life cycle:
  - The iconic Kevin Mitnick
- The social engineering life cycle:
  - Reconnaissance
  - Target selection
  - Pretext development

- Engagement
- Exploitation or elicitation
- Execution (post-exploitation)

• How to stay protected

Technical requirements

There are no technical requirements for this chapter.

Disclaimer

All characters in the screenshots are fictional characters.

The screenshots are inspired by real attacks; therefore, the language used (including spelling and grammatical errors) was done on purpose.

The history of the social engineering life cycle

Social engineering attacks are intricately linked to the evolution of human communication, and they increase as new ways of communication are used by humans.

In fact, the foundation of social engineering can be traced back to hundreds of years ago when individuals utilized deception and manipulation to gain advantage.

More recent examples include spies assuming false identities, using disguises, or employing persuasive tactics to gather information or achieve their objectives.

Over time, these attacks were perfected, and *social engineering attacks became an art*. This art is in constant evolution, and we have witnessed how these attacks evolve as technology evolves, from basic attacks of dumpster diving to more sophisticated attacks that now leverage the latest technologies such as the metaverse and even generative AI to better craft the attacks.

Now, as part of this evolution, social engineering attacks have grown in sophistication and frequency, and security professionals and researchers have begun to formalize the stages and methodologies of social engineering attacks. This has led to the development of a structured framework known as the social engineering life cycle.

Now, as part of this evolution, we can determine the stages that most attackers follow when executing a social engineering attack. The combination of those stages is what is known as the social engineering life cycle.

This life cycle is aimed at providing a systematic understanding of the various phases involved in a social engineering attack, from reconnaissance and target selection, all the way to execution of the attack.

Depending on the author, the number of stages may vary from four to even nine stages, but in most cases, it is the same method—either super concentrated on four stages or overextended in nine stages.

> **Note**
> As mentioned, social engineering is an art; therefore, each attacker may execute the attack in their own way, sometimes combining several steps into a single interaction or, in more elaborated attacks, splitting a single stage into multiple iterations to enhance the impact and success of the attack.

In this case, and based on our combined experience in the field (working with *Fortune 100* companies) and academia (doing research studies, patents, and publications), we concluded that a life cycle of six stages is the perfect balance to successfully explain the life cycle of most social engineering attacks.

The iconic Kevin Mitnick

In the 1990s, Kevin Mitnick became a prominent hacker who showcased the power of social engineering through several exploits that made him the *first person to be on the FBI's most wanted list for cyber attacks*.

Mitnick utilized various tactics such as pretexting (creating false scenarios), impersonation, and exploiting trust to manipulate individuals into divulging sensitive information or granting unauthorized access to computer systems. He also demonstrated how dumpster diving (gathering information from the trash of top technology companies) can be a great source of information.

The way he mastered social engineering tactics and techniques to successfully access the system of top technology companies and even government agencies gave him the title of "the father of social engineering."

He was also the inspiration of many cybersecurity enthusiasts and experts through his stories, which are well documented in his books (which we highly recommend you read), listed here:

- *The Art of Deception*
- *The Art of Intrusion*
- *Ghost in the Wires*
- *The Art of Invisibility*

His activities helped to raise awareness of the impact of social engineering and how those attacks can impact even major corporations.

With the recognition of social engineering as a significant threat to organizational security, industries began acknowledging the need to address the human factor in cybersecurity. Here, the social engineering life cycle gained recognition as a valuable tool for assessing vulnerabilities, designing effective training programs, and implementing countermeasures.

The social engineering life cycle

The social engineering life cycle is a systematic approach that describes the stages involved in a social engineering attack. It provides a comprehensive framework for understanding and mitigating the tactics employed by attackers who manipulate human behavior to gain unauthorized access, extract information, or exploit individuals or organizations for personal gain.

The social engineering life cycle involves several stages, as listed here and also demonstrated in *Figure 9.1*:

- **Reconnaissance**: Gathering information about the target
- **Target selection**: Carefully choosing individuals or groups to exploit
- **Pretext development**: Creating a believable and trustworthy persona
- **Engagement**: The attacker works on building a relationship and gaining the target's trust
- **Exploitation or elicitation**:
  - **Exploitation**: Manipulating the victim to perform a plurality of actions desired by the attacker
  - **Elicitation**: The discrete gathering of information from the victim without explicitly asking for it
- **Execution (post-exploitation)**: Exploiting the gained information or access to execute a cyber attack

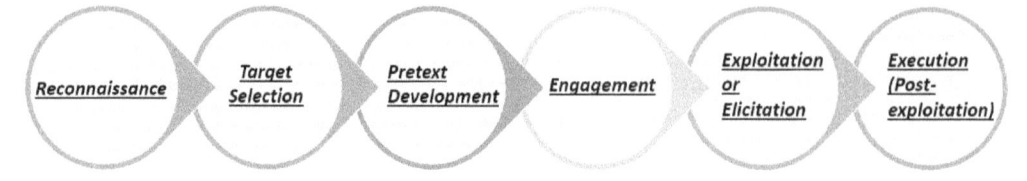

Figure 9.1 – Social engineering life cycle stages

It's important to note that the stages of the social engineering life cycle are not always linear or discrete. They can overlap, repeat, or occur in different sequences based on the attacker's strategy and the unique characteristics of each attack.

Understanding the social engineering life cycle helps organizations develop robust countermeasures, including security awareness training, policy enforcement, and technological safeguards, to mitigate the risks associated with social engineering attacks. Let's now look at each stage in more detail.

Reconnaissance

In the social engineering life cycle, reconnaissance is the initial stage of the attack process. During this phase, attackers gather information about their target or organization. They employ various methods, such as **Open Source Intelligence** (**OSINT**) gathering, social media analysis, dumpster diving, or phishing to collect valuable data.

The purpose of reconnaissance is to identify potential vulnerabilities, key individuals, and relevant details necessary for executing a social engineering attack. By acquiring information about the target, including their organizational structure, technology systems, employee roles, and communication patterns, the attacker can better tailor their approach and increase the chances of success.

> Note
> Reconnaissance provides the foundation for the subsequent stages of a social engineering attack, allowing the attacker to make informed decisions during target selection, establish trust, exploit vulnerabilities, execute the attack, cover their tracks, and maximize the value derived from a successful campaign.

It's important to note that reconnaissance can also be conducted by defenders to identify and mitigate potential social engineering risks. By proactively understanding the information available about their organization and potential attack vectors, defenders can implement measures to strengthen security and raise awareness among employees to reduce the probability and impact of social engineering attacks.

As seen in *Figure 9.2*, a simple social media profile may inadvertently disclose sensitive information that could be leveraged by an attacker to craft a social media attack:

Figure 9.2 – Example of the reconnaissance stage

Target selection

Target selection is a crucial stage in the social engineering life cycle, following the reconnaissance phase. Once an attacker has gathered information about potential targets or organizations, they carefully assess and choose individuals or groups they intend to exploit. During target selection, several factors are considered to maximize the effectiveness of the social engineering attack. These factors may include the following:

- **Roles and access privileges**: The attacker identifies individuals with roles or positions that provide them with access to valuable information or resources.
- **Psychological vulnerabilities**: The attacker looks for traits such as trustworthiness, gullibility, willingness to help, or susceptibility to manipulation.
- **Susceptibility to influence**: Targets who are more likely to be influenced or persuaded by external factors, such as authority figures or social norms, may be preferred.
- **Relevance to the attack objectives**: The attacker selects targets based on their relevance to the overall objectives of the social engineering attack. For example, if the goal is to gain access to a specific system, the targets may include individuals who have direct or indirect control over that system.

Target selection is a critical step as it allows the attacker to focus their efforts on individuals who can provide the necessary information or facilitate the desired actions. On the defensive side, organizations can mitigate the risk of social engineering attacks by identifying potential target profiles and implementing robust security measures. This could involve conducting security awareness training, implementing access controls, and establishing protocols to verify requests or actions involving sensitive information.

As seen in *Figure 9.3*, an attacker may choose their target based on their job role, type of access to the system, or their company and industry:

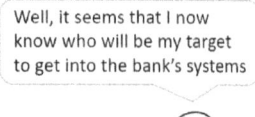

Figure 9.3 – Example of the target selection stage

Pretext development

Pretext development is an essential stage in the social engineering life cycle, following target selection. It involves the creation and refinement of a plausible and convincing pretext or scenario that the attacker will use to manipulate the target. The goal of pretexting is to establish a believable reason for the attacker's interaction with the target. By crafting a compelling story or situation, the attacker aims to lower the target's guard and increase their willingness to cooperate or provide the desired information. During pretext development, attackers take into account several factors, as follows:

- **Contextual relevance**: The pretext must align with the target's environment, role, or circumstances and should be tailored to fit the specific industry, organization, or individual being targeted
- **Emotional appeal**: Pretexts often leverage emotions such as urgency, fear, curiosity, or empathy to manipulate the target's behavior
- **Credibility and consistency**: The pretext should be supported by consistent details and information that can be verified if the target decides to investigate
- **Knowledge of the target**: The attacker researches the target's background, interests, or affiliations to personalize the pretext and make it more convincing

Once a pretext is developed, the attacker employs it during interaction with the target. This could occur through various channels such as phone calls, emails, in-person meetings, or online interactions. The attacker skillfully presents the pretext, adapts it based on the target's responses, and guides the conversation toward their desired outcome, which could involve extracting information, gaining access to systems, or influencing the target's behavior.

As seen in *Figure 9.4*, the information gathered in the previous stages is often used to craft a convincing pretext:

Figure 9.4 – Example of the pretext development stage

Engagement

Engagement is a critical stage in the social engineering life cycle, occurring after the pretext development phase. It involves actively interacting with the target to create rapport and gain the victim's trust. During the engagement stage, the attacker leverages the established pretext and applies various techniques to engage and control the target. Here are some key aspects of engagement:

- **Building a rapport**: The attacker focuses on establishing a rapport and creating a sense of trust with the target
- **Exploiting human vulnerabilities**: The attacker leverages social engineering concepts to exploit common human tendencies and vulnerabilities
- **Manipulating actions**: The attacker will leverage a plurality of manipulation techniques to gain the trust of the victim
- **Maintaining control**: An interesting fact is that throughout the engagement, the attacker will try to keep control of the interaction, ensuring that the target remains unaware of the manipulation by controlling the flow of conversation

The engagement stage requires a combination of interpersonal skills, psychological manipulation techniques, and adaptability to effectively influence the target's behavior.

As seen in *Figure 9.5*, the attacker will leverage the information gathered during the previous steps to engage the user and earn their trust:

Hi Tina, I am the president of the Dog welfare association.
We want to make a donation in your area, and I was wondering if you can help us find the right group

Hi, oh that is Awesome!
And yes, I know several groups that can benefit from that

Figure 9.5 – Example of the engagement stage

Exploitation or elicitation

Now that the attacker has engaged the victim and gained their trust, they will then leverage that trust to either *elicit* the desired information from the victim or *exploit* that trust to convince the victim to execute a given task.

Therefore, *exploitation* involves capitalizing on the trust gained from the victim to achieve the attacker's objectives. Here are some example cases:

- Make the victim disable the antivirus or any other cybersecurity control
- Motivate the victim to perform a restricted action (such as sharing a password)
- Manipulate the victim into downloading and or executing a malicious file
- Manipulate the victim into accessing sensitive data
- Convince the victim to delete some data
- Persuade the victim to execute a given command that negatively impacts the infrastructure (such as shutting down a server)

It is important to note that exploitation can occur through various channels, including online interactions, phone calls, in-person interactions, or a combination of these methods, as seen in *Figure 9.6*, where the first iteration is by phone:

Figure 9.6 – Example of the exploitation stage

Figure 9.6 also illustrates how an attacker can convince their victim to execute an action (download and open a file) and even provide an excuse to influence the victim to bypass any security control that may arise.

It is important to highlight that the only effective way to mitigate the risk of exploitation is to implement a comprehensive employee awareness program.

Regular security training and simulated social engineering exercises will help employees recognize and resist exploitation attempts, enhancing the overall resilience of the organization against such social engineering attacks.

Elicitation can be described as the act of discreetly extracting information from the victim without their knowledge. Of course, this involves several skills from the attacker, including the following:

- **Strategic questioning**: The attacker uses carefully crafted questions to extract information from the target. These questions may start with innocuous and non-threatening topics, gradually progressing toward more sensitive areas.

- **Active listening**: By actively listening to the target's responses, the attacker can identify valuable pieces of information and opportunities for further exploitation.

- **Establishing common ground**: The attacker establishes a sense of rapport and commonality with the target to foster a comfortable and open dialogue.

- **Exploiting psychological factors**: The attacker leverages psychological techniques such as reciprocity (offering something in return) and authority (positioning themselves as knowledgeable or influential) to manipulate the target's behavior and elicit desired information.

- **Timing and framing**: The attacker carefully chooses the timing and framing of their questions to maximize the chances of obtaining valuable information.

- **Exploiting human curiosity**: The attacker may leverage the target's natural curiosity to elicit information.

By skillfully employing these elicitation techniques, an attacker can extract sensitive information and confidential details that can be leveraged by them to perform further attacks.

As illustrated in *Figure 9.7*, an attacker can easily elicit information from the victim without the victim realizing they are giving away sensitive information:

Figure 9.7 – Example of the elicitation stage

As with exploitation, the best way that organizations can defend against elicitation attacks is by promoting a culture of security by creating cybersecurity awareness campaigns, providing constant training to employees, and establishing clear protocols to identify and report potential social engineering attacks.

Execution (post-exploitation)

Post-exploitation is the last phase in the social engineering life cycle and occurs after the successful manipulation of the victim to perform a given task or unwillingly provide some information.

This is a key step, as here is where the attacker executes the final attack against the victim. That attack could be carried out in several ways; let's explore some of them here:

- **Selling of data/data monetization**: The attacker may seek to monetize the obtained information by selling it on the black market or to interested parties. This could include selling sensitive data, financial information, trade secrets, or **intellectual property** (**IP**).

- **Financial fraud**: This is one of the most common methods in which the attacker leverages information gathered from the victim to steal their financial assets. This normally involves the following: unauthorized purchases of goods and services, transfer of money to other accounts, manipulating financial records, or even requesting bank services on your behalf.

- **Persistence and further exploitation**: The social engineer may use the obtained information or access as a foothold for further and more complex attacks. This could include launching subsequent social engineering campaigns, targeting other individuals or systems within the organization, or leveraging the gained privileges to escalate the scope of their attacks.

- **Extortion and blackmail**: In some cases, the attacker may attempt to blackmail the target or the organization by threatening to expose sensitive information or disrupt operations. This could involve demanding a ransom or using the acquired assets as leverage to exert pressure on the victim.

- **Intelligence gathering**: The obtained information could be used for intelligence purposes, providing the attacker with valuable insights about the target organization, its operations, vulnerabilities, or future targets. This intelligence could be leveraged for strategic planning, to refine future social engineering attacks, or to perform any other sophisticated attack.

- **Disrupting operations**: The attacker can exploit access gained to the system to execute additional attacks to disrupt the operations of the target company.

As seen in *Figure 9.8*, one common cause of ransomware infection is social engineering attacks that trick the victim into opening a malicious file that may infect the entire corporate network:

Figure 9.8 – Example of post-exploitation

With regard to mitigation, mitigating the risks associated with post-exploitation requires organizations to implement robust security measures. This includes comprehensive **incident response** (**IR**) protocols, ongoing monitoring for suspicious activities, regular system audits, and employee training on recognizing and reporting potential post-exploitation activities. Additionally, organizations should focus on strengthening their overall security posture, including implementing strong access controls, encryption, and regular vulnerability assessments, to prevent and detect these attacks.

How to stay protected

As you already saw, you can implement several techniques to reduce the risk in each of the stages of the social engineering life cycle.

However, let's summarize those methods, techniques, and controls that you can implement through the different stages of the social engineering life cycle.

Control your social media posts

One of the most common sources for attackers to start harvesting data is social media platforms, so remember that *"Think before you post"* is one of the best pieces of advice to avoid sharing data that an attacker may use against you.

Configure your privacy settings on social media

Limit access to only people you know to prevent strangers from accessing your pictures, posts, and so on.

Also, the more granularly you configure privacy settings, the more control you will have over your data.

Beware of fake profiles

Attackers may clone the profile of one of your friends to trick you into accepting their friend request.

Most of the time, the attacker will use an excuse such as: "*My old profile was closed or hacked*" to trick the victim into accepting the new request, so be aware of this technique.

Be cautious

Be cautious when approached by an unknown person (in person or using any digital media) offering something that seems to be too good to be true—for example, an offer to sponsor an event, a charity donation, and so on.

Be careful with dating sites

Dating sites are becoming the favorite places for attackers to elicit information. Here, attackers can use their "charm" to gain the victim's trust and gather personal information from the victim.

Most of the time, attackers will use fake images (including images generated using generative AI technologies) as part of their strategies to "catch" the victim's attention and create a rapport.

Avoid social media bragging

Depicting an eccentric or expensive lifestyle on social media could make you become a potential target for attackers, so as mentioned before, make sure you keep your social media as private as possible and avoid publications that could make you a target for attackers.

Be mindful of your posts

An apparently innocent post such as "*Enjoying the beach at Guiro hotel*," followed by another post stating "*Here in paradise for the rest of the week*" may provide too much data for attackers. In this case, the attacker already knows where you went for vacations, when, and even with whom (by checking the tags). All that information could be used by attackers to create a more tailored and dangerous attack.

Remove image metadata

When you take a picture of your lovely vacation, the camera may also include some additional data (metadata) in the picture, including the location of where the picture was taken. This information could be used by attackers in several stages of a social engineering attack; therefore, as a good practice, you should remove all metadata before sharing your pictures. This is how you can easily do it on a Windows machine:

1. Right-click over the image and go to **Properties**.
2. Select **Details**.

3. Click on **Remove Properties and Personal Information**.
4. Select if you want to create a copy of the files without the metadata or just remove it from the actual file.
5. Done—you successfully removed the metadata from your image.

Implement awareness campaigns

One of the most successful strategies to prevent social engineering attacks is the implementation of awareness campaigns. They are aimed at introducing the audience to the topic and making them aware of how such attacks are executed. This greatly reduces the probability of people falling victim to such attacks.

Summary

In this chapter, we embarked on a journey to gain a deep understanding of the social engineering life cycle. By way of introduction, we understood how this life cycle was developed and its evolution over the years.

Then, we explored each of the stages that comprise this life cycle, from doing a passive recognition and selection of the victim to the last stage in which the attacker leverages information elicited from the victim to execute the attack (for example, gaining unauthorized access to the victim's bank accounts).

We also provided a number of screenshots that illustrated each of the stages of the attack, and we hope that these will also serve as an inspiration for you to create your own images to illustrate the different stages of attacks during your awareness campaigns.

To close the chapter, we also provided you with a list of tips and techniques to reduce the probability and impact of social engineering attacks across the stages of their life cycle.

And now, get ready to unlock the secrets to safeguard your digital fortress as we delve into the next chapter, *Defensive Strategies for Social Engineering*, where you will learn the art of outsmarting attackers using social engineering.

10
Defensive Strategies for Social Engineering

In this chapter, we explore the importance of defensive strategies in combating social engineering threats. By recognizing red flags, conducting employee awareness campaigns, implementing countermeasures against phishing, engaging in practical exercises such as **Capture the Flag** (CTF), enhancing cybersecurity training, and learning from real-world case studies, organizations can establish a robust defense.

By implementing and embracing defensive strategies, organizations significantly reduce their vulnerability to social engineering threats. This involves cultivating a security-conscious culture, empowering employees to recognize red flags, deploying technical countermeasures, providing practical training opportunities, and drawing lessons from past incidents. The objective of this chapter is to offer valuable insights and guidance for developing robust defensive strategies against social engineering attacks.

In this chapter, we will cover the following main topics:

- Importance of defensive strategies
- Recognizing social engineering red flags
- Employee awareness campaigns
- Phishing campaigns and countermeasures
- CTF exercises
- Enhanced cybersecurity training
- Case studies and lessons learned:
    - Analyzing real-world social engineering incidents
        - Extracting valuable lessons from past experiences

Technical requirements

There are no technical requirements for this chapter.

Disclaimer

All characters in the examples are fictional characters.

The examples are inspired by real attacks; therefore, the language used (including spelling and grammatical errors) has been used on purpose.

Importance of defensive strategies

Defensive strategies in the context of social engineering are of utmost importance in protecting individuals and organizations from manipulative tactics employed by malicious actors. These strategies are critical in combating social engineering attacks, which exploit human vulnerabilities rather than technical weaknesses, by helping individuals and organizations develop a robust defense against manipulative tactics employed by attackers seeking to deceive, trick, or exploit human trust and behavior.

Firstly, defensive strategies provide awareness and education. By educating individuals about the various social engineering techniques and tactics employed by attackers, defensive strategies empower them to recognize warning signs and potential red flags. This knowledge equips individuals with the ability to discern and resist manipulation attempts, enhancing their overall security posture.

Furthermore, these strategies emphasize the importance of skepticism and critical thinking. They encourage individuals to question requests, verify the authenticity of communication channels, and validate the legitimacy of information or requests before taking any actions. By fostering a healthy skepticism, defensive strategies help individuals avoid falling victim to social engineering schemes.

The implementation of strong policies and procedures is another crucial aspect of defensive strategies. Organizations can establish guidelines and protocols that dictate how sensitive information is handled, shared, and accessed. These policies can include strict authentication measures, clear procedures for verifying identities, and guidelines for sharing information only with authorized parties. Such measures act as a strong deterrent against social engineering attempts and ensure that employees are equipped with a framework for secure behavior.

Defensive strategies also prioritize the importance of ongoing training and awareness programs. Regular training sessions and simulated social engineering scenarios can help employees recognize and respond appropriately to manipulative tactics. By exposing individuals to realistic simulations, defensive strategies enable them to practice and refine their responses, making them more resilient to social engineering attacks in real-world situations.

In the next paragraphs, we are going to cover several best practices that companies can (and should) leverage to enhance their security strategies and prevent social engineering attacks.

In terms of the implementation, our recommendations can be implemented in-house by an internal IT or security department, by a third-party vendor that provides some of those services, or by a joint combination of internal teams and support from specialized vendors that can enhance the program with specialized tools, experience, and expertise in the field.

It is also important to highlight that each company should develop its own implementation strategy based on its unique environment (budget, company culture, industry, etc.).

Recognizing social engineering red flags

Recognizing social engineering red flags is crucial in protecting yourself and organizations from manipulation and deceptive tactics employed by malicious actors. By being vigilant and attentive to certain indicators, individuals can identify potential social engineering attempts and take appropriate action to safeguard their interests. Here are some key aspects of recognizing social engineering red flags:

- **Urgency and pressure**: Social engineers often create a sense of urgency to compel individuals to make hasty decisions without careful consideration. Requests for immediate action, threats of negative consequences, or promises of extraordinary rewards can indicate a manipulative approach.
- **Authority and trust**: Attackers may impersonate figures of authority, such as supervisors, executives, or trusted individuals, to gain compliance. Unusual or unexpected requests from these sources, particularly if they bypass regular channels or protocols, should raise suspicion.
- **Information gathering**: Social engineers often engage in extensive information gathering to personalize their approach and gain credibility. Unsolicited requests for personal or sensitive information, especially when combined with seemingly innocuous conversations or friendly interactions, can indicate a social engineering attempt.
- **Inconsistencies or discrepancies**: Pay attention to inconsistencies or discrepancies in communications or requests. These can include discrepancies in email addresses, phone numbers, or official documentation. If something doesn't add up or seems out of place, it may be a red flag.
- **Unusual or unfamiliar methods of communication**: Be cautious of unexpected or unusual communication channels. Social engineers may reach out through unfamiliar platforms, social media, or personal messaging instead of official channels. This can be an attempt to bypass security measures and gain trust.
- **Emotional manipulation**: Social engineers may use emotional manipulation to exploit empathy, sympathy, or fear. They may create sob stories, share distressing situations, or invoke a sense of urgency to elicit a desired response. Beware of emotional appeals that seem disproportionate or suspicious.

- **Unsolicited offers or too-good-to-be-true opportunities**: Be wary of unsolicited offers, especially if they promise substantial rewards or benefits. Social engineers often use attractive offers to lure individuals into sharing information, performing actions, or making financial commitments without proper verification.

- **Poor grammar or spelling errors**: While not definitive proof, emails or messages with noticeable grammar or spelling mistakes can be a sign of a social engineering attempt. Many attackers operate from regions where English may not be the first language, leading to linguistic errors.

- **Requests for confidential information or login credentials**: Requests for sensitive information, account credentials, or financial details through unexpected or suspicious channels should raise an alarm. Legitimate organizations typically have established procedures for handling such requests.

- **Trust your instincts**: If something feels off or raises suspicions, trust your instincts. Social engineers often rely on creating confusion, distractions, or doubt to manipulate their targets. If a situation doesn't feel right, take the time to verify, seek additional opinions, or consult the appropriate authorities before taking any action.

Remember, recognizing social engineering red flags is an ongoing process that requires vigilance and awareness. By staying informed, exercising caution, and being proactive in verifying requests and information, individuals can significantly reduce their susceptibility to social engineering attacks.

Employee awareness campaigns

Employee awareness campaigns for social engineering are comprehensive initiatives designed to educate and empower employees to recognize, prevent, and respond effectively to social engineering attacks. These campaigns aim to create a culture of heightened awareness, promote responsible behavior, and establish a strong defense against manipulative tactics employed by malicious actors. Here are in-depth descriptions of employee awareness campaigns for social engineering:

- **Objectives and scope**:

    Employee awareness campaigns for social engineering have clear objectives that encompass both individual and organizational goals. These objectives may include the following:

    - Educating employees about various social engineering techniques, tactics, and their potential consequences
    - Enhancing employees' ability to recognize and respond to social engineering red flags
    - Promoting a security-conscious culture that prioritizes vigilance and responsible behavior
    - Mitigating the risks associated with social engineering attacks, including data breaches, unauthorized access, and financial losses

- Encouraging reporting and swift action when employees encounter suspicious incidents

The scope of these campaigns can vary based on organizational needs, industry-specific risks, and the complexity of social engineering threats faced.

- **Comprehensive training programs**:

  Employee awareness campaigns typically feature comprehensive training programs that cover a range of topics related to social engineering. These programs may include the following:

  - **General awareness sessions**: Interactive sessions that provide an overview of social engineering concepts, common tactics, and real-life examples to increase awareness and understanding
  - **Phishing simulations**: Simulated phishing campaigns that expose employees to realistic phishing scenarios, allowing them to practice identifying and reporting suspicious emails or links
  - **Role-specific training**: Tailored training modules for specific job roles or departments, addressing unique social engineering risks and best practices relevant to their responsibilities
  - **Ongoing training**: Continuous education initiatives that reinforce knowledge, provide updates on emerging threats, and refresh employees' understanding of social engineering trends and mitigation strategies

- **Real-life scenarios and case studies**:

  To enhance the practical understanding of social engineering, employee awareness campaigns often include real-life scenarios and case studies. These illustrate how social engineering attacks have occurred within the organization or industry, emphasizing the potential consequences and highlighting lessons learned. Real-life examples create relatability and help employees apply their knowledge to their own work environment.

- **Best practices and mitigation strategies**:

  - **Employee awareness campaigns**: These provide clear guidelines and best practices to help employees mitigate social engineering risks effectively. These may include the following:
  - **Strong password management**: This involves encouraging employees to use complex passwords, enable two-factor authentication, and avoid reusing passwords across multiple accounts
  - **Information handling protocols**: This includes clearly defining procedures for sharing sensitive information, verifying the legitimacy of requests, and reporting suspicious incidents
  - **Secure communication practices**: These include promoting the use of secure channels for sharing confidential data, avoiding public Wi-Fi for sensitive tasks, and encrypting sensitive emails or attachments

- **Physical security measures**: These include educating employees about physical security risks, such as tailgating or unauthorized access, and reinforcing the importance of identity verification and adherence to access control procedures

- **Continuous communication and engagement**:

  Employee awareness campaigns foster a culture of continuous communication and engagement. This includes the following:

  - **Regular reminders and updates**: Periodic communication channels, such as newsletters, email reminders, or intranet posts, to reinforce key messages, provide updates on emerging threats, and celebrate employee achievements in recognizing and reporting suspicious incidents
  - **Awareness materials**: Provide employees with easily accessible resources, such as posters, infographics, or digital handouts, that highlight social engineering risks, red flags, and best practices
  - **Open lines of communication**: Encourage employees to report suspicious incidents or share concerns without fear of repercussions, and provide clear reporting channels for prompt action and investigation

- **Leadership support and accountability**:

  Employee awareness campaigns require strong leadership support and accountability. Executives and managers should actively participate, endorse initiatives, and lead by example. This includes the following:

  - Demonstrating commitment to security and setting clear expectations for responsible behavior
  - Allocating resources for training, awareness materials, and technology solutions that aid in detecting and mitigating social engineering attacks
  - Recognizing and rewarding employees for their vigilance, reporting incidents, and actively engaging in security practices
  - Establishing accountability mechanisms to monitor the effectiveness of the awareness campaigns and regularly assess the organization's overall readiness to combat social engineering threats

In conclusion, employee awareness campaigns for social engineering play a crucial role in equipping employees with the knowledge and skills necessary to recognize, prevent, and respond to manipulative tactics. By fostering a security-conscious culture, organizations can significantly reduce their vulnerability to social engineering attacks, protecting sensitive information, maintaining trust, and safeguarding their reputation.

Phishing campaigns and countermeasures

Phishing campaigns are malicious attempts to deceive individuals or organizations into divulging sensitive information, such as login credentials, financial details, or personal data. These campaigns typically involve deceptive emails, messages, or websites that mimic legitimate entities, aiming to trick recipients into taking actions that benefit the attackers. Implementing effective countermeasures against phishing campaigns is crucial to protect individuals and organizations from falling victim to these fraudulent schemes. Here are in-depth descriptions of phishing campaigns and countermeasures:

- **Understanding phishing campaigns**:

    Phishing campaigns employ various techniques to manipulate individuals and create a false sense of trust. Key characteristics of phishing campaigns include the following:

    - **Spoofed identities**: Attackers impersonate trusted entities, such as banks, online services, or colleagues, by using deceptive email addresses, domain names, or forged branding elements.
    - **Urgency and fear tactics**: Phishing emails often create a sense of urgency or fear to pressure recipients into immediate action, such as account suspension, security breaches, or pending consequences.
    - **Deceptive URLs and links**: Phishing emails contain links that direct recipients to fake websites designed to resemble legitimate ones. These URLs may use subtle variations, misspellings, or hidden redirects to deceive users.
    - **Social engineering techniques**: Phishing campaigns exploit human psychology by leveraging social engineering techniques, such as emotional manipulation, curiosity, or appealing to recipients' desire for rewards or assistance.

- **Phishing countermeasures**:

    Implementing effective countermeasures can significantly reduce the risk of falling victim to phishing campaigns. These countermeasures include the following:

    - **Employee awareness and training**: Regular, comprehensive training programs educate employees about the various forms of phishing attacks, red flags, and safe practices. This empowers employees to recognize and report phishing attempts promptly.
    - **Email filtering and anti-phishing tools**: Deploying robust email filtering solutions can automatically detect and block phishing emails based on known patterns, suspicious senders, or malicious URLs. Anti-phishing tools can provide real-time warnings and analysis of email content and attachments.
    - **Multi-factor authentication (MFA)**: Enabling MFA adds an extra layer of security by requiring additional verification steps beyond usernames and passwords. This mitigates the risk of compromised credentials being used in phishing attacks.

- **Secure browsing practices**: Encouraging employees to use secure web browsers with built-in phishing protection features, such as anti-phishing extensions or warning mechanisms, helps detect and prevent access to phishing websites.

- **URL inspection and verification**: Training employees to hover over links to inspect the actual URL before clicking can reveal discrepancies or suspicious domains. Educating users about the importance of manually typing URLs or using bookmarks instead of relying solely on email links enhances security.

- **Incident reporting and response**: Establishing clear reporting channels and incident response procedures enables employees to report suspicious emails, links, or websites promptly. This allows for swift investigation, mitigation, and dissemination of information to prevent further damage.

- **Regular security updates and patch management**: Keeping operating systems, applications, and security software up to date ensures that known vulnerabilities are patched, reducing the likelihood of successful phishing attacks.

- **Security policies and procedures**: Implementing and enforcing robust security policies and procedures that outline guidelines for handling sensitive information, verifying requests, and reporting incidents provides a framework for secure behavior and reduces the risk of falling victim to phishing.

• **Continuous monitoring and assessment**:

Phishing threats constantly evolve, requiring continuous monitoring and assessment of phishing campaigns and their countermeasures. This includes the following:

- **Threat intelligence**: Staying informed about emerging phishing techniques, new attack vectors, and evolving trends through threat intelligence sources helps organizations proactively adapt their defenses.

- **Regular assessments and simulations**: Conducting periodic phishing simulations and vulnerability assessments provides insights into the organization's susceptibility to phishing attacks. These assessments help identify areas for improvement, tailor training programs, and measure the effectiveness of existing countermeasures.

- **Incident analysis and lessons learned**: Analyzing phishing incidents and sharing lessons learned within the organization helps refine security protocols, update training materials, and enhance the overall resilience against future phishing campaigns.

Implementing effective countermeasures against phishing campaigns requires a combination of employee awareness, technical solutions, secure practices, and continuous monitoring. By integrating these countermeasures, organizations can significantly reduce the risk of falling victim to phishing attacks, safeguard sensitive information, and maintain a robust security posture.

CTF exercises

CTF exercises are dynamic and interactive cybersecurity training events that immerse participants in simulated environments to test their skills, knowledge, and problem-solving abilities. These events are designed to replicate real-world scenarios, allowing participants to experience the challenges faced by cybersecurity professionals in a controlled and educational setting.

During CTF exercises, participants engage in a series of challenges that span various domains of cybersecurity, such as cryptography, network security, web application security, reverse engineering, and forensics. These challenges are carefully crafted to reflect the latest trends and techniques used by cyber attackers, ensuring participants gain practical insights into emerging threats and vulnerabilities.

Setting up and conducting CTF events for employees requires careful planning and coordination. The challenges must be meticulously designed to strike a balance between being challenging enough to stimulate critical thinking and solvable enough to encourage active participation. The event organizers need to create a diverse range of challenge categories that cater to different skill levels and provide opportunities for participants to apply their expertise and learn new techniques.

To promote teamwork and skill development, CTF events often encourage participants to form teams and collaborate to solve challenges. This fosters a sense of camaraderie and allows participants to leverage each other's strengths and expertise. Effective communication and information sharing among team members are vital for successful collaboration, as participants must work together to dissect complex challenges and solve them collectively.

Incorporating social engineering scenarios in CTF challenges adds an additional layer of realism and complexity. These scenarios simulate social engineering attacks, such as phishing or impersonation attempts, where participants must analyze suspicious communication, identify red flags, and take appropriate actions to mitigate the risks. By including social engineering elements, CTF exercises raise awareness of the human aspect of cybersecurity and highlight the importance of vigilance and skepticism when dealing with potential threats.

CTF exercises not only provide a platform for employees to enhance their technical skills and knowledge but also promote critical thinking, creativity, and resourcefulness. They encourage participants to think like attackers, analyze systems and networks from multiple perspectives, and develop effective strategies to protect against cyber threats. By participating in CTF events, employees gain practical experience, identify areas for improvement, and strengthen their ability to detect and respond to cybersecurity incidents effectively.

Overall, CTF exercises offer a dynamic and engaging approach to cybersecurity training, empowering employees to become more proficient in their roles, enhancing teamwork and collaboration, and equipping organizations with a stronger defense against evolving cyber threats.

Enhanced cybersecurity training

Enhanced cybersecurity training is a transformative approach that goes beyond the surface-level understanding of basic security practices. It delves into the intricacies of cyber threats and equips employees with the necessary skills and knowledge to become proactive defenders against ever-evolving risks. By immersing participants in comprehensive training experiences, organizations can foster a culture of cybersecurity excellence and empower their workforce to navigate the complex landscape of cyber threats effectively.

At the core of enhanced cybersecurity training lies a deep understanding of the threat landscape. It goes beyond simply educating employees about the existence of cyber threats and instead provides them with an in-depth comprehension of the motivations, techniques, and tactics employed by malicious actors. By delving into the psychology and strategies behind social engineering, phishing attempts, and other prevalent threats, employees gain a deeper awareness of potential vulnerabilities and are better equipped to identify and respond to sophisticated attacks. Traditional methods of information dissemination are transformed into dynamic and engaging learning experiences. Employees participate in simulated scenarios, role-playing exercises, and hands-on simulations that mirror real-world cyber threats. This immersive approach enhances critical thinking, decision-making, and problem-solving skills, empowering participants to make informed choices when faced with potential security incidents.

Tailoring training to address social engineering threats specifically takes the depth of cybersecurity training to a higher level. Social engineering attacks exploit human psychology and trust, making them highly effective and difficult to detect. By focusing on this specific threat vector, training programs can equip employees with the ability to recognize manipulation techniques, spot red flags in communication, and develop a healthy skepticism toward suspicious requests or activities. With specialized modules and interactive exercises centered around social engineering, employees gain the confidence and expertise needed to thwart such attacks.

Enhanced cybersecurity training is not a one-time event but a continuous journey of learning and improvement. It recognizes that the threat landscape is constantly evolving and organizations must adapt accordingly. Regular updates, refresher courses, and ongoing education keep employees informed about emerging threats, evolving attack vectors, and the latest defensive strategies. By fostering a culture of lifelong learning, organizations can stay resilient and agile in the face of new and emerging cyber risks.

By embracing enhanced cybersecurity training, organizations elevate their cybersecurity posture and create a workforce that is vigilant, knowledgeable, and proactive in defending against cyber threats. It fosters a sense of ownership and responsibility among employees, empowering them to play an active role in protecting sensitive information, preserving the organization's reputation, and safeguarding valuable assets. Ultimately, enhanced cybersecurity training cultivates a cyber-resilient organization that can effectively navigate the digital landscape and stay one step ahead of cybercriminals.

Assessing the effectiveness of existing cybersecurity training programs

In the rapidly evolving landscape of cyber threats, organizations must regularly evaluate the effectiveness of their cybersecurity training programs. This assessment provides valuable insights into the impact and efficacy of the training initiatives and allows organizations to identify areas for improvement. By assessing training effectiveness, organizations can ensure that their employees are equipped with the necessary knowledge and skills to effectively recognize and respond to cyber threats, including social engineering attacks.

Assessing training effectiveness involves various measures, such as evaluating participant feedback, conducting assessments or quizzes, monitoring security incident trends, and analyzing performance metrics. Feedback from participants provides valuable insights into the relevance, clarity, and engagement level of the training content. Assessments and quizzes help gauge the retention and understanding of the training material, allowing organizations to identify areas where further clarification or reinforcement may be needed.

Monitoring security incident trends before and after implementing training programs can offer a quantitative assessment of their impact. A decrease in incidents related to social engineering or an increase in incident reporting can indicate the effectiveness of the training in raising awareness and improving incident response.

Performance metrics, such as the success rate of simulated phishing exercises or the speed of incident resolution, can provide tangible measures of training effectiveness. These metrics help organizations track progress over time and identify areas where additional support or training may be required.

Regularly assessing the effectiveness of cybersecurity training programs is crucial in the dynamic landscape of cyber threats. It allows organizations to stay proactive, adapt their training strategies, and address emerging challenges effectively.

Identifying gaps and areas for improvement

Identifying gaps and areas for improvement is a critical process in enhancing an organization's cybersecurity posture. It involves conducting thorough assessments and analyses to identify weaknesses, vulnerabilities, and shortcomings within existing security measures. By recognizing these gaps, organizations can take proactive steps to address them and strengthen their overall security defenses.

In the evolution of the landscape of cybersecurity, organizations must constantly strive to improve their defenses and stay one step ahead of malicious actors. Identifying gaps and areas for improvement is a vital part of this proactive approach. Identifying gaps serves as a reality check, shedding light on areas where the organization may be at risk or not fully meeting industry best practices. This could include gaps in policies and procedures, outdated technologies, insufficient employee training, or ineffective incident response protocols.

The benefits of identifying gaps and areas for improvement are manifold:

- Firstly, it allows organizations to allocate resources effectively by prioritizing efforts where they are most needed. By focusing on the specific areas identified as gaps, organizations can optimize their investments and ensure that limited resources are allocated to the most critical security needs.

- Secondly, it enables organizations to enhance their security posture and reduce the likelihood of successful cyber-attacks.

- Moreover, identifying gaps fosters a culture of continuous improvement within the organization. It encourages ongoing evaluation and refinement of security measures, ensuring that the organization stays agile and responsive to emerging threats.

- Lastly, identifying gaps and areas for improvement contributes to overall risk mitigation and regulatory compliance. By identifying vulnerabilities and taking action to address them, organizations demonstrate their commitment to safeguarding sensitive data, protecting customer trust, and complying with industry regulations and standards.

In conclusion, identifying gaps and areas for improvement is a fundamental aspect of effective cybersecurity management. It empowers organizations to proactively address weaknesses, allocate resources wisely, enhance their security posture, foster a culture of continuous improvement, and mitigate risks.

Case studies and lessons learned

In this section, we will explore case studies and the valuable lessons learned from real-world social engineering incidents, shedding light on the tactics employed by attackers and the measures organizations can take to defend against such attacks.

Analyzing real-world social engineering incidents

Analyzing real-world social engineering incidents is a crucial aspect of understanding the tactics, techniques, and impact of these attacks. By studying and dissecting such incidents, organizations can gain valuable insights into the vulnerabilities they exploit, the methods used, and the potential consequences. Here are the key steps involved in analyzing real-world social engineering incidents:

1. **Incident identification**: Identify and collect information about social engineering incidents that have occurred in real-world contexts. This can include incidents reported within the organization, incidents from industry sources, or publicly disclosed cases.

2. **Incident documentation**: Document the details of each incident, including the target, the type of social engineering attack employed, the attack vector used (for example, a phishing email, phone call, or physical impersonation), and any known or suspected impacts.

3. **Incident reconstructions**: Reconstruct the sequence of events leading up to the incident. This involves analyzing the attack vectors, such as email headers, call recordings, or surveillance footage, to understand how the attack unfolded and how the attacker gained access to sensitive information.

4. **Analysis of social engineering techniques**: Analyze the social engineering techniques employed in the incident. This includes understanding the psychological manipulation tactics used by the attacker, such as exploiting authority, urgency, fear, or personal relationships, to deceive the target.

5. **Vulnerability assessment**: Identify the vulnerabilities or weaknesses that allowed the social engineering attack to be successful. This can include factors such as a lack of employee awareness, inadequate security policies and procedures, or technical vulnerabilities that were exploited.

6. **Impact assessment**: Assess the impact of the social engineering incident on the organization, individuals, or systems involved. This can include financial losses, data breaches, reputational damage, or operational disruptions.

7. **Lessons learned and recommendations**: Extract key insights from the analysis and develop recommendations to prevent future incidents. This may involve strengthening employee awareness and training programs, enhancing security controls, implementing MFA, or improving incident response protocols.

8. **Sharing knowledge and best practices**: Share the findings and recommendations with relevant stakeholders within the organization and the wider community. This can help raise awareness, promote information sharing, and improve collective defense against social engineering attacks.

9. **Continuous monitoring and adaptation**: Continuously monitor and adapt security measures based on emerging social engineering trends and new attack techniques. Regularly reassess the organization's vulnerability to social engineering attacks and update defense mechanisms accordingly.

Analyzing real-world social engineering incidents provides organizations with valuable insights into the evolving threat landscape and helps them develop effective countermeasures. It enables them to identify weaknesses, improve security awareness and practices, and mitigate the risks associated with social engineering attacks. By learning from real-world incidents, organizations can strengthen their defenses and better protect themselves and their employees from social engineering threats.

Extracting valuable lessons from past experiences

Case studies and lessons learned from social engineering incidents provide valuable insights into real-world scenarios, highlighting the tactics used by attackers, the vulnerabilities exploited, and the resulting consequences. Here are a few examples of social engineering case studies and the lessons learned from them:

Case study – the targeted phishing attack

In this case, an organization fell victim to a targeted phishing attack. Attackers sent highly convincing emails to employees, posing as a trusted colleague, and requested sensitive information. Several employees unknowingly divulged their credentials, leading to a data breach and unauthorized access to critical systems.

Lesson learned: Employee awareness and training are vital in combating phishing attacks. Organizations should educate employees about the risks of phishing, teach them to identify red flags, and emphasize the importance of verifying email requests through secure channels before sharing sensitive information.

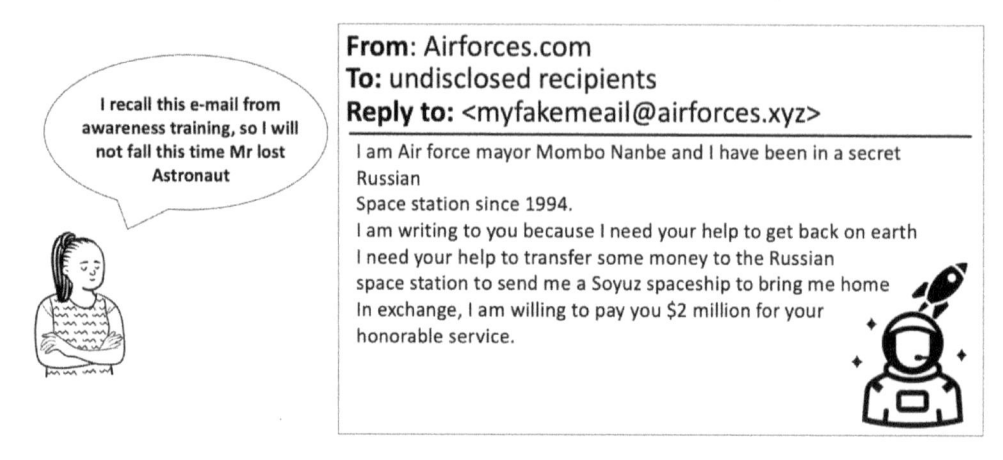

Figure 10.1 – Example of Targeted phishing attack

As seen in *Figure 10.1*, awareness campaigns are one of the best methods to keep your organization secure against this type of threat.

Case study – the impersonation scam

In this case, an attacker posed as a company executive and contacted an employee, claiming to be in urgent need of financial assistance. The employee, believing the request was genuine, transferred a significant amount of funds to the attacker's account.

Lesson learned: Implement strict verification procedures for financial transactions and establish clear protocols for verifying requests, particularly those involving large sums of money. Employees should be trained to validate unusual or urgent requests through multiple channels before taking any action.

Figure 10.2 – Example of impersonation scam

As seen in *Figure 10.2*, implementing strict verification procedures for financial transactions and always verifying the caller and the request is the best way to be protected against this type of attack.

Case study – the physical impersonation attack

In this case, an attacker gained unauthorized access to a secure facility by posing as a maintenance worker. The attacker exploited the lack of strict identity verification procedures and used social engineering techniques to convince employees to provide access codes and sensitive information.

Lesson learned: Physical security measures must include robust identity verification protocols. Employees should be trained to challenge unfamiliar individuals in restricted areas and to report any suspicious activity immediately. Regular audits of access control systems and employee training on physical security best practices are essential.

Figure 10.3 – Example of physical impersonation attack

As seen in the *Figure 10.3*, we need to be careful to always report inappropriate behavior or actions.

Case study – social media manipulation

In this case, an attacker gathered publicly available information from the social media profiles of employees and used it to impersonate colleagues. The attacker then used this trust to deceive employees into revealing sensitive information or clicking on malicious links.

Lesson learned: Encourage employees to be cautious about sharing personal or work-related information on public platforms and adjust privacy settings accordingly. Implement social media usage policies that raise awareness about the risks of social engineering and educate employees about the importance of privacy and security online.

Figure 10.4 – Example of social media manipulation attack

As seen in *Figure 10.4*, posting sensitive or private information on social media can be used by attackers to craft an attack against you or people that you know, so be aware of your social media posts.

These case studies illustrate the diverse methods employed by attackers and the importance of employee awareness, training, and stringent security measures to mitigate social engineering risks. By studying such incidents and implementing the lessons learned, organizations can strengthen their defenses and reduce the likelihood of falling victim to social engineering attacks.

Summary

In this chapter, you have learned key skills to establish a robust defense against social engineering threats. Recognizing social engineering red flags is crucial, as it enables individuals to identify suspicious behaviors and tactics used by attackers to manipulate people into compromising security.

The chapter has emphasized the importance of conducting employee awareness campaigns, which involve designing effective training programs to educate employees about social engineering techniques and foster a culture of security awareness. Implementing countermeasures, such as MFA and access controls, helps mitigate social engineering risks.

The chapter also highlighted the value of organizing CTF exercises, which provide employees with simulated scenarios to practice identifying and responding to social engineering attacks. Enhancing cybersecurity training was another essential skill we discussed, which involves staying up to date with the latest attack techniques and best practices.

Lastly, the chapter emphasized the significance of learning from real-world case studies to gain insights into the methods used by attackers and vulnerabilities exploited. By acquiring these skills, organizations can significantly reduce their vulnerability to social engineering attacks and establish a stronger defense against these insidious threats.

As we delve deeper into the realm of social engineering, the next chapter unveils a comprehensive exploration of applicable laws and regulations that serve as crucial safeguards against the deceptive tactics employed by cybercriminals. Join us as we navigate the legal landscape, uncovering the protective measures and regulatory frameworks designed to combat social engineering and ensure the security of individuals and organizations alike.

11
Applicable Laws and Regulations for Social Engineering

This chapter delves into two crucial aspects of the battle against social engineering: the laws and regulations established worldwide to safeguard individuals' privacy and cybersecurity, and the lessons learned from notable convictions related to social engineering. By examining these intertwined elements, we gain insights into the legal landscape and the implications of social engineering on individuals and society as a whole.

Firstly, we will explore a range of laws and regulations from different countries that address the multifaceted challenges posed by social engineering. From the groundbreaking **General Data Protection Regulation (GDPR)** in the **European Union (EU)** to the **California Consumer Privacy Act (CCPA)** in the United States, we will navigate through a tapestry of legal frameworks designed to protect personal data, enhance privacy, and mitigate the risks associated with social engineering techniques. These examples illustrate the global efforts to establish legal structures that strike a balance between enabling innovation and safeguarding individuals' rights and security.

Additionally, we will delve into notable convictions stemming from social engineering cases, which serve as cautionary tales and provide valuable lessons for understanding the legal consequences of such activities. From the exploits of infamous hackers such as Kevin Mitnick, who employed social engineering to gain unauthorized access to computer systems, to the case of Albert Gonzalez, responsible for massive data breaches that compromised countless individuals' financial information, we will examine the repercussions faced by those who engage in social engineering-driven cybercrimes. These real-world examples shed light on the gravity of the offenses, the impact on victims, and the criminal justice system's response.

By studying the interplay between laws, regulations, and convictions, we gain a comprehensive understanding of the legal landscape surrounding social engineering. We explore the motivations, methodologies, and consequences of social engineering techniques and assess how legal frameworks have evolved to counter these threats. Through this exploration, we aim to equip you with knowledge and insights that can aid in combating social engineering, protecting personal information, and strengthening cybersecurity practices.

Join us on a journey through the intricate web of laws, regulations, and convictions, as we unravel the complexities of social engineering, examine legal approaches from around the world, and draw invaluable lessons from notable cases. Together, we can forge a safer and more resilient digital future.

In this chapter, we will cover the following main topics:

- Examples of laws and regulations around the world
- Convictions for social engineering – lessons learned from notable cases

Technical requirements

There are no technical requirements for this chapter.

Examples of laws and regulations around the world

Social engineering, the art of manipulating human behavior to deceive and exploit individuals, presents significant challenges in the realm of cybersecurity and privacy. While no specific laws exclusively target social engineering techniques, various legal frameworks around the world encompass provisions that address the risks associated with this deceptive practice.

It is important to highlight that laws and regulations change depending on your location, your industry, and even the location of your customers; therefore, it is imperative that you invest time in understanding the laws and regulations that are relevant to your business.

Also, make sure to get advice from your legal counsel to better understand the applicable laws and regulations regarding data privacy and cybersecurity in your region.

> **Note**
> Laws and regulations is a very serious topic that involves other teams such as legal departments and **human resources** (**HR**). Therefore, those teams must always be included when addressing this topic.

The following examples highlight key laws and regulations from different countries that tackle social engineering concerns:

- **GDPR – EU:**

The GDPR, effective since May 2018, is a landmark data protection regulation applicable to all EU member states. It aims to harmonize data protection laws within the EU and enhance the rights and privacy of individuals. The regulation applies to organizations that process personal data of EU residents, regardless of the organization's location. Key provisions of the GDPR include the following:

- **Consent**: It requires organizations to obtain clear and affirmative consent from individuals for the processing of their personal data
- **Data breach notification**: Organizations must report data breaches to the relevant supervisory authority within 72 hours of becoming aware of the breach unless the breach is unlikely to result in a risk to individuals' rights and freedoms
- **Right to access**: Individuals have the right to request access to their personal data held by organizations and obtain information about how their data is being processed
- **Right to erasure**: Also known as the *right to be forgotten*, it allows individuals to request the deletion of their personal data in certain circumstances

- **CCPA – United States:**

The CCPA, effective from January 1, 2020, is a comprehensive privacy law applicable to businesses that collect and process the personal information of Californian residents. Key aspects of the CCPA include the following:

- **Right to know**: Individuals have the right to know what personal information is being collected and how it is being used or shared
- **Right to opt out**: Individuals can opt out of the sale of their personal information to third parties
- **Right to deletion**: Individuals can request the deletion of their personal information held by businesses, subject to certain exceptions
- **Non-discrimination**: Businesses cannot discriminate against individuals who exercise their privacy rights

- **Personal Data Protection Act (PDPA) – Singapore:**

Singapore's PDPA governs the collection, use, and disclosure of personal data by organizations. Key provisions of the PDPA include the following:

- **Consent obligations**: Organizations must obtain individuals' consent for the collection, use, or disclosure of personal data, and inform individuals of the purposes for such processing
- **Protection of personal data**: Organizations must implement reasonable security measures to protect personal data from unauthorized access, collection, use, disclosure, copying, modification, disposal, or similar risks

- **Access and correction**: Individuals have the right to access their personal data and request corrections if necessary
- **Data breach notification**: Organizations are required to notify the **Personal Data Protection Commission** (**PDPC**) of any data breach that poses a risk of significant harm to affected individuals

• **Telecommunications Act 1997 – Australia:**

Australia's Telecommunications Act 1997 includes provisions related to privacy and security within the telecommunications sector. Key elements of the Act include the following:

- **Unauthorized access**: The Act prohibits unauthorized access to telecommunications networks and facilities
- **Interception of communications**: Intercepting or accessing communications without proper authorization is an offense under the Act
- **Protection of personal information**: Telecommunications providers must take reasonable steps to protect personal information from unauthorized access or disclosure
- **Notification of security incidents**: Telecommunications providers are required to notify the **Australian Communications and Media Authority** (**ACMA**) of any significant security incidents affecting their networks

• **Cybersecurity Law – China:**

China's Cybersecurity Law, implemented in 2017, aims to safeguard national cybersecurity and protect citizens' rights in cyberspace. Key provisions of the law include the following:

- **Personal information protection**: Network operators must obtain individuals' consent when collecting personal information, clearly specifying the purpose, method, and scope of collection, and ensuring proper security measures
- **Security incident reporting**: Network operators are required to promptly report cybersecurity incidents to the relevant authorities and cooperate with investigations
- **Critical Information Infrastructure (CII) protection**: Operators of CII must adopt measures to ensure secure and reliable operations, conduct regular security assessments, and establish emergency response plans
- **Cross-border data transfers**: For operators of CII, critical data must be stored within mainland China unless a security assessment deems it necessary for business purposes to transfer data abroad

These examples demonstrate the commitment of various jurisdictions to address privacy, security, and data protection concerns arising from social engineering techniques. However, *it's important to review the full texts of the laws and consult legal experts to understand the detailed provisions and implications in each jurisdiction.*

Convictions for social engineering – lessons learned from notable cases

In the realm of cybercrime, social engineering has emerged as a formidable tactic, exploiting the vulnerabilities of human psychology to gain unauthorized access, deceive individuals, and perpetrate fraudulent activities. While specific convictions solely for social engineering may be challenging to find, there have been notable cases where individuals were convicted for offenses related to manipulation, deception, and unauthorized access. Examining these cases provides valuable insights into the legal consequences and lessons learned from such actions. Let's look at these now:

- **Kevin Mitnick – unmasking the hacker extraordinaire**

    In the annals of cybersecurity, the name Kevin Mitnick reverberates as one of the most infamous hackers. Mitnick employed various social engineering techniques to infiltrate computer systems, leaving a trail of unauthorized access and compromised data in his wake. His relentless pursuit of technological exploits eventually led to his conviction and imprisonment. Mitnick faced charges including wire fraud, computer fraud, and unauthorized access to computer systems. His case shed light on the legal repercussions of social engineering tactics and their potential impact on individuals and organizations.

- **Albert Gonzalez – unveiling the mastermind behind massive breaches**

    Albert Gonzalez, known by his online alias *soupnazi*, orchestrated a series of high-profile hacking incidents that rocked the cybersecurity landscape. Through social engineering methods, Gonzalez and his accomplices infiltrated the security defenses of major retail companies, leading to the theft of millions of credit and debit card details. The consequences of his actions were severe, as unsuspecting individuals fell victim to identity theft and financial losses. Gonzalez's conviction for computer fraud, wire fraud, and identity theft demonstrated the significant legal penalties awaiting those who engage in social engineering-driven cybercrimes.

- **Adrian Lamo – a homeless hacker's tale of intrigue**

    Adrian Lamo, famously dubbed the *homeless hacker* employed his skills in social engineering to gain unauthorized access to various computer systems and networks. His exploits, including breaching the security of *The New York Times*, thrust him into the spotlight. However, Lamo's actions did not go unpunished. Following his eventual self-surrender, he faced legal consequences for computer crimes, including unauthorized network access and information theft. Lamo's case highlighted the ethical and legal boundaries crossed by social engineers and underscored the potential repercussions of their actions.

- **Mathew Bevan and Richard Pryce – hacking pioneers amid controversy**

    During the nascent days of widespread computer network adoption, Mathew Bevan, also known as *Kuji*, and Richard Pryce, known as *Datastream Cowboy*, made headlines for breaching the security of military and government computer systems. Their exploits involved social engineering tactics, resulting in concerns over national security. Although neither Bevan nor Pryce was ultimately convicted, their cases ignited debates surrounding the legality and ethics of hacking, as well as the evolving nature of cybercrime legislation.

These notable cases demonstrate that social engineering as a tactic carries substantial legal risks. The convictions and legal outcomes serve as cautionary tales for those tempted to exploit the vulnerabilities of human trust and psychological manipulation. They highlight the importance of robust cybersecurity measures, user awareness, and stringent legal frameworks to counter social engineering-driven cybercrimes. By studying these cases, individuals, organizations, and policymakers can gain a deeper understanding of the legal consequences associated with social engineering and work toward building a safer and more secure digital ecosystem.

Summary

Through this chapter, you are now equipped with the knowledge and insights necessary to navigate the legal landscape surrounding social engineering. You are empowered to protect personal information, uphold privacy rights, and contribute to building a safer and more secure digital ecosystem. By unraveling the intricacies of laws and regulations, alongside the lessons derived from notable convictions, you become active participants in the ongoing battle against social engineering, driving us toward a more resilient digital future.

Index

A

account hijacking 112
account suspension scam 58
Ace Ventura scam 45
advance-fee fraud 38
adware attack 98
   preventing, considerations 99
AI-assisted social media manipulation attacks 140, 141
   algorithmic exploitation 141
   automated content generation 141
   bot networks 141
   influencer impersonation 141
   micro-targeting 141
   protecting against 142
AI-driven social engineering techniques 125
   deepfake technology 125
   natural language processing (NLP) 125
   voice cloning 125
AI-enhanced social engineering attacks
   protecting against 127, 128
   strategies, for combating 125-130

AI-powered phishing attacks 137, 138
   advanced social engineering 138
   AI-enhanced impersonation 138
   automated spear phishing 138
   protecting against 139, 140
   real-time adaptation 139
   security measures, evading 139
   smarter targeting 138
America Online (AOL) attack 55
app-based attacks 103
app permissions, exploiting for data access
   app permissions and user consent 106
   consequences of exploitation 107
   exploitation techniques 107
   risks and concerns 106
Arduino-Based Attack Vector 157
artificial intelligence (AI)
   advantages, to social engineering 124, 125
   in social engineering attacks 124
artificial intelligence (AI) voice cloning tool 65
attack vectors 159

Index

B

Bad USB 70
baiting 70
  cyber baiting 71
  physical baiting 70, 71
  protecting from 71
Business Email Compromise (BEC) scam 48, 49

C

calendar hijacking 66
calendar phishing 66, 67
  detecting 68
  fake appointment 67
  malware attack 67
  protecting from 68
  ransomware attack 67
  spoofed event 67
California Consumer Privacy Act (CCPA) 197
  key aspects 199
Capture the Flag (CTF) 179
CEO fraud 59
clickbait attack 108, 109
  protecting against 110
cloned fake web page
  example 56
convolutional neural networks (CNNs) 131
crypto mining 76
crypto scam
  and social engineering 28-34
CTF exercises 187
cyber baiting 71
cybersecurity
  Social Engineering Toolkit (SET), importance 147

Cybersecurity Law - China 200
  key provisions 200, 201

D

dark web services 63
deepfake audio 133
  detecting 135, 136
  detection challenges 134
  dubbing and localization 134
  ethical considerations 134
  fraud and social engineering 134
  impersonation and misuse 134
  voice conversion 134
  voice synthesis 134
deepfakes 125, 130
  data collection and training 131
  deep learning algorithms 131
  facial recognition and mapping 131
  hardware and computing power 131
  image and video processing 131
  implications, for social engineering attacks 136
  preventing 136, 137
  voice synthesis 131
deepfake videos 132
  detecting 133
deep fake voicemail scam 65
defensive strategies 180
  importance 180, 181
distribution channels, malicious apps
  app update mechanisms 105
  drive-by downloads 105
  file-sharing platforms and websites 104
  official app store 104
  phishing and malicious websites 104
  pre-installed apps 105

social engineering and messaging
platforms 105
Third-Party app stores 104
**Domain-Based Message
Authentication, Reporting, and
Conformance (DMARC)** 62
DomainKeys Identified Mail (DKIM) 62
dumpster diving attack 19, 72
protecting from 72

E

email phishing attacks 59
detecting 60, 61
protecting from 61, 62
spear phishing 60
whaling 59
empathy 13
using, to bypass security controls 14
employee awareness campaigns 182
best practices 183, 184
comprehensive training programs 183
continuous communication
and engagement 184
leadership support and accountability 184
mitigation strategies 183, 184
objectives 182
real-life scenarios and case studies 183
scope 183
engagement
key aspects 172
enhanced cybersecurity training 188
benefits, for identifying gaps and
areas for improvement 190
existing cybersecurity training
programs, assessing 189
gaps and areas for improvement,
identifying 189, 190

enhanced social engineering attacks 81
evil wife 46
exploitation (elicitation) 173, 174
attacker skills 174

F

Facebook 19
face swapping 131
fake advertisements 25
fake appointment 67
fake investment 23-25
fake job offers attack 74, 75
fake login attacks 84, 85
preventing, considerations 86
fake news attacks 116
protecting against 118
working, through mechanisms 117
fake page attack 89-91
preventing, considerations 91, 92
fake update attacks 86, 87
preventing, considerations 87
false charities 75
favor to favor attacks. *See* **quid
pro quo attacks**
federal government grant attack 21
fake agent 21
link 21
forex attacks
fake forex brokers 119
fake trading signals and analysis 119
Forex fraud schemes 119
manipulation of forex prices 119
pump and dump schemes 119
pyramid schemes 119
unauthorized trading 119
forex scams 119
protecting against 120

forum-based attacks 95-97
  preventing, considerations 97, 98
fraud compensation 49, 50
free software to download attack 74
free tech support attack 73

G

gaming-based attacks 94
  preventing, considerations 95
GDPR - EU
  key provisions 199
General Data Protection Regulation (GDPR) 197, 199
generative adversarial networks (GANs) 131
Google attack 57, 58
Graphics processing units (GPUs) 131

H

hacking-ware attack 93, 94
  preventing, considerations 94
high-value target attacks 79
high-value targets
  identifying 81, 82
HTML Application (HTA) 155
human resources (HR) 198

I

impersonation attacks 65
impersonation scam 192
incident response (IR) protocols 176
indicators of compromise (IoCs) 162
Infectious Media Generator 155
influence, for defensive security
  authority 14
  scarcity 14
  social proof 14

inheritance scam 44
inline frame (iframe) 154
Instagram based attacks 112, 113
  protecting against 113, 114
intellectual property (IP) 175
international transfer 44
Intrusion Detection and Prevention systems (IDPS) 160
investor scam 48

K

Kali
  installing, with VM 148
  installing, with Windows Subsystem for Linux (WSL)/WSL2 148
  reference link 148
keylogging 19

L

lost passport attack 19, 20
lottery scam 44

M

magic-ware attacks 92, 93
  preventing, considerations 93
malicious apps 103
  distribution channels 104, 105
  risks, prevention and mitigation 105, 106
  types 103, 104
malicious app types
  fake apps 104
  grayware 104
  malware-infected apps 103
malware 19
malware attack 67

malware distribution 112
man in the middle attack 19
Mass Mailer Attack 156
Miley Cyrus Dead clickbait attack 109
mitigation and defense against SET
    attacks, best practices 160
  access controls, implementing 161
  continuous monitoring and
    response 161, 162
  email and web filtering solutions,
    implementing 161
  IR plan, developing 161
  least-privilege principles, implementing 161
  technical controls 160
  TI feeds, incorporating 161
  user awareness and training 160
  vulnerability management 160
Mitnick, Kevin 167
Multi-Factor Authentication
    (MFA) 86, 127, 161, 185

N

natural language processing (NLP) 125
Nigerian astronaut 46, 47
Nigerian prince 44
Nigerian scam (419 scam) 38, 39
  avoiding 47
  funny scams 45
  history 39, 40
  identifying 41-44
  types 44
Nigerian Space Research and Development
    Agency (NASRDA) 46

O

OMG cable 70

Open Source Intelligence
    (OSINT) 79, 82, 169
  methods, examples 83
  tools 82, 83
  tools, examples 82
  use cases 84

P

PayPal attack 58, 59
Penetration Testing (Fast-Track) menu 159
permission elevation and root
    access, on Kali Linux
  reference link 150
Personal Data Protection Act
    (PDPA) – Singapore
  key provisions 199
persuasion, principles
  authority 9
  commitment and consistency 8
  liking 9, 10
  reciprocity 7
  scarcity 10, 11
  social proof 8
phishing 19, 112
phishing attacks 55
  calendar phishing 66-68
  email phishing 59-62
  Google attack 57, 58
  history 55, 56
  PayPal attack 58, 59
  SMS phishing (smishing) 62-64
  technical support scam 68, 69
  voice phishing (vishing) 64-66
  Yahoo! attack 56, 57
phishing campaigns 184, 185
  continuous monitoring and assessment 186
  countermeasures 185, 186

phishing links 62
physical baiting 70, 71
physical impersonation attack 193, 194
piggybacking. *See* tailgating attack
Pizzagate 116
Powershell Attack Vectors 158
pretext development 171
   factors 171
pretexting 74
   fake job offers 74, 75
   false charities 75
prize scamming 62

Q

QRCode Generator Attack Vector 158
quid pro quo attacks 73
   free software to download 74
   free tech support 73
   protecting from 74

R

ransomware attack 67
rapport
   tactics, for developing 11-13
real-world social engineering incidents
   analyzing 190, 191
reconnaissance 169
referral scams 96
robocall scam 65
role-based access control (RBAC) 128
romance scam attack 21
   avoiding 22
   working 22

S

scam 38
scambaiting 50
scareware attacks 87, 88
   preventing, considerations 88
security information and event management (SIEM) 161
security operations center (SOC) 161
Sender Policy Framework (SPF) 62
SET installation
   system requirements 148
sextortion 114, 115
   protecting against 115, 116
SMS interception 63
SMS phishing (smishing) attacks 62
   dark web services 63
   detecting 63, 64
   inadequate security, for multi-factor authentication (MFA) 63
   phishing links 62
   prize scamming 62
   protecting from 64
   SMS interception 63
   spoofed SMS 62
   urgent SMS 63
social engineering 3, 4, 7, 19
   and crypto scam 28-35
   convictions 201, 202
   laws and regulations, examples 198, 199
   legal consequences 201, 202
   through mobile applications 102, 103
   via malicious apps, mitigating 108
social engineering attacks
   baiting 70, 71
   detecting 17, 18
   dumpster diving 72
   examples 5, 6

phishing 55-69
pretexting 74, 75
quid pro quo 73, 74
tailgating 73
watering hole 76
Social-Engineering Attacks menu
Arduino-Based Attack Vector 157
Create a Payload and Listener module 155
Infectious Media Generator 155
Mass Mailer Attack 156
Powershell Attack Vectors 158
QRCode Generator Attack Vector 158
Spear-Phishing Attack Vectors 152-154
Third Party Modules 158
Website Attack Vectors 154, 155
Wireless Access Point Attack Vector 157
social engineering incidents, case studies 191
impersonation scam 192
physical impersonation attack 193, 194
social media manipulation 194
targeted phishing attack 192
social engineering lifecycle 168
engagement 168, 172
execution (post-exploitation) 168, 175, 176
exploitation (elicitation) 168, 172, 173
history 166
pretext development 168, 171
reconnaissance 168, 169
security best practices 176-178
stages 168
target selection 168, 170
social engineering red flags
recognizing 181
recognizing, aspects 181, 182

social engineering techniques, in fake advertisements
reciprocity 27
scarcity 27
social proof 26
social engineering, through mobile applications 102, 103
app-based attacks 103
app-based attacks, identifying challenges 107
app permissions, exploiting for data access 106, 107
malicious apps 103
malicious apps, mitigating 107
Social Engineering Toolkit (SET) 145-147
benefits 147
components 150
downloading 148
executing 149, 150
importance, in cybersecurity 147
installing 148, 149
modules 150
Social Engineering Toolkit (SET), menu options
Help, Credits, and About 160
Penetration Testing (Fast-Track) 159
Social-Engineering Attacks 152
Third Party Modules 159
Update SET configuration 160
Update the Social-Engineer Toolkit 160
social engineering, via social networks 108
clickbait attack 108, 109
Instagram based attacks 112
WhatsApp based attacks 110
social media attacks 18
fake advertisements 25-28
fake investment 23-25
federal government grant 21

    lost passport 19-21
    romance scam 21, 22
    romance scam, avoiding 22, 23
spear phishing attack 60
Spear-Phishing Attack Vectors 152-154
spoofed event 67
spoofed SMS 62

T

tailgating attack 73
targeted attacks 80
    customizing ways 82
    high-value targets, identifying 81, 82
targeted phishing attack 192
target selection 170
    factors 170
technical support scam 68
    protecting from 69
Telecommunications Act 1997 – Australia 200
    key elements 200
Third Party Modules 158, 159
time-based one-time passwords (TOTPs) 64
two-factor authentication (2FA) 113

U

urgent calls 65
urgent SMS 63
USB human interface devices (USB HID) 157
USB Ninja 70

V

voice cloning 125
Voice Conversation (VoCo) 135
voice phishing (vishing) attacks 64, 134
    deep fake voicemail scam 65
    detecting 66
    impersonation attacks 65
    protecting from 66
    robocall scam 65

W

watering hole 76
    crypto mining 76
web-based attacks 84
    adware attack 98
    fake login 84, 85
    fake page attack 89-91
    fake update attacks 86, 87
    forum-based attacks 95-97
    gaming-based attacks 94
    hacking-ware attack 93, 94
    magic-ware attacks 92, 93
    scareware attacks 87, 88
Website Attack Vectors 154, 155
whaling 59
WhatsApp based attacks 110
    protecting against 111, 112
Windows Subsystem for Linux
    reference link 148
Wireless Access Point Attack Vector 157

Y

Yahoo! attack 56, 57

‹packt›

Packtpub.com

Subscribe to our online digital library for full access to over 7,000 books and videos, as well as industry leading tools to help you plan your personal development and advance your career. For more information, please visit our website.

Why subscribe?

- Spend less time learning and more time coding with practical eBooks and Videos from over 4,000 industry professionals
- Improve your learning with Skill Plans built especially for you
- Get a free eBook or video every month
- Fully searchable for easy access to vital information
- Copy and paste, print, and bookmark content

Did you know that Packt offers eBook versions of every book published, with PDF and ePub files available? You can upgrade to the eBook version at packtpub.com and as a print book customer, you are entitled to a discount on the eBook copy. Get in touch with us at customercare@packtpub.com for more details.

At www.packtpub.com, you can also read a collection of free technical articles, sign up for a range of free newsletters, and receive exclusive discounts and offers on Packt books and eBooks.

Other Books You May Enjoy

If you enjoyed this book, you may be interested in these other books by Packt:

Effective Threat Investigation for SOC Analysts

Mostafa Yahia

ISBN: 978-1-83763-478-1

- Get familiarized with and investigate various threat types and attacker techniques
- Analyze email security solution logs and understand email flow and headers
- Practically investigate various Windows threats and attacks
- Analyze web proxy logs to investigate C&C communication attributes
- Leverage WAF and FW logs and CTI to investigate various cyber attacks

Practical Threat Detection Engineering

Megan Roddie, Jason Deyalsingh, Gary J. Katz

ISBN: 978-1-80107-671-5

- Understand the detection engineering process
- Build a detection engineering test lab
- Learn how to maintain detections as code
- Understand how threat intelligence can be used to drive detection development
- Prove the effectiveness of detection capabilities to business leadership
- Learn how to limit attackers' ability to inflict damage by detecting any malicious activity early

Packt is searching for authors like you

If you're interested in becoming an author for Packt, please visit `authors.packtpub.com` and apply today. We have worked with thousands of developers and tech professionals, just like you, to help them share their insight with the global tech community. You can make a general application, apply for a specific hot topic that we are recruiting an author for, or submit your own idea.

Share Your Thoughts

Now you've finished *The Art of Social Engineering*, we'd love to hear your thoughts! Scan the QR code below to go straight to the Amazon review page for this book and share your feedback or leave a review on the site that you purchased it from.

`https://packt.link/r/1804613649`

Your review is important to us and the tech community and will help us make sure we're delivering excellent quality content.

Download a free PDF copy of this book

Thanks for purchasing this book!

Do you like to read on the go but are unable to carry your print books everywhere?

Is your eBook purchase not compatible with the device of your choice?

Don't worry, now with every Packt book you get a DRM-free PDF version of that book at no cost.

Read anywhere, any place, on any device. Search, copy, and paste code from your favorite technical books directly into your application.

The perks don't stop there, you can get exclusive access to discounts, newsletters, and great free content in your inbox daily

Follow these simple steps to get the benefits:

1. Scan the QR code or visit the link below

    `https://packt.link/free-ebook/9781804613641`

2. Submit your proof of purchase
3. That's it! We'll send your free PDF and other benefits to your email directly

Milton Keynes UK
Ingram Content Group UK Ltd.
UKHW031348220724
42UKWH00064B/892